Dilemmas and Challenges in Islamic Finance

The phenomenal growth of Islamic finance in the last few decades has been accompanied by a host of interesting questions and challenges. One of the critical challenges is how Islamic financial institutions can be motivated to participate in the 'equity-like' profit-and-loss sharing (PLS) contracts. It is observed that Islamic banks are reluctant to participate in the pure PLS scheme which is manifested by the rising concentration of investment on *murabaha* or mark-up financing. This phenomenon has been the hotbed of academic criticism on the contemporary practice of Islamic banking. This book explains the '*murabaha* syndrome' in light of the incentive provided by the current institutional framework and what are the changes required in the governance structure to mend this anomaly.

Yasushi Suzuki is Professor at the Ritsumeikan Asia Pacific University, Japan.

Mohammad Dulal Miah is Assistant Professor at the University of Nizwa, Oman.

T0382739

Islamic Business and Finance
Series Editor: Ishaq Bhatti

There is an increasing need for western politicians, financiers, bankers, and indeed the western business community in general to have access to high quality and authoritative texts on Islamic financial and business practices. Drawing on expertise from across the Islamic world, this new series will provide carefully chosen and focused monographs and collections, each authored/edited by an expert in their respective field all over the world.

The series will be pitched at a level to appeal to middle and senior management in both the western and the Islamic business communities. For managers with a western background the series will provide detailed and up-to-date briefings on important topics; for the academics, postgraduates, business communities, or managers with western or Islamic backgrounds the series will provide a guide to best practice in business in Islamic communities around the world, including Muslim minorities in the west and majorities in the rest of the world.

Islamic Financial Economy and Islamic Banking
Masudul Alam Choudhury

God-Conscious and the Islamic Social Economy
Masudul Alam Choudhury

Labor in an Islamic Setting
Edited by Necmettin Kizilkaya and Toseef Azid

Islamic Macroeconomics

A Model for Efficient Government, Stability and Full Employment
Raja Almarzoqi, Walid Mansour and Noureddine Krichene

Dilemmas and Challenges in Islamic Finance
Looking at Equity and Microfinance
Edited by Yasushi Suzuki and Mohammad Dulal Miah

For more information about this series, please visit www.routledge.com/Islamic-Business-and-Finance-Series/book-series/ISLAMICFINANCE

Dilemmas and Challenges in Islamic Finance

Looking at Equity and Microfinance

Edited by Yasushi Suzuki and Mohammad Dulal Miah

Routledge
Taylor & Francis Group

LONDON AND NEW YORK

First published 2018
by Routledge
2 Park Square, Milton Park, Abingdon, Oxon OX14 4RN

and by Routledge
605 Third Avenue, New York, NY 10017

First issued in paperback 2020

Routledge is an imprint of the Taylor & Francis Group, an informa business

British Library Cataloguing-in-Publication Data
A catalogue record for this book is available from the British Library

Library of Congress Cataloging-in-Publication Data
A catalog record for this book has been requested

ISBN 13: 978-0-367-50426-7 (pbk)
ISBN 13: 978-1-138-09540-3 (hbk)

Typeset in Galliard
by Apex CoVantage, LLC

Contents

Figures

Tables

Contributors

Editors and contributors

Yasushi Suzuki is Professor at the Ritsumeikan Asia Pacific University, Japan.

Mohammad Dulal Miah is Assistant Professor at the University of Nizwa, Oman.

Contributors

Nahid Afroz is a graduate student at University of Chittagong, Bangladesh.

Saiful Anwar is Vice Director of the Postgraduate Program on Islamic Finance at STIE Ahmad Dahlan, Jakarta and member of Risk Oversight Committee of PT. Bank Rakyat Indonesia Syariah, Indonesia.

Asif Nawaz Chowdhury is a graduate student at University of Chittagong, Bangladesh.

A. K. M. Kamrul Hasan is a doctoral student at the Ritsumeikan Asia Pacific University, Japan.

Mohammad Hashim Kamali is Professor and founding CEO of International Institute of Advanced Islamic Studies (IAIS), Malaysia.

Sigit Pramono is Chairman of SEBI School of Islamic Economics and Lecturer at University of Indonesia, Indonesia.

Oni Sahroni is Lecturer at SEBI School of Islamic Economics and member of Dewan Syariah Nasional (National Syari'ah Board) at the Majelis Ulama Indonesia (Indonesian Ulama Council), Indonesia.

Trisiladi Supriyanto is *Shari'ah* board member of Koperasi Syariah Benteng Mikro Indonesia and Lecturer at Universitas Ibnu Khaldun, Indonesia.

Helal Uddin is a doctoral student at the Ritsumeikan Asian Pacific University, Japan.

S. M. Sohrab Uddin is Professor at University of Chittagong, Bangladesh.

Foreword

Islamic finance has been growing at an amazing pace since the time of its inception on a larger scale in the mid-1970s. According to the Islamic Financial Services Industry Stability report, the assets with Islamic financial institutions (IFI) grew to US$ 1.89 trillion as of the first quarter of 2017. The upsurge of Islamic finance can be attributed to the increased popularity of Islamic banking not only in the Arab or Islamic countries but also in some Western countries including the UK, the US, and Singapore. Besides Islamic banks, conventional banks are also offering Islamic banking services by either opening new branches tagged after 'Islamic banking branch' or opening a new window labelled 'Islamic banking window'. Numerous reasons have been cited as the causes of rising popularity of this distinct model of finance. The primary among them is the desire of the Muslim population to embrace the Islamic faith in their economic and social lives.

Although modern Islamic finance began its journey in the 1970s in the Middle Eastern countries, the Malaysian government took it to a new height by taking pragmatic and goal-oriented long-term strategic plans. Specially, in the commercial banking and *Sukuk* market, the country introduced innovative products to meet the market demand. Several governmental agencies' initiatives like introducing comprehensive Islamic banking regulations, allowing the conventional banks to open Islamic banking windows, establishing educational institutes to promote the research on Islamic finance, developing *Shari'ah*-approved stock and so forth made Malaysia as an international Islamic finance hub. It also attracts many Middle East financial groups to start operations in Malaysia.

My vision was to bring the Islamic financial system as a parallel to the Western financial model. In so doing, we have been challenged to resolve several dilemmas facing the Islamic financial system. The field of Islamic finance is expanding rampantly in the Muslim countries and beyond due to its relevance to development and social justice. This phenomenal growth has accompanied a host of interesting questions and challenges some of which are sorted out and refuted in this book. Readers interested to know about these challenges and dilemmas and the way to resolve them may find this book worth reading.

Tun Abdullah Ahmad Badawi
The 5th Prime Minister of Malaysia

Foreword

Professor Yasushi Suzuki, a post-Keynesian economist by training, is an avid reader and enthusiastic scholar of Islamic finance. His enthusiasm on the subject is shown by his many contributions to the field, which are also well received by scholars and specialists in the field. Professor Suzuki recently visited the International Institute of Advanced Islamic Studies (IAIS) Kuala Lumpur, Malaysia and Yusof Ishak Institute (ISEAS) Singapore as a visiting research scholar where he had the opportunity to exchange views with different stakeholders of Islamic finance. It was during his stay at IAIS Malaysia that I had the opportunity to know him and gain closer familiarity with his works. As a passionate researcher in the field, he raises questions and engages the reader in issues and challenges Islamic finance are facing at present. He has evidently felt it essential to answer some of these questions in the midst of many issues of wider interest in Islamic finance. Professor Suzuki has travelled to many Muslim countries, including Malaysia, Bangladesh and Indonesia, and communicated with researchers in these countries who are currently engaged with a variety of issues of topical interest in Islamic banking and finance. The current book is a result, to a large extent, of these endeavors.

Islamic finance, through its journey in the last four decades or so, has expanded into various branches and areas. Although the beginning was marked solely by the presence of Islamic banking, the field has expanded over the years into such other areas as venture capital, microfinance, cooperative enterprises, and Islamic bonds or *Sukuk*. However, the banking segment still dominates the Islamic financial system, contributing to about three-fourths of the total Islamic financial assets. Thus, any success and failure of this distinct financial model is bound to be largely attributed to the Islamic banking system. But the reality is that Islamic banks like their conventional counterparts are profit-seeking institutions. They attempt to maximize their return by investing within the permissible areas of Islamic law, and the given boundaries of the applied laws of the land. This strategy has led them towards the concentration of particular modes of finance, which have generated, in turn, extensive academic debates as well as public criticisms.

Professor Suzuki and the fellow contributors of this volume have delved into these discussions and criticisms to unravel the causes and rationales behind them. They have set their goals clearly at the outset of this book, and were able to convincingly achieve them by following scientific methodologies. It is apparent from the tenor of their analyses that the book has not fallen short of achieving the goals it has set for itself. Prospective readers will thus find the book interesting and informative, and a product also of inquisitive yet mature scholarship in the field.

Professor Dr Mohammad Hashim Kamali
Founding CEO, International Institute of Advanced Islamic Studies (IAIS)

Foreword

The rise of Islamic finance in the last couple of years has heralded the importance of this particular discipline to the socio-economic lives of the Muslim population. Islamic finance has penetrated in countries with a majority Muslim population but it has also marked its presence in countries lacking large Muslim populations, which manifests that this distinct financing model possesses some social and economic benefits to offer. To single out a particular benefit, Islamic finance has been playing a critical role in propelling economic growth by including a segment of the population that remained out of conventional finance mainly due to their belief in the Islamic faith.

In its remarkable journey in the past few decades, Islamic finance has received not only applauded acceptance from society but also some criticisms. Most criticisms, however, are pointed towards ameliorating some apparent inconsistencies or critical deficiencies of the model. Thus, they deserve to be addressed for the greater interest of Islamic finance. This effort requires, first, a clear understanding about the challenges Islamic finance is facing at present followed by a coherent analysis about the available means to overcome these challenges. The current book is well positioned for this academic colloquium. It brings forth a host of interesting questions in a clear and concise academic manner and attempts to answer them logically backed by practical evidence.

The book is fresh in ideas and diverse in analytical perspectives. Readers interested to know about the existing practice of Islamic financial institutions would find it helpful in refreshing their views in Islamic finance and what to expect in the future.

Datuk Dr Mohd Daud Bakar
Founder and Group Chairman, Amanie Group

Preface

The book is divided into three parts. Part I deals with dilemmas and challenges on the prohibition of *riba* and *gharar*. We aspire to explain the economics of Islamic finance linking the central thesis of Islamic finance to some prominent schools of economic thought. Part I also offers a comprehensive analysis of the acceptable level of *gharar* through the lens of New Institutional and Post-Keynesian Economics. Part II argues on the issues as to who should challenge participatory finance as instructed by Islamic *Shari'ah*. This part, the central part of the book, focuses on various mechanisms and options for participatory finance including Islamic venture capital firms, *Sukuk*, and Islamic microfinance institutions. Part III looks at the current challenges and dilemmas Islamic financial institutions are facing now and the ways to address them for a sustainable and resilient Islamic financial system. One potential avenue which has been emphasized is that the governance structure should be designed in such a way that is conducive for the overall growth and prosperity of Islamic finance.

The diversification and absorption of risk and uncertainty embedded in incubating innovative start-ups and empowering marginalized people is a great challenge for the Islamic financial system as a whole. However, it is not easy to design a mode of finance which aims at achieving a delicate balance between mobilizing funds from risk-averse depositors *and* creating as well as accumulating enough wealth in society for incubating risk-neutral investors or donors who would be willing to absorb various risks and uncertainty exposed to innovative start-ups or to empower marginalized people. Apart from an idealistic view, this book suggests, from a view point of Institutional Political Economy, that the Islamic financial system should take a trial-and-error process to evolve upon the 'specialization' and 'division of work' in credit risk screening activities and financial intermediary functions. We would be more than happy if this book encourages further studies in the Institutional Political Economy of Islamic finance.

Yasushi Suzuki and Mohammad Dulal Miah
November 2017

Acknowledgements

The editors would like to thank Routledge/Taylor & Francis Asia Pacific for their guidance and continuous support towards the publication of this book. *Yasushi* would like to acknowledge that his work was supported by JSPS Grant-in-Aid for Scientific Research (C), Grant Number 15K03374. He would like to thank Akiko Suzuki for her constant support and inspiration, and Mohammad Hashim Kamali, Mohamed Azam Mohamed Adil, Mohd Daud Bakar, and Muhammad Hakimi Bin Mohd Shafiai for their encouragement and support. *Mohammad Dulal* would like to convey his gratitude to Professor Suzuki Yasushi for his continuous guidance and support to successfully complete this project. He would also like to express his sincere gratitude to Mir Ferdousi for her constant support and motivation. Special thanks go to Dr S. Arockiasamy for his encouragement to be involved with research. Many thanks are due to Dr Gholamreza Chabokrow, Shamshudheen Arumathadathil, and Syed Mahbubur Rahman.

Introduction

Yasushi Suzuki and Mohammad Dulal Miah

One of the salient characteristics of Islamic finance that distinguishes it from the conventional financing model is that the former complies, in objectives and operations, with *Shari'ah* (Islamic law). Two major prohibitions – prohibition of *riba* (interest) and prohibition of *gharar* (uncertainty) – underlie the basic *Shari'ah* principles. Qur'an (2: 275–76) clearly states that dealing with *riba* is 'sinful'. Instead, *Shari'ah* norms and principles encourage 'profit-and-loss sharing' (PLS) financial transactions. Islamic financial institutions have evolved to offer financial products which comply with Islamic *Shari'ah*. Some of these products are designed with features resembling participatory finance (*musharaka*) and trust-based finance (*mudaraba*) which are equity-like PLS-based contracts while others are characterized by sale- or leased-based mark-up transactions (*mudaraba, ijara, bai bithman ajil, bai salam* etc.). As of the first quarter of 2017, equity-like PLS contracts accounted for less than 5 percent of the total financing of Islamic banks. In contrast, mark-up or cost-plus financing combined more than 71 percent in the same period. This manifests that Islamic banks are reluctant (or discouraged) to participate in equity-like PLS schemes.

We note, first, that *murabaha* is a *Shari'ah*-compliant product, but many Islamic economists insist that it does not fully embody the spirit of PLS financing. This issue has been still controversial in the academic discussion. Islamic idealistic economists are of the view that Islamic banks should practice equity-like PLS-based financing otherwise their *raison d'être* is difficult to justify. This is, indeed, a critical challenge which Islamic finance scholars must explain. In refuting this challenge one must confront a dilemma. Islam encourages equity-like PLS contracts which are embedded in risks and fundamental uncertainty. In other words, increasing equity-like PLS-based investment in the portfolio of Islamic banks means embracing more risk as well as uncertainty, as well as exposing them to occasionally 'excess' uncertainty (*gharar*) which is prohibited by Islamic *Shari'ah*. This is a dilemma which seeks to be explained convincingly. The existing literature of Islamic finance rightly identifies the dilemma but pays much less attention to unfolding the paradox.

Second, it is suggested that agency problems should be mitigated if Islamic economies really wish to witness a surge in equity-like PLS-based financing (Maurer, 2002; Khalil et al., 2002; Farooq, 2007). In so doing, Islamic banks should initiate tighter screening and monitoring policies for participatory financing (trust-based financing may entail different dimensions in financing). This pre-scription is important but secondary only as far as Islamic banking is concerned. The primary concern centres on the question of what extent should Islamic banks be allowed to accept risks involved with participatory or trust-based financing.

Banks are financial intermediaries. They collect funds by selling deposits to the mass population and lending (investing) these funds to borrowers (entrepreneurs) who employ them in different projects. The payback of depositors' funds thus critically depends on the success of these projects that are subject to fundamental uncertainty. Although tighter screening and prudential monitoring as suggested by Islamic economists can be effective tools for resolving adverse selection and moral hazard problems, these tools are unlikely to be effective in eliminating uncertainty involved with entrepreneurial projects.

Both Islamic and conventional banks face the same uncertainty of entrepre-neurs but at a varying degree. Conventional banks usually enter into a debt-contract with their clients. Debt-contracts unlike equity contracts allow banks only a limited interest on a firm's stake. However, debt-contracts in most cases are secured by the collateral. Even in the case of unsecured loans, debt-contracts enti-tled to be preferred over the residual owners in case of a firm's liquidation. This implies that debt-like contracts are more secure than equity contracts. In contrast, equity holders as partners are, in general, ranked at an advantageous position to have direct access to the information on the firm. Therefore, higher risk in equity financing is linked with higher expected return. Should Islamic banks be allowed to take more risk for higher return? The answer to this question would help us understand the extent to which Islamic banks should be involved with participa-tory finance and why *murabaha* concentration is a logical choice for Islamic banks under the existing institutional underpinnings.

Third, Islamic financial institutions, besides their typical role of providing finance following *Shari'ah* principles, are also expected to make a positive contri-bution in poverty alleviation by fulfilling the socioeconomic objectives of 'social justice' in accordance with the objectives of *Shari'ah*. Altruism and reciprocity are highly encouraged by Islamic teaching and may contribute to setting up various financial institutions including Islamic angel investors and microfinance institu-tions to finance start-ups and microenterprises. However, strong reciprocity – a propensity to cooperate and share with others similarly disposed even at personal cost – may create a dilemma. For instance, strong reciprocity may force altruists to withdraw their support when they perceive that the person receiving the help does not sincerely try enough to be self-sufficient or uphold moral upstanding. Since these attributes of human beings are intangible and cannot be easily measured, altruists may abstain from altruistic contributions based on his self-assessment, which sometimes may prove wrong. This is again a conundrum which needs to be resolved for a broader development of Islamic finance.

The current literature has given much less emphasis on these contemporary issues and, thus, falls short of providing a comprehensive explanation for resolving these dilemmas and challenges. Furthermore, the anatomy of Islamic equity and microfinance has not been given adequate attention in Islamic finance literature. Although some noteworthy theoretical contributions are prevalent in the existing literature, theoretical arguments in most cases are not supplemented well by empirical analyses. This edited volume is a humble attempt to bridge this gap. It aims to unfold critical dimensions of these issues for a rigorous academic discussion so that pragmatic solutions can be agreed upon. Keeping this in mind, chapters for this book have been carefully selected with the aim of offering a balanced discussion between three major issues of Islamic finance: (1) dilemmas and challenges on the prohibition of *riba* and *gharar*, (2) issues in Islamic equity finance and microfinance, and (3) dilemmas and challenges in governance structure.

The book is divided into three parts. Part I deals with 'dilemmas and challenges on the prohibition of *riba* and *gharar*'. This part consists of three chapters. **Chapter 1** aspires to explain the economics of Islamic finance linking the central thesis of Islamic finance to some prominent schools of economic thought. The authors briefly describe the current financial architecture which is marked by the shift of the economic epicenter from industrial production to financial capitalism. This change has facilitated the rise of a new class called the 'rentier' class that derives major income from exploiting the scarcity value of capital. Drawing evidence from the Keynesian and Marxian analyses, this chapter links the economics underlying the prohibition of interest and uncertainty of Islamic finance to investment and employment as well as social equality and justice. In the Marxian theory, the circulation from 'idle' money to 'interest-bearing' capital for production is drawn as engines for the mode of capitalism. On the other hand, the Marxian school is very concerned about inequitable distribution of wealth and income resulting from the concentration of financial capital. Similarly, to achieve full employment by ensuring sufficient investment, Keynes advocated the realization of a low rate of interest for seeking 'social justice'. While this line of argument is compatible with Islamic philosophy, the authors point out the dilemmas and difficulties faced by Islamic finance in mediating and accumulating idle money to capital for production in the process of industrialization.

Islamic financial institutions particularly banks have designed their products complying with *Shari'ah* principles. *Murabaha* is one but noteworthy among them. In a typical *murabaha* contract, Islamic banks purchase the goods to be supplied to clients at a 'cost-plus' or 'mark-up' price. Clients may pay a lump sum amount instantly and the remaining on a deferred installment basis. Since sale-based transactions are permitted in Islam, *murabaha* is a *Shari'ah*-compliant product. The mark-up price of *murabaha* is pre-fixed which helps banks avoid uncertainty involved with PLS-based transactions.

However, there is a huge outcry in regard to the rising concentration of *murabaha* financing. The logic of the criticism relies on the fact that *murabaha*, although *Shari'ah*-compliant, does not uphold the spirit of equity-like PLS financing. Islamic principles encourage PLS-based transactions so that associated risks and uncertainties can be shared between participating parties. Many Islamic 'idealist' economists insist that the current practice of Islamic banks is a detour from this spirit. **Chapter 2** offers an elaborate discussion as to why Islamic banks prefer *murabaha* financing to equity-like PLS financing. The authors are of the view that the gross criticism against *murabaha* concentration is unfair. They argue that the encouragement towards equity-like PLS-based financing which is associated with higher risk and uncertainty and the parallel prohibition of *gharar* may have created a dilemma leading to the rise of so-called *murabaha* syndrome. Based on this understanding they argue that, under the existing institutional framework, *murabaha* syndrome can be ironically justified and compatible with the incentives provided by the system. This particular finding is interesting and deserves further analysis for designing appropriate institutions conducive for a vibrant Islamic financial system.

Although *gharar* is instructed to be avoided, there should be a realm of acceptable level of it because contracts are inevitably incomplete, which implies that some level of uncertainty exists in every transaction. Thus, financial institutions have to deal with their clients in a state of incomplete contract or in the presence of uncertainty. To what extent should Islamic banks deal with *gharar* so that depositors' interest (welfare) on the bank is adequately protected? **Chapter 3** attempts to answer this question. In so doing, it offers a comprehensive analysis of the acceptable level of *gharar* through the lens of New Institutional and Post-Keynesian Economics. The chapter is well equipped evidently and very interactive analytically to demark that realm. The authors draw their analysis of both Islamic jurisprudence and contemporary economic thought and argue that *gharar* is not prohibited wholesale but rather transactions that involve too much or excessive uncertainty should be prohibited. The authors further contend that Islamic financial institutions should challenge even *major* uncertainty if it is associated with 'enterprises', while they should avoid even *minor* uncertainty on 'speculations'.

Who should challenge participatory finance as instructed by Islamic *Shari'ah*? This issue permeates Part II of this book. This central part of the book focuses on different mechanisms and options for participatory finance including Islamic venture capital firms, *Sukuk*, and microfinance institutions. **Chapter 4** sheds an analytical light on the feasibility and dilemmas of mobilizing Islamic equity funds for the particular mode of participatory finance. The authors first derive some important motivating factors including altruism and reciprocity which are emphasized in the Muslim scriptures to be adopted by the believers. Islam as a religion encourages followers to maintain trust and reciprocity. At the same time, it strongly prohibits the actor's opportunistic behavior. The virtue of altruism and reciprocity should encourage Muslim capitalists to finance those entrepreneurs who are financially stranded. On the other hand, the element of trust should work as a guidepost for entrepreneurs not to behave opportunistically. If properly maintained, these social lubricants can overhaul the drawbacks resulting from incomplete contracting. The authors, however, are prompt to remind that trust and other moral virtues of actors are intrinsic and difficult to preserve. As a consequence, these virtues should be supplemented by tangible regulations.

While **Chapter 4** enumerates a broader venture capital (VC) environment, **Chapter 5** provides evidence on various aspects encountered by Islamic VC firms. The authors analyze two large VC firms each from Indonesia and Bahrain. One of the salient contributions of the chapter is that it develops some typology based on their extended analysis of these cases. The authors show that VC firms particularly in matured economies explore innovative venture seeds, challenging 'high risk' but 'high return' profit opportunities whereas banks' patronized VC firms are shown to be very conservative in financing entrepreneurs. Also, some VC firms evolve to target the real estate financing because they lack basic knowledge and skills to absorb projects' versatile risk. There are other VC firms which are backed by the government. They merely facilitate funds mainly from the state to enterprises without challenging the risky ventures much. This typology would help policymakers develop VC strategies appropriate for macroeconomic characteristics.

Typical Islamic indirect financial products are not highly suitable for sovereign debt or large-scale corporate financing demand. This drawback has largely facilitated the evolution of *Sukuk* or Islamic bond, a comparatively recent addition to the line of Islamic financial products. Unlike the conventional bond in which the holders of the bond are simply the creditors and receive periodic fixed interest, *Sukuk* gives the owner undivided ownership of some tangible assets underlying the debt and receive profit earned from the investment of the *Sukuk* amount. Although *Sukuk* is not an equity-based product it has, however, the hybrid nature of debt and equity. The fixed income provision of *Sukuk* makes it a debt-like instrument whereas the ownership of assets or the perpetual *Sukuk* appears to have an equity-like nature. Due to its advantage of having access to a large pool of liquidity in many Muslim countries, *Sukuk* issuance has increased significantly in the recent period. Alzaharani and Megginson (2017) report that *Sukuk* markets have experienced an average growth of 27 percent per year in the last two decades. The industry amounted to $318.5 billion at the end of 2016 (IFSB, 2017).

Malaysia has sustained itself as the largest *Sukuk* outstanding market in 2016, accounting for 46.4 percent of the total market, declining from 50.6 percent in 2015. The share of Saudi Arabia accounts for 17.4 percent followed by the UAE (10.5 percent) and Qatar (5.9 percent). These statistics show that Malaysia offers itself as an example for other countries that aim to develop their national *Sukuk* market. In this regard, **Chapter 6** can be of particular interest which provides a comprehensive analysis of the Malaysian *Sukuk* market and the governance structure underlying it. Comparing the *Sukuk* markets in Bangladesh and Malaysia the authors argue that the differences between these two *Sukuk* markets can be attributed to differences in the legal and regulatory framework, availability of *Sukuk* instruments, awareness of corporations about the benefits of *Sukuk* etc. Based on their in-depth analysis the authors argue that emerging economies can materialize the benefits of this innovative Islamic product but such an attempt requires proper planning and coordination among regulatory authorities, Islamic banks, Islamic financial institutions, *Shari'ah* scholars, and other market participants. What makes the chapter more interesting is that it examines the genesis and development of the J-*sukuk* (Japan *Sukuk*) market. Although the issuance of J-*sukuk* is yet to be seen, readers interested to know about the regulatory frameworks evolving in a region that is lacking large Muslim populations to encourage a financial product originally based on ethical concerns of Islam may find it worth reading.

It is evident that Islamic banks follow the suit of conventional banks as far as ventures and Small and Medium sized Enterprises (SME) financing are concerned. Both clusters of banks prefer financing large firms which have established reputations and historical track records as well as which possess significant tangible assets that can be made collateral against borrowing. This strategy of Islamic banks is logical from the perspective of their limited risk absorbing capacity. SMEs lack sufficient information required for a comprehensive assessment of the borrowers' creditworthiness. Thus, Islamic banks limit their exposure to such firms. However, marginalized borrowers of SMEs are deprived of the necessary financing. Historically, microfinance institutions and cooperative enterprises have catered the financing needs of these SMEs and marginalized borrowers to a large extent. The last two chapters of Part II bring various dimensions of these issues.

Chapter 7 offers a comparative study between conventional and Islamic microfinance in Bangladesh. Needless to say, Grameen Bank (GB), a renowned microfinance institute which originated in Bangladesh, is known worldwide for its pivotal role in eradicating poverty through financing the marginal borrowers. The model is thus followed by many developing countries across the world. The authors in this chapter are keen to check the feasibility of the GP model to be adopted by Islamic microfinance providers. In so doing, they analyze in detail the Rural Development Scheme (RDS), an Islamic microfinance institution (IMFI) under the auspices of Islami Bank Bangladesh Ltd. and identify some critical constraints to its growth. It has been found that the shortage of funds, improper regulatory infrastructure, and asymmetry of information restrict the growth of IMFI. Taking into consideration the nature of operational differences between GB and RDS, the authors are very cautious in suggesting what RDS can learn from the success story of GB. In particular, market information and funds recovery method of GB can be of particular interest to RDS. The authors add an additional dimension by showcasing the problems and prospects of some IMFIs in Pakistan.

Islamic Saving–Loan and Financing Cooperatives (KSPPS) of Indonesia are one example which was modelled after the GB with some modifications. This cooperative was later converted to a *Shari'ah*-compliant microfinance institution. **Chapter 8** discusses the target of KSPPS on poverty alleviation. The authors estimate how many of KSPPS' clients are likely to live under the poverty line upon the international standard, the national standard in Indonesia, and the KSPPS target, respectively. The authors point out that the national standard is a bit indulgent. Simultaneously, the authors find that, even upon the KSPPS standard, more than three-quarters of the respondents are likely to live under the poverty line. The outreach of Islamic Saving–Loan and Financing Cooperatives to marginalized clients is perhaps very limited in Indonesia. This chapter also makes a methodological contribution to the existing scientific method of impact assessment of microfinance by introducing the concept of 'artificial neural networks'. To facilitate the discussion on how well or poorly Islamic finance could contribute to poverty alleviation, the method of impact assessment should be critically assessed for its improvement.

The current challenges and dilemmas for Islamic financial institutions need to be addressed for a sustainable and resilient Islamic financial system. To accomplish this objective, governance structure should be designed in such a way that is conducive for the overall growth and prosperity of Islamic finance. Part III of this book takes this issue into consideration. In particular, **Chapter 9** explicates the governance structure of the *Shari'ah* board and proposes what is further required to make the board *Shari'ah* minded as well as knowledgeable about modern economics and finance. This chapter analyzes various principal–agent relations involved with the Islamic financing paradigm. In addition to conventional agency problems, Islamic financial institutions encounter one additional layer in their governance structure, the *Shari'ah* board, which is appointed and remunerated by the concerned financial institution. The *Shari'ah* board thus appointed may have maintained their *de facto* independence (in practice) but they lack the independence *de jure* (in appearance). Thus, the authors propose remedies to make a board independent both *de facto* and *de jure*. A distinct characteristic of this chapter lies in the authors' attempt to tell an insider's story about the nature and functions of a *Shari'ah* board, echoing the tone of a *Shari'ah* board member having versatile experiences in serving different *Shari'ah* boards. Their solid suggestions in this chapter are also substantiated by discussing the corporate governance codes of the UK. Although different in nature, the authors find these particular codes a great learning tool to remodel the *Shari'ah* board.

From the perspective of *Shari'ah* independence, two roughly distinct models – separated vs. independent – are noticed in the Islamic world. For instance some countries follow a separated model in which the *Shari'ah* board has been bestowed with a high degree of independence. In contrast, an integrated version which is modelled upon the harmonization among different entities related to banking regulations and operations is followed by a cluster of countries. **Chapter 10** offers a detailed analysis of integrated vs. separated models of *Shari'ah* boards and their distinctive characteristics. The authors then check if the integrated or separated model suits well to the available Islamic financial infrastructure in Bangladesh. Upon analyzing the existing practice of the governance structures the authors find that the model currently practiced in Bangladesh consists of a few country-specific features which make it distinct from the two widely used models. These distinctive features have been elaborated in this chapter along with their related pros and cons.

The current mode of profit-and-loss sharing provides, in practice, an idea of the difficulty for Islamic banks in assuming equity-based financing. It is impractical to expect the acceleration of participatory financing without preserving much higher margins of security to cover further profit-and-loss sharing risk. *Shari'ah* scholars, the regulatory authority, and other professionals need to design an appropriate financial architecture which can create different (and socially acceptable) levels of margin opportunities for Islamic banks to avail the benefit from the variety of Islamic financing as declared by *Shari'ah*. The final chapter, **Chapter 11**, takes these issues into consideration. In light of the challenges and dilemmas covered in this book, the chapter suggests some mechanisms which are believed to be helpful for policymakers in designing an appropriate policy framework conducive for PLS-based Islamic finance.

The authors specifically propose a model based on 'specialization' and 'division of work'. In so doing, they highlight the sensitivity of the banking industry to any adverse economic and financial shocks. Since banks deal with depositors' funds, they must be very cautious in exposing themselves to excessive risks and uncertainties. From this vantage point the authors argue that it won't be so sensible to suggest Islamic banks be involved extensively with equity-like PLS-based financing. Given that *murabaha* is a *Shari'ah*-compliant product and receives a high demand from Muslim societies, Islamic banks' concentration on *murabaha* financing is rational. The authors thus suggest that Islamic banks should limitedly be involved in *musharaka* financing. On the other hand, entrepreneurs financing needs based on PLS contracts should be catered by venture capital firms whereas microfinance institutions can meet the demand for marginalized borrowers. To materialize this integrated PLS-based Islamic financial model, some institutional constraints identified in this chapter should be wiped out.

Part I

Dilemmas and challenges on the prohibition of *riba* and *gharar*

1 Heterodox vs. Islamic views on interest and uncertainty

Commonalities and contradictions

Yasushi Suzuki and Mohammad Dulal Miah

1. Introduction

One of the dominant principles of Islamic finance is the prohibition of '*riba*' or interest and '*gharar*' or uncertainty. For the people in the Abrahamic monotheistic faith, in particular, for Muslims, this is a divine rule and in principle believers of this faith should accept the rule for their benefits in this world and the world hereafter. Despite the fact that we cannot assess the benefits of the life hereafter, some worldly benefits derived from the prohibition of *riba and gharar* should be logically explained from the perspective of economic and social circumstances.

No doubt, interest is an essential element of finance and is embedded in our financial systems. In the absence of interest, financial architectures of most capitalist economies might have been different from what they are today because modern economies are increasingly tending towards a financial system where risks and uncertainties are modeled to be quantified as premiums which are traded in the financial markets. Such a practice, nevertheless, has accompanied perils and promises. On the promise side, increased quantification of risks has made investment in the financial markets easier than ever before, which in turn helps attract a large base of investors. Firms in shortage of funds can capitalize on issuing new innovative securities (repackaged mortgages, complex derivatives and so forth) to these investors. On the contrary, innovation in the financial products may also prove to be catastrophic. Lohmann (2011, p. 650) asserts "the latest attempt to keep things moving by expanding credit has meanwhile led to an unlimited, and ultimately catastrophic, expansion of risk."

Islam as a religion does not stand alone in prohibiting interest and uncertainty. Other major contemporary religions in the past barred paying and receiving interest although all religions except Islam have gradually detoured from this practice (Lewis, 2007). Similarly, some philosophical thoughts have emerged which explicitly explain the functions of interest in the economy and their ultimate consequence on society. One such view is the heterodox school of economics which contrasts itself from the neoclassical orthodox school of self-centric (rational) individualism. The heterodox view of Keynes and Marx is of particular interest in this regard because the Marxian and Keynesian traditions shoot a skeptical look towards those rentier-functionless investors who earn and accumulate wealth through financing means upon interest without directly taking part in productive activities. We find Islamic prohibition of interest and uncertainty compatible, to a good extent, with this heterodox thesis. This chapter aims to link the heterodox perspective on functionless investors to the Islamic prohibition of *riba* and *gharar*. The chapter also takes into account the benefits interest-free transactions may offer to society in regard to justice and equity, as well as the challenges faced by Islamic and heterodox views.

The chapter has been structured as follows: Section 2 describes the Islamic principles of prohibition of *riba* and *gharar* whereas Section 3 discusses the heterodox view underlying the concept of interest and uncertainty. Section 4 sheds an analytical light on the relevance of heterodox and Islamic views in this particular context. In doing so, an emphasis is placed on the role of functionless investors in the economy and how their activities invite welfare-reducing impacts on society. However, the idea of interest-free transactions is not free from challenges. The primary challenge evolves from the fact that, in the absence of interest, mobilization of idle funds accumulated by risk-averse investors may be infeasible. This point along with other critical challenges and how Islamic finance in particular plans to deal with these challenges will be discussed in Section 5. Section 6 offers an interim conclusion.

2. Islamic principles of interest and uncertainty

There are various verses revealed in the Holy Qu'ran prohibiting *riba*. According to Siddiqi (2004) there are a total of 12 verses in the Qu'ran which deal with *riba* and the word *riba* directly appears eight times. Chapter 2, Verse 275 states:

> Those who practice usury and interest, (their condition is such as) they will not be able to stand except like the standing of one who has lost his reason under the influence of Satan (devil). That is so because they say, "Trade is just like usury and interest". Whereas Allâh has made trade lawful and made interest unlawful. Then whosoever has received (this) admonition from his Lord and keeps away (from usury and interest) he may keep whatever (interest) he has taken in the past. His matter rests with Allâh. As for those who revert (to the practice of usury and interest) it is these who are the fellows of the Fire, therein shall they live for long.

Some other verses also explicitly mention various aspects of *riba*. For instance, Verse 276 (of Chapter 2) states, "Allâh annuls usury and interest and promotes charity" and Verse 278 reads, "O you who believe! Take Allâh as a shield and forgo all outstanding gains from usury and interest if you are indeed believers." Strong provision for punishment is promulgated for those who deal with *riba*. Verse 279 states, "But if you do (it) not, then beware of war from Allâh and His Messenger. But if you turn away (from such an unlawful transaction) then you shall have your principal (without interest) back." In collecting the sum, a provision has been stated favoring the debtors. For instance, Verse 280 reads:

> If any (debtor) be in straitened circumstances there shall be respite (for him) till (his circumstances) ease. But that if you remit (the debt) by way of charity (for the sake of God), it is better for you, if you only knew.

The above verses clarify some important points about *riba*. First, *riba* is prohibited outright without any reservation. Second, *riba* is defined as the excess of principal. Third, severe punishment is provisioned for those who, despite knowing, deal with *riba*. Fourth, trade is solemnized and is separated from *riba*.

Islam is a religion born in the Arabian Desert, where trade constituted the most important, "perhaps even the sole economic activity, favors merchants, property rights, free trade and market economy" (Çizakça, 2011, p. xv). As such, Islam is called the religion for merchants (Ayub, 2007; Çizakça, 2011). The business ethics in the Islamic mode of transactions are related to the civilized urban way of life at the birth of Islam. The holy Prophet had spent half of his life working as a merchant in Mecca, where the urban culture flourished and the values for facilitating fair transactions among merchants in equal positions were shared. The holy Prophet mentioned that trade constituted nine-tenths of the livelihood of early Muslims. In fact, of the four righteous Caliphs, Abu Bakr was a cloth merchant and Uthman was an importer of cereals (Çizakça, 2011, p. xiv).

The values being shared among merchants have developed the concept of contracting and the importance of respecting mutual property rights in the Muslim community. Islam recognizes the role of the market and the freedom of individuals in business and trade while restraining the freedom to engage in business and financial transactions on the basis of a number of prohibitions, ethics and norms. It is widely known that the prohibition of *riba*, *gharar* and *maisir* (gambling) is the most strategic factor that defines invalid and voidable contracts and demarcates the overall limits which should not be crossed (Ayub, 2007, p. 12).

Islam as a religion did not stand alone in the past in prohibiting *riba*. An examination of the world's dominant religions shows that they all prohibited interest. The Abrahamic faith traditions – Judaism, Christianity and Islam – took initial strides to prevent adherents from charging any interest on loans (Looft, 2014). While the Jewish and Christian faiths have both evolved to draw distinctions between acceptable interest and usury, Islam still explicitly forbids charging any interest on loans. Usury is referred to as a rate of interest greater than that which the law or public opinion permits (Looft, 2014). Looft (2014) points out that, nevertheless, there are still voices within Christian communities that deride all forms of interest as usury, referring to the following poem written by Peter Maurin who co-founded the Catholic Worker Movement in 1933: (i) Before John Calvin people were not allowed to lend money at interest, (ii) John Calvin decided to legalize money-lending at interest in spite of the teachings of the Prophets of Israel and the Fathers of the Church, (iii) Protestant countries tried to keep up with John Calvin and money-lending at interest became the general practice, (iv) And money ceases to be a means of exchange and began to be a means to make money, (v) So people lent money on time and started to think of time in terms of money and said to each other: "Time is money" '(Looft, 2014, pp. 114–115). Islam has not relented to pressures from the market and has continued to maintain its stance that charging interest on loans is usurious and a violation of Islamic law. Now the important question is why Islam relentlessly adheres to the prohibition of *riba*.

It is difficult to get explicit Qur'anic text on the logic as to why interest is prohibited because the rationales are more implicit than explicit. Also, there is a possibility that the contemporary stock of knowledge may not have adequately decoded the logics implied in the Qur'an. Albeit, Siddiqi (2004) analyzing the context of various Qur'anic verses summarizes five broader reasons; (i) interest corrupts society, (ii) interest implies improper appropriations of others' property, (iii) interest slows down the growth of real sectors, (iv) interest demeans and diminishes human personality and (v) interest is simply unjust. As we mentioned earlier, the Qur'an does not provide detailed analysis of the rationale of prohibition of interest. The rationales outlined earlier in the chapter are identified and articulated by Islamic scholars, who are subject to error. The only rationale in regard to the provision of *riba* that can be sensed from the Qur'anic verse is related to 'exploitation' or 'injustice'. It is stated in the Qur'an as, "deal not unjustly (by asking more than your principal) and you shall not be dealt with unjustly" (Chapter 2, Verse 279).

Different aspects of exploitation have been discussed in the existing literature. For instance, Al-Qaradawi (2013) who summarizes the explanation from an earlier Islamic scholar (Imam Fakhr al-Din al-Razi, 1149–1209 AD) takes a general view that in a lender–borrower relation, the former is usually wealthy whereas the latter is poor. This disparity may lead to exploitation of the latter by the former. K. Ahmad (1980) refers to Sayyid Abul A'la Mawdudi who supports the view that interest is indeed a means of exploitation. Mawdudi further notes that interest can be considered a way of transferring wealth towards the favor of haves which results in inequality. Similarly, Farooq (2009) argues that many Muslims have resorted to interest-free Islamic banking not merely because it is Islamic, but because it would help society to be free from exploitation. In the same token, Looft (2014) stresses that lending money at interest without any means of sharing risk between lenders and borrowers creates a relationship where weak and vulnerable individuals can be easily exploited by more powerful ones. Chapter 3, Verse 130 of the Qur'an reads, "O you, who believe, consume no *riba* doubled and multiplied." Similarly, Chapter 30, Verse 39 reveals, "And whatever you give for *riba* to increase within the wealth of (other's) people will not increase with Allah." Farooq however, raises a concern about the deficiency of modern Islamic literature in casting a focused attention to the issue of exploitation from the perspective of interest. Farooq (2012) argues that while the traditional arguments on prohibition of interest are indicative of an apparent anti-exploitation concern, the reality is that the intellectual and theological framework within which this discourse is framed does not demonstrate a genuine and adequate understanding of the extent and nature of exploitation in the contemporary world.

Although deficient in an appropriate analytical model, the above Qur'anic verses prove that Islam treats interest as a means of expropriation of the disadvantaged by the capitalists with the intent to increase the latter's accumulation. This in turn creates inequality in society leading to oppression, chaos and anarchy, which undermine the social peace and amity. However, solid empirical assessment of these rationales, which requires comparative analysis, cannot be performed because currently no country can be found which follows pure Islamic rules. Second, institutional-level analysis is infeasible owing to the fact that the current mode of Islamic financing is dominated by *murabaha* or mark-up financing instead of *musharaka* and *mudaraba* (this aspect is also the major concern of this book).

Like *riba*, avoiding *gharar* is another salient principle of Islamic finance. In the Islamic mode of investment and financial intermediation, excessive uncertainty is perceived in two dimensions; one refers to the lack of clarity in the terms and essence of the contract, the other refers to the uncertainty in the object of the contract (Ayub, 2007; El-Gamal, 2006). Complete contracting is intrinsically impossible. Therefore, some measure of uncertainty is always present in contracts. El-Gamal (2006, p. 58) notes that "jurists distinguished between major or excessive *gharar*, which invalidates contracts, and minor *gharar*, which is tolerated as a necessary evil." Also, the uncertainty in the object of the contract cannot be avoided in any business. The problem, however, "was that the extent of uncertainty making any transaction *Haram* had not been clearly defined" (Ayub, 2007, p. 58). Ayub (2007) refers to *gharar-e-kathir* and *gharar qalil* (too much and nominal uncertainty) and agrees that only those transactions that involve too much or excessive uncertainty in respect to the subject matter should be prohibited. Al-Saati (2003) suggests that the *Hadith* (which prohibits *gharar*) does not intend to prohibit all *gharar*, but intends to prohibit *gharar* which can cause dispute and cannot be tolerated.

Basically, Islamic principles of economics focus on clarity and lack of ambiguity, just and fair treatment for all and care for the rights of others (Ayub, 2007). So far as these principles are necessarily ethical, incubating small- and medium-sized enterprises (SMEs) would be acceptable to an extent in which the associated major uncertainty can be shared and absorbed in the community through an adequate profit–loss sharing (PLS) agreement (Suzuki, 2013). Ayub mentions:

> for a more efficient economy, we must promote systems in which people work in productive pursuits rather than unproductive ones. Change the system to relate it with real sector activities and all those clever dealers who earn huge profits out of thin air could become doctors, industrialists, business people and teachers instead.
>
> (n.d., p. 2)

This provides the evidence that engagement in enterprise rather than speculation seems to be preferable in the Islamic mode of investment. In addition, the prohibition of *gharar* embedded in speculation is considered the wisdom for minimizing the potential periodic financial disaster.

3. Heterodox perspective on interest and uncertainty

In order to compare and contrast the heterodox view with the Islamic logic of the prohibition of *riba* and *gharar*, it would be worthwhile to focus on the context in which Islam restricts *riba* and *gharar*. As mentioned earlier, the prohibition of *riba* in Islam is fueled by the spirit of social justice whereas the prohibition of *gharar* aims at reducing potential conflicts or disagreements regarding qualities or incompleteness of information. The heterodox view of Marx and Keynes is compatible with the idea of restricting interest as well as uncertainty.

Differentiating itself from the dominant neoclassical ideology of methodological individualism, the heterodox school explains the economic system by its relationship between and among parties engaged in producing goods and services for society. Lee (2009, p. 8) elaborates that heterodox economics is "concerned with explaining the process that provides the flow of goods and services required by society to meet the needs of those who participate in its activities". This means that it is the social analysis that underlies the heterodox view (Lawson, 2006). Social analysis constitutes social structures which deal with the structures of production (the use of inputs to produce the output), social-economic classes (capitalist vs. workers) and the capitalist state (Lee and Jo, 2011). These elements of social analysis owe a lot to the contribution of Marx and Keynes.

Marx's analysis of interest is rooted in his analysis of the production system. In the Marxian production process, money [M] is first accumulated and converted into means of production which are transformed into commodities [C]. Commodities are then sold and reconverted into money again with surplus [M' = M + ΔM; where ΔM is the surplus]. Or in other words, the M-C-M' is the ideal production circuit where M stands for industrial capital as it is employed by its owner to the production process. In the circuit, the 'idle' or 'stagnant' money accumulated in society is collected and mediated by financial intermediaries as 'interest-bearing capital'. Marx (1959) postulated that the exchange of interest-bearing capital is confined merely to the exchange of hands between money capitalists and functioning capitalists. But it is not a phase by which commodity metamorphosis or even reproduction of capital takes place. The latter is achieved when interest-bearing capital "is expended a second time, in the hands of the active capitalist who carries on trade with it, or transforms it into productive capital" (Marx, 1959, p. 231). Since the functioning capitalist produces some surplus in the production process [ΔM] utilizing the capital lent by the money capitalist, the former shares a portion of the surplus with the latter which is known as 'interest'. Marx (1959, p. 230) contended, "he (functioning capitalist) would thereby pay the use-value, the use-value of its function as capital, the function of producing a profit; (and) part of the profit paid to the owner is called interest."

In the parlance of Marxian analysis, maximum magnitude of interest [i] can be equal to the magnitude of the profit [ΔM] generated through the production process because interest is merely a part of profit paid by the industrial capitalist to the money capitalist. In this relation, we can sense an inverse relation between interest and profits [Π] of enterprises. However, variations in interest rate does not necessarily affect the value or the price of commodities (from which surplus is derived) but only have an effect on the distribution of surplus value or total profits between money capitalists and functioning capitalists. Given that C, the labor value of non-labor means of production, is constant, the rate of profit is therefore determined by the real wage rate [W]. Marx considered the rate of profit to be determined by the distribution conflict between capital and labor [ΔM = M' − (C + W)]. The rate of interest (r) influences only the distribution of surplus between money capitalists and functioning capitalists and makes the rate of profit of enterprise [Π] a residual variable [Π = ΔM − r].

For Marx, interest is an alien to the movements of industrial capital, the rate of which is determined by the class struggle between money capitalists and industrial capitalists. "It is only the competition between these two kinds of capitalists which creates the rate of interest" (Marx, 1959, p. 252). If a large number of capitalists wish to convert their accumulation into money capital, the rate of interest would fall due to the comparative abundance of money capital compared to industrial capital. The money capitalist would find interest income insufficient to live by which would force some of them to transform into industrial capitalists. As soon as money capital is lent out to industrial capitalists, interest on it grows, fulfilling the most ardent desire of the hoarder.

Marx further related the magnitude of interest to the cycle of economy in which he mentioned that a low rate of interest corresponds to the period of prosperity or extra profit. The reason is that in the period of prosperity the regularity of handsome returns can adequately fulfill the increased demand for industrial capital and prevents the level of interest from rising. In contrast, "a maximum of interest up to a point of extreme usury corresponds to the period of crisis" (Marx, 1959, p. 243) because during the crisis period money is borrowed even at an extreme rate to meet the payment requirement.

Besides the natural demand and supply, Marx also stressed that the interest rate may rise due to speculative use of credit. Marx argued:

> The supply of an article can also fall below average, as it does when crop failures in corn, cotton, etc., occur; and the demand for loan capital can increase because speculation in these commodities counts on further rise in prices and the easiest way to make them rise is to temporarily withdraw a portion of the supply from the market. But in order to pay for the purchased commodities without selling them, money is secured by means of the commercial "bill of exchange operations." In this case, the demand for loan capital increases, and the rate of interest can rise as a result of this attempt to artificially prevent the supply of this commodity from reaching the market. The higher rate of interest then reflects an artificial reduction in the supply of commodity-capital.
>
> (1959, pp. 369–370)

Marx further noted that a capitalist society is featured by the main relationship of exploitation and class between worker and capitalist. In societies where this is an example of dominant relation, there exists a relation of indebtedness arising in the credit market. Marx argued referring to the pre-capitalist society that the class struggle resulted from the conflict between debtor and creditor. The usurer's capital which has the mode of exploitation of capital without its mode of production was pervasive in that stage of society (Eslter, 1986, p. 86). Exploitation through usurer's capital or financial capital, according to Marx, gives no impetus to the development of productive forces. In other words, such a functionless investor has neither the incentive nor the opportunity to improve the methods of production because he is not necessarily seeking ways to further residual return. From this perspective, Marx argued that it is unfair that some should be able to earn an income without working, whereas others must accept the toil. Capitalist extraction of surplus value is therefore equivalent to theft, embezzlement, robbery and stealing (Eslter, 1986, p. 95). Marx (1959, p. 399) noted:

> Talk about centralisation! The credit system, which has its focus in the so-called national banks and the big money-lenders and usurers surrounding them, constitutes enormous centralisation, and gives to this class of parasites the fabulous power, not only to periodically despoil industrial capitalists, but also to interfere in actual production in a most dangerous manner – and this gang knows nothing about production and has nothing to do with it. . . . These bandits . . . are augmented by financiers and stock-jobbers.

On the other hand, Keynes (1936, p. 150) stated that the rate of interest is not the price "which brings into equilibrium the demand for resources to invest with the readiness to abstain from present consumption (savings)" but rather it is the price "which equilibrates the desire to hold wealth in the form of cash with the available quantity of cash". This implies that it is 'liquidity' rather than 'saving' which is the function of the interest rate. A lower rate of interest means less reward for parting with liquidity or cash. At this circumstance, people will have less incentive to sacrifice their liquid position and *vice versa*. For Keynes, liquidity preference (L) along with the quantity of money (M) determines the actual rate of interest (r) in a given circumstance. The fundamental speculative demand for money among them can be stated as $M = L(r)$.[1]

Keynes established the arbitrary relationship between savings upon swinging propensity to save, investment upon expectations and rate of interest upon changing liquidity preference. On the other hand, as his philosophical speculations for seeking an ideal society, Keynes advocated for the realization of a low rate of interest: "It is to our best advantage to reduce the rate of interest to that point relatively to the schedule of the marginal efficiency of capital at which there is full employment" (Keynes, 1936, p. 343). The question is: How low should be the rate of interest? Should it ultimately be zero?

From Keynes's perspective upon his concept of social justice, so far as full employment is achieved, a much lower rate of interest would be desirable. According to Keynes, the scale of investment depends on the relation between the rate of interest and the schedule of the marginal efficiency of capital (MEC). In theory, a lower rate of interest, zero rate of interest at the extreme case, upon the ample availability of loanable funds, which is independent of interest rate, would encourage the borrowers (mainly enterprises) to make more investments so far as their prospective yield of the investments remains at a satisfactory level (the MEC in the general theory depends on the relation between the replacement cost [the supply price of a capital asset] and its prospective yield).

Like Marx, Keynes viewed the inequality of income that results from enterprise is desirable; however, inequality of income that results from ownership of wealth is undesirable (Minsky, 1975). The rentier class retains the cumulative oppressive power and uses it to exploit the scarcity value of liquid capital. But economic growth could be better satisfied if capital ceases to be scarce.

It is worth noting that the MEC, based on which the rate of interest is to be determined targeting the full employment, is subject to the subjective swings of mood of the borrower. The swings of mood stem from general uncertainty. Similarly, individual preference for liquidity is subject to the condition of uncertainty as to the future of the rate of interest, which is also fixed by mass psychology. This postulates that the Keynesian analysis of interest rate is linked greatly to his analysis of uncertainty. Keynes stated:

> By uncertain knowledge, let me explain, I do not mean merely to distinguish what is known for certain from what is only probable. The game of roulette is not subject, in this sense, to uncertainty; nor is the prospect of a Victory bond being drawn. Or again, the expectation of life is only slightly uncertain. Even the weather is only moderately uncertain. The sense in which I am using the term is that in which the prospect of a European war is uncertain, or the price of copper and the rate of interest twenty years hence, or the obsolescence of a new invention, or the position of private wealth owners in the social system in 1970. About these matters there is no scientific basis on which to form any calculable probability whatever. We simply do not know. Nevertheless, the necessity for action and for decision compels us as practical men to do our best to overlook this awkward fact and to behave exactly as we should if we had behind us a good Benthamite calculation of a series of prospective advantages and disadvantages, each multiplied by its appropriate probability waiting to be summed.
>
> (1937, pp. 213–214)

Uncertainty makes our decision processes complex and volatile and thereby can have an important impact on the demand for an investment. Since the level of investment and the rate of interest were determined largely by expectation, uncertainty would also matter to determine both the MEC and liquidity preference schedules. They tend to put less weight on the matters which are highly uncertain than the factors about which they "feel somewhat confident, even though they may be less decisively relevant to the issue than other facts about which our knowledge is vague and scanty" (Keynes, 1936, p. 33). This point reflects the current trend of mounting *financialization* in which uncertainties embedded in complex financial products are codified using sophisticated models and hence positively influence investors' confidence towards accepting excess financial leverages, which gradually leads to financial fragility.

The relevance of the heterodox view on interest and uncertainty to the modern financial architecture is to be deduced. An increased role of rentiers has been particularly noted along with its adverse consequences of *financialization*. Increased commoditization of complex financial products owing to the innovation of sophisticated financial modeling which helped reducing embedded uncertainty with these products apparently seemed to increased actors' favorable expectations about the future outcome. This in turn prompted actors to engage with financial speculation, leading to mounting levels of indebtedness and financial fragility.

4. Relevance of interest and uncertainty to the current financial world

The core issue to the prohibition of interest lies in the exploitation by money capitalists and/or the people being engaged in the financial industry. An opportunity to earn interest encourages economic agents to accumulate wealth and earn income even without engaging in productive activities. Accumulation of wealth through financial channels (particularly surplus and interest) other than the traditional means of production and exchange of commodity has resulted in the shift of the economic epicenter from industry to finance (Foster, 2007). As a consequence, the financial market has become the pace-setter of all markets as wealth effect, positive and negative, plays a crucial role in economic cycles, in which "gambling with analysis, advice, appraisal, advertising, and commission-charging becomes a major growth industry" (Dore, 2000, p. 6). More functionless investors who seem to exploit profit margins in the process of financial flows are growing.

The dominance of finance in the economy, especially in capitalist economies, began to grow at a noticeable scale in the final quarter of the twentieth century when industries in those economies faced tremendous competitive pressure from the rest of the world owing to the nascent pace of globalization. In response to this threat, firms started shifting their investment and operations from production to finance. Such a shift has helped the financial industry contribute a larger share to the GDP. Epstein and Power (2003) report that the rise of rentier income between the periods of the 1960s–1970s and the 1980s–1990s was tremendous. In the 1950s, profit earned by US financial corporations as a proportion of national income averaged 9.5 percent which rose to 45 percent in 2002 (Mukunda, 2014). Mukunda further reports that profits earned by finance and insurance industries accounted for 37 percent of the profit all other sectors combined in 2013. This means that more than one-third of dollars earned in the US economy go to the financial institutions. Including the financial activities of non-financial firms would make the estimation unbelievably high. In the 2000s, Ford's income from selling loans was more than its income from selling cars, while GE Capital generated approximately half of GE's total earnings (Mukunda, 2014). On the other hand, financial costs to non-financial firms increased manifold. Crotty (2005) shows that the payments to financial sectors in the form of interest, dividends and share buybacks by non-financial firms as a proportion to cash flow accounted for 20 percent in the 1960s, 30 percent in the 1970s and 75 percent in 1990. As the cycle goes on gearing up more financial activities and profit thereof, available funds for investment in tangible assets are drained from real to financial markets.

In contrast to the prohibition of interest, the core issue to the prohibition of (excess) uncertainty lies in the reality in which the future is not knowable by human beings. Frank Knight distinguishes between risk and uncertainty in which he defines risk as a future event that can be assigned a probability, whereas uncertainty cannot be quantified objectively. However, the innovation of sophisticated financial models has presumably attempted to turn entrepreneurs' uncertainty into risk. These models have been given enormous importance as objective, or at least objectifiable, measures of risk assessment tools. It seems that the current financial world has deliberately ignored the heterodox (post-Keynesian) view on the difficulty of dealing with fundamental uncertainty embedded in economic activities. Pacces (2010) argues that the neoclassical economic theory, including financial modeling, has traditionally neglected the Knightian distinction due to its mathematical intractability. This detour from the basic economic principles has repeatedly paved the way for an unsustainable rise of finance and the resulting financial crisis.

Recurrent financial crisis in the capitalistic system construes that crises in the financial markets are systemic in which investment is more or less exposed to fundamental uncertainty. An analysis of financial crises reveals that most waves of financial bubbles are the result of excessive risk-taking by lenders' optimism. Stiglitz (2012) argues that in the post Glass–Steagall era some banks have shouldered the amount of risk that they are practically unable to absorb. Similarly, Calomiris and Haber (2014) show that in the post-Second World War period banks in the worlds' most developed economies became excessively leveraged and maintained smaller amounts of low-risk assets. Financial and non-financial institutions were engaged heavily with the trading of toxic financial products such as financial derivatives, leading to excessive (or uncertain) risk exposures of enterprises.

We emphasize that the excessive risk-taking underlies the swings of mood – optimistic or occasionally opportunistic behavior – in decision-makers under the conditions of uncertainty. Intermediaries and brokers have taken packaging and repackaging of securities so far and ambiguously that the final investors could rarely trace the origin of cash flows on which payment on securities he/she holds depends. It is ultimately the cash flows generated by the investors or entrepreneurs who, as mentioned earlier, are subject to fundamental uncertainty. Pacces (2010) argues that wholesale investors accepted to finance banks dealing with securitization because they disregarded the uncertainty of the liquidity they were generating. Ostensibly sophisticated financial models, which were believed to predict flawlessly the default probability of entrepreneurs, helped boost investors' confidence in this particular regard. In reality, these models' predictive accuracy was proved to be illusionary rather than the representation of the real scenario. For instance, predictions sometimes appeared to be so unrealistic that the default rates for CDO tranches calculated by top rating agencies exceeded projections, on average, by 20,155 percent (Nelson and Katzenstein, 2014, p. 377). This proves that uncertainty cannot be treated like risk. Both Islamic and heterodox views issue strong cautionary notes for dealing with uncertainties whereas the new classical models increase investors' confidence and attract agents to embrace uncertainty to such an extent that they are financially unable to absorb it.

5. Challenges to Islamic and heterodox views

Modern capitalism, albeit its setbacks resulting from the excessive reliance on finance, throws serious challenge to the view which heterodox and Islamic economics endorse in regard to risk and uncertainty. Keynes (1936, p. 344) argues that "the owner of capital can obtain interest because capital is scarce . . . but there are no intrinsic reasons for the scarcity of capital." For Keynes, interest cannot be the price of financial capital because the rate of interest depends on the monetary supply and the demand which are based upon the income level and the liquidity preference of holders. Therefore, interest can be kept minimum, even zero at the extreme case, so far as a state of full employment is achieved.

However, it is worth noting that the scale of investment is not always promoted by a low rate of interest as assumed in the general theory. Despite the availability of sufficient funds, screening and monitoring activities by (functional) lenders and investors still matter in order to respond to the general uncertainty from which lenders suffer, and thereby contribute to the optimal allocation of risk funds. For banks as financial intermediaries, their nominal net profit from lending (particularly in the case of lending upon 'floating rate') is not affected by the change in the market reference rate as the funding rate for banks, so far as the spread margin as risk premium towards their borrowers remains unchanged and the loan exposure to them remains the same. In other words, banks' net profit from lending upon the floating rate is affected only if (i) banks consider their borrowers' lowered funding costs to reasonably lower their probability of default (to increase their probability of success), then banks are willing to increase the loan exposure towards their borrowers when risk-adjusted returns are expected to be increased; and (ii) the borrowers increase the demand of fund-raising for their investment. The above (i) is related to banks' subjective judgment of screening and monitoring, while the above (ii) depends on the borrowers' subjective sentiment of investment. Both are, by nature, arbitrarily determined.

Second, we should ask how a low rate of interest can attract the ultimate fund providers. In the Marxian tradition, the analysis of banking credit and interest is undertaken on the basis of Marx's approach such that stagnant (or idle) money is systematically generated in the course of industrial accumulation, transformed into interest-bearing capital by the credit system and returned to accumulation to receive a share of surplus value (Itoh and Lapavitsas, 1999, p. 61). The money capital accumulated through the sale of commodity capital as well as the hoard of temporarily idle money of the industrial and commercial capitalists (workers, the state or anyone else) are collected and centralized in the financial institutions, and transformed into potential money capital available to industrial capital (Fine and Saad-Filho, 2004). Needless to say, a lower (or zero) rate of interest would be less attractive to the idle money holders. Less money capital available to industrial capital would be less contributing to the capital accumulation for society. In respect to Marx's theory, the circulation of M-C-M' or M-M' in the interest-free mode where expected incomes are not pre-determined is considered slower than that in the capitalist mode where a certain interest margin is offered. On the one hand, Islamic principles are contributing to squeezing functionless financiers by giving them less opportunities of exploiting. Similarly, in the process of squeezing functionless financiers, the functional financiers who are expected to have the partner's strategy in participatory financing for incubating new industries are also possibly squeezed.

Islamic banks mobilize deposits on the basis of PLS agreement and to some extent on the basis of *wakalah* (agency) against pre-agreed service charges or agency fees. While sharing profit or loss arising on investments, they earn a return on their trading and leasing activities by dint of the risk and liability undertaken and adding value in real business activities (Ayub, 2007). We note the following threat and sanctions mechanisms which encourage prudent screening and monitoring in the Islamic mode of banking. First, *Shari'ah* rules are considered the cornerstone of Islamic financial products and services. If depositors or customers become aware that the products they have in their portfolios are not *Shari'ah* compliant, it would seriously undermine customer confidence in the Islamic bank concerned or, on a larger scale, in the Islamic financial services industry as a whole (Bhambra, 2007, pp. 204–5). Second, a conservative credit screening policy is pursued from the perspective of loss aversion. Risk-averse depositors will look for low-risk forms of financing, for instance, *murabaha* and other similar asset-backed financing. El-Gamal (2006) refers to what Islamic finance practitioners call 'displaced commercial risk'. This may arise if Islamic bank depositors suffer a loss compared to the conventional bank depositors and therefore withdraw their funds from the Islamic bank (El-Gamal, 2006, p. 155). A conservative credit screening policy is also pursued from the perspective of avoiding the risk. Third, strict practice of PLS principle is a rarity in Islamic banking operations and in most cases the return for the depositors is homogenous for all banks irrespective of their scales of profitability (Chong and Liu, 2009; Farook and Farooq, 2011, Zaher and Hassan, 2001).

It is highly likely that some Islamic banks are hesitant to share losses with their depositors maintaining their franchise value as prudent monitors to avoid the displaced commercial risk. Credit risk is similar to conventional banking, but credit risk management and recovery process are far more complicated in the Islamic banking system than in conventional banking (El Tiby, 2011). Unlike conventional banks, Islamic banks have to absorb not only the credit risk but also the risk associated with the compliance of Islamic *Shari'ah*, that is, *Shari'ah* risk. Accordingly, within the difference between the rates of profit received and profit paid (borrowing rate and lending rate, respectively, in conventional banking), Islamic banks need to reserve a cushion to absorb the unexpected loss and the transaction costs associated with the *Shari'ah* compliance to maintain the franchise value.

In parallel, we should note that under the prohibition of *gharar* and the PLS framework, it may have created a dilemma of the so-called *murabaha* syndrome leading to the financial disintermediation (particularly the drain of long-term funds) for hampering the potential of SMEs. Long-term growth may suffer as a result. Suzuki (2013) suggests that on the condition that the best effort to avoid the incompleteness of the contract is made, it should be acceptable, to an extent in which the associated uncertainty in *enterprises* can be shared and absorbed in the community through an adequate PLS agreement, to incubate small and medium enterprises in agricultural and industrial sectors (see Chapter 3 of this book). However, the issue on the acceptable or unacceptable level of *gharar* is still controversial. How Islamic financial institutions will tackle the *murabaha* syndrome while improving the financial intermediation to industrial potentials entails further argument (see Chapter 2 of this book).

As is argued earlier in this chapter, it is possible that the prohibition of *riba* makes it difficult to collect and centralize the temporarily idle money in order to transform it into potential money capital available to industrial capital. Çizakça (2011) laments that the difficulty of collecting deposits without offering interest results in the rise of Islamic banking dominated by merely *Shari'ah*-compliant asset-based financing including *murabaha* rather than by the dominance of profit-and-loss sharing *mudaraba* (trust-based contract) and *musharaka* (partnership/equity-based contract) that are developed by the divine rules prescribed in Islamic *Shari'ah*. However, the current PLS mode gives Islamic banks less incentives to assume equity-like financing along with higher credit risk. As Suzuki and Uddin (2014) point out, it is impractical to expect the acceleration of participatory financing without preserving much higher bank rent opportunities for Islamic banks to compensate for *Shari'ah* PLS risk. The dilemma in the Islamic mode of mobilizing financial resources can be analyzed from the Marxian political-economy view on money and credit.

From the Marxian political-economy perspective, capital is considered the sum total of social relations between capitalists and workers, but also the ceaseless movement of value in pursuit of self-expansion.

> The latter is best thought of as a circular flow; capital value starts as money, becomes material inputs for production through market purchases (means of production and labor power), turns into finished commodities through production, and returns to money (augmented by surplus value generated in production, i.e. profit) through sale of finished commodities.
>
> (Lapavitsas, 2003, p. 67)

In the trend of *financialization*, interest-bearing capital (IBC) as represented by the M-M' circuit where money stands apart from the production process is also considered the ceaseless movement of value in pursuit of self-expansion. On the other hand, IBC represents a claim on surplus value that has yet to be produced. In this light, since there can be no guarantee of production and appropriation of surplus value, it is hardly surprising that the financial sector should be capable of financing overproduction and generating spectacular speculative bubbles and equally spectacular crashes. Nor is it surprising that the possibility of fraud is ever present, even though 'fictitious capital' of this kind has become increasingly necessary for real accumulation (Fine and Saad-Filho, 2004).

If this Marxian view is held, it seems infeasible to eliminate the role of functionless financiers in the movement, while maintaining appropriate incentives to the functional financiers. Or, in other words, we cannot tame the spirit of *finan-cialization* without simply killing 'the golden goose' – the rentier; and at the same time, continuous *financialization* is engulfing the real economy.

Perhaps, this dilemma can rationalize the partnership strategy upon the PLS between industrial capitalists and money capitalists (fund providers) widely observed in Islamic finance. Islam does not allow rentier income from interest; rather it encourages profit-and-loss sharing financial contracts so that uncertainty involving with the future income is shared by contracting parties. However, it is a great challenge for Islamic banks and depositors to diversify and absorb the general uncertainty.

Under the recent trend of ugly neologisms – "*marketization plus financializa-tion*" (Dore, 2000; Dore, 2008; Dore, 2011), the orthodox and traditional con-ceptualization of the decision-making process under 'measurable' uncertainty or risk has gained a total domination of the subject. The post-Keynesian and hetero-dox view on the decision-making under 'unmeasurable' uncertainty *a la* Knight is nearly dead particularly among the practitioners in financial markets. Since the consequences of actions extend into the future, accurate forecasting is essential for making objectively rational choices. But in the real world, most choices take place under conditions of uncertainty. The screening and monitoring actors (the banks as lenders and the investors as fund providers) are working under condi-tions of uncertainty. This means that monitoring activities are not mechanical, and that they are intrinsically based on subjective judgments that are often extremely difficult. The fundamental implication of Keynes's uncertainty is that all economi-cally meaningful behavior derives from agents' efforts to protect themselves from uncertainty (Dymski, 1993). While the functional financiers who deal with vari-ous ranges of credit risk under conditions of uncertainty are required for our soci-ety, it makes sense of the emergence of the functionless financiers who pay their efforts to protect themselves from uncertainty. How can we expect the Islamic mode of financial intermediation to transcend this dilemma?

6 Concluding comments

In this chapter we have attempted to explain the economics of the Islamic prohi-bition of *riba* and *gharar* and the compatibility of this principle to the heterodox perspective on interest and uncertainty. Islam strictly forbids dealing with profits on loans irrespective of interest or usury. Severe punishment has been provisioned in the Islamic teaching for those who violate this principle. Since religion is a spiritual element of human life the benefits of complying with religious princi-ples cannot be objectively measured. Nevertheless, some implications of religious teaching should be reflected in our social and economic life. In this pursuit, we find the economics of Keynes and Marx compatible with the Islamic prohibition of interest and uncertainty.

Key rationale that underpins the interest-free argument lies in the prevention of exploitation. In a lending relationship, the person who is poor usually borrows (debtor) from the wealthy individuals or merchants (creditors). Since the debtor is already poor, the burden of extra payment would lead his financial position to further deterioration, perhaps entangling him in a vicious cycle of poverty. In contrast, the creditor who does not take part in any real activities would enjoy a pre-determined return just because of postponing his current consumption to the future. Can the ethics in the mode of interest-free lending including *musharaka*, *mudaraba* and *wakalah* avoid this cumbersome situation? This ethics may draw a prescription for modern capitalism where the lending relationship is dominated by the entrepreneurial class as debtor and the surplus depositors as creditors. Although the modern concept of entrepreneur-lender replaces the typical poor-rich relation in lending activities, the opportunity of exploitation remains in place. This opportunity has been analyzed from the context of the heterodox school. It is argued that the capitalist mode of production and distribution, as it stands today, relies heavily on financing activities leaving the real economy behind (crowding-out effect). This trend has paved the way for the emergence of a capitalist class which artificially attempts to make capital scarce and hence hikes exorbitant interest as its use-value, which according to the Keynesian school should not exist. Keynes, instead, argued as his philosophical speculation that interest rate at the minimum should be lower if it ensures full employment. Similarly, Marx finds capital to be a machine for exploitation (as well as an engine for the mode of capitalism). In exchange of supplying capital in the production system, capitalists exploit the surplus value produced by the working class, which according to Marx is opposite to the spirit of equality and social justice.

In a similar fashion, it is argued that modern capitalism has put tremendous effort to accurately model uncertainty using some probabilistic theories. Such an endeavor has undoubtedly created enormous opportunities for economic agents to profit from engaging with trading securities in the financial markets. In addition, such models at times provided regulators with greater legitimacy for their decisions although the tendency of commoditizing risk and uncertainty as well as sophistication of financial products created over-optimism about the financial markets and products. Over-optimism created by the innovation of financial products and risk management models facilitated the formation of bubbles. Eventual burst of a bubble in the past left a lot of scary marks in the economy including decline in consumer wealth and prolonged unemployment.

However, an interest-free world upon the PLS is not so easy to implement at a time where interest is embedded in every sphere of our economy. In this regard, attempts have also been made to highlight the challenges the interest-free school often faces in the context of the capitalistic mode of financing. Keynesian logic for a lower interest rate is very restrictive because the argument that a lower interest rate leads to higher investment as well as employment is conditional upon other economic variables. In the same token, the Islamic prohibition of interest suffers from a dilemma. For instance, the existence of uncertainty on the one hand and the non-existence of interest on the other make it difficult for Islamic financial institutions to mobilize deposits and expand loans. This has resulted in the concentration of Islamic *murabaha* financing instead of true PLS contracts. Some of these challenges and their possible explanations are discussed in detail in the following chapters.

Note

1 In the general theory, Keynes distinguishes the transactions, precautionary and speculative motives for holding money. Keynes wrote the demand for money as: $M = L_1(Y) + L_2(r)$, where L_1 is the liquidity function corresponding to and income Y and L_2 is the liquidity function of the rate of interest r. In this formulation L_1 reflected the transactions motive and L_2 the speculative motive (Minsky, 1975).

2 A critique to a naïve critique to *'murabaha' 'tawarruq'* syndrome

Mohammad Dulal Miah and Yasushi Suzuki

1. Introduction

Islamic banks are prohibited from dealing with interest (profits on loans) and excess uncertainty, the two dominant features embedded in conventional banking practices. Instead, the Islamic mode of banking is required to offer various financial products complying with *Shari'ah* principles. *Shari'ah* principles endorse a profit-and-loss sharing (PLS)-based mode of financing instead of interest-based loans. In particular, *musharaka* (participatory finance) and *mudaraba* (trust-based finance) are considered purely PLS-based financing. Under this financing paradigm, assets and liabilities of Islamic banks are integrated in the sense that borrowers share profits and losses with the banks which, in turn, share profits and losses with the depositors. There are other financial contracts permissible in Islam and are practiced by Islamic banks across the world. For example, *murabaha* (mark-up) financing is most popular among Islamic banks whereas *ijarah* (leasing), *bai bithman ajil* or *bai muajjal* (variant of *murabaha*), *bai salam* (forward sale contract), and *istisna* (commissioned or contract manufacturing) are also offered by Islamic banks. These products, although permitted in Islam, are, according to the classification by Çizakça (2011), the *Shari'ah*-compliant financing, rather than the purely *Shari'ah*-based financing.

Although many Islamic banks claim to invest and finance complying with Islamic principles, scholars however dissent in opinion as to whether Islamic banks are really Islamic. For instance, Chong and Liu (2009) comparing the deposit rates between Islamic and conventional banks conclude that the deposit of Islamic banks is not interest free (in passing, it is worth noting that Islamic banks offer *'hidah'* rate for *wadi'ah yad-dhomanah* (saving account holders, and 'indicative profit rate' for *mudharabah* saving account holders. We will discuss this issue later). Ariff and Rosly (2011) argue in the context of the Malaysian banking system that Islamic banking is not very different from conventional banking. Similarly, Aggarwal and Yousef (2000) and Khan (2010) contend that Islamic banking activities in most instances are still functionally indistinguishable from conventional banking. In the same token, Dusuki (2007) contends that the current practices of Islamic banking entail that this model of banking in reality is not different from conventional banking practices since the net result of Islamic banking operations is the same as that of conventional banking.

In contrast, Beck *et al.* (2013), drawing evidence from a large number of banks worldwide, find that Islamic banking activities are different from conventional banking although the difference is limited. They particularly show that the fee income, which they consider an indicator of difference, is higher for Islamic banks than the conventional banks. Similarly, Miah and Uddin (2017) find in the context of GCC countries that the operation of Islamic banks is different from the conventional banks. Salient features of Islamic banks that distinguish this model from the conventional banking model are also documented in many studies (see Metwally, 1997; Olson and Zoubi, 2008).

Critics of Islamic banking support their arguments drawing evidence from the analysis of investment patterns of Islamic banks. Suzuki *et al.* (2017) analyze income from different financing activities of Islamic banks of Malaysia, Indonesia, Pakistan, and Bangladesh. They find that although Islamic banks comply with *Shari'ah* principles their mode of investment is dominated by *murabaha* or mark-up lending which is close to conventional banks' lending. Similarly, Aggarwal and Yousef (2000) drawing evidence from a large number of banks find that *murabaha* and *ijara* constituted about 52 percent of the total financing of Islamic banks in 1994 which increased slightly to 56 percent in 1995. In contrast, *musharaka* and *mudaraba* combined 20 percent in 1994 which also increased slightly to 23 percent in 1995. Yousef (2004) provides relatively recent evidence on the concentration of mark-up financing of Islamic banks. His analysis shows that mark-up financing comprises 86 percent of the total financing of Islamic banks in the Middle East, 70 percent in East Asia, 92 percent in South Asia, and 56 percent in Sub-Saharan African countries.

In this chapter we aim to critically evaluate the naïve critic of *murabaha* concentration. In so doing we provide some recent data collected from the audited financial statements of banks in the GCC countries to check the status of *murabaha* concentration in the region. We then assess if there is any change in the financing pattern of Islamic banks over the years. Finally, we refute some criticisms aimed at *murabaha* concentration. We argue that the preference of Islamic banks for debt-like financing over the participatory mode of investment is a rational choice given the current financial set-up.

The chapter has been structured as follows: Section 2 briefly describes the *Shari'ah*-based and *Shari'ah*-compliant banking products. Section 3 highlights the *murabaha* concentration in the GCC countries whereas Section 4 critically evaluates the critics of *murabaha* concentration which is followed by a brief conclusion.

2. *Shari'ah*-based vs. *Shari'ah*-compliant banking products

Although the spirit of Islamic finance is rooted in the PLS mode of financing such as *musharaka* and *mudaraba* which are purely *Shari'ah*-based 'participatory' products, the evidence provided in the previous section shows that most Islamic banks prefer to deal with products which are akin to debt-like instruments. *Murabaha, ijarah, tawarruq, bai bithman ajil* (*bai muajjal*) are some examples which are not based on participatory financing but they comply with Islamic *Shari'ah*. We briefly describe the salient features of these products.

2.1 Shari'ah-*based products*

Musharaka: The Arabic root of the word *musharaka* is *shirkah* which means being a partner or sharing. In the Islamic banking context, *musharaka* refers to a joint partnership in which a bank and an entrepreneur join together for the purpose of a business. According to the general contract rule, all the necessary preconditions of a valid contract must be present. Partners contribute capital and manage the business jointly. Also, partners share profit according to a specific ratio, while the loss is shared according to the ratio of the contribution of capital.[1] It is to be noted that the ratio of profit for each partner must be determined in proportion to the actual profit earned by the business; hence, it is not allowed to fix a lump sum amount for any one of the partners, or any rate of profit tied up with his investment. Moreover, the contract will be void in the absence of a predetermined profit-sharing ratio.

Musharaka is an independent legal entity and the bank may terminate the joint venture gradually after a certain period of time or upon the fulfilment of certain conditions. According to the *musharaka* principles every partner has the right to take part in its management and to work for it. However, upon the consent of contracting partners, a single partner can take care of the *musharaka* on behalf of others. In such a case the sleeping partner shall be entitled to profit only to the extent of his investment, and the ratio of profit allocated to him should not exceed the ratio of his investment. However, if all the partners agree to work for the joint venture, each one of them shall be treated as the agent of the other in all matters of business. Any work done by one of them in the normal course of business shall be deemed as authorized by all partners.

There are two types of *musharaka* according to Islamic *Shari'ah*, *Shirkat-ul-Mulk* and *Shirkat-ul-Aqd*. In *Shirkat ul-Mulk*, partners are involved with joint partnerships of certain properties voluntarily (such as the purchase of an asset upon mutual agreement) or partners join in the venture automatically (in the case of inheritance). *Shirkat-ul-Aqd* on the other hand can literally be translated as a partnership effected by mutual contract or a joint commercial enterprise. The basis of joint partnerships can be capital (*Shirkat Ul-Mal*), expertise or labor (*Shirkat ul-a'mal*), or it can be based on credit such as purchasing at deferred price and selling at spot price (*Shirkat Ul-Wujuh*). Since it is purely a PLS-based contract, *musharaka* is considered an ideal alternative to interest-based financing.

Mudaraba: *Mudaraba* is also another type of PLS-based contract which can be translated as trust finance, profit sharing among trustees, and equity sharing and profit-sharing basis (Haron and Azmi, 2009). Kettell (2011) argues that the *mudaraba* contract is established as being permissible by the consensus of the Islamic scholars and is not based on primary sources of the *Shari'ah*.

In a *mudaraba* contract, one partner who provides the required funds is called '*rabb-ul-mal*' whereas the partner who is entrusted with the money and managing the business is known as the agent or '*mudarib*'. Although *mudaraba* seems to be similar to *musharaka*, Hasan (2014) points out differences between these two types of contracts. First, *mudaraba* is suitable for short-term projects or projects for specific purposes such as constructions whereas *musharaka* is based on equity participation in an ongoing business. Second, the profit-sharing ratio may have no relation with the loss sharing ratio in *mudaraba* whereas in *musharaka* the profit-and-loss sharing ratio can be identical. In *mudaraba*, the '*rabb-ul-mal*' provides the capital and only the '*mudarib*' participates in managing the business, whereas in *musharaka* all the parties provide capital and reserve the right to participate in management. Thus, the capital provider bears all the losses and the '*mudarib*' earns a profit share, if the project is profitable.

As the fund provider, the *rabb-ul-mal* may specify a particular business for the *mudarib* if the former is interested to invest in a particular business. If the *mudarib* agrees to participate in this particular business, the resulting *mudaraba* is called '*al-mudaraba al-muqayyadah*' (restricted *mudaraba*). But if the *rabb-ul-mal* leaves the option to *mudarib* to undertake whatever business he wishes, the *mudarib* shall be authorized to invest the money in any business he deems fit. This type of *mudaraba* is called '*al-mudaraba al-mutlaqah*' (unrestricted *mudaraba*).

Islamic banks most often use two-tier *mudaraba*. In the first-tier, the bank and the depositors agree on a *mudaraba* contract in which depositors supply the fund (*rabb-ul-mal*) and the bank acts as manager (*mudarib*). The depositors place their money in the bank without any guarantee that they would receive return of the principal. Like the ordinary *mudaraba* contract, the depositors bear any losses. Also, they share profits with the Islamic bank in accordance with a pre-agreed ratio. In the second-tier, the bank agrees with a customer or an entrepreneur to supply necessary funds (*rabb-ul-mal*) for projects which the entrepreneur would manage (*mudarib*). Here, the bank bears all the losses and shares profits resulting from the normal course of business according to a pre-agreed ratio. It reflects that in a two-tier *mudaraba*, the bank plays the role of an intermediary between depositors and customers. Banks bear all the losses in the second-tier contract which they must transfer to the depositors, though, in practice, the so-called displaced commercial risk discourages Islamic banks to fully transfer the losses to the investment account holders. Even if they could fully transfer all the losses, this may have an adverse effect on the deposit collection compared to the conventional banks. Thus, Islamic banks must ensure that investment portfolios are sufficiently diversified. Otherwise, Islamic banks are discouraged to be engaged as the owner of '*mudaraba*' capital.

2.2 Shari'ah-*compliant products*

Murabaha: Murabaha is the dominant mode of finance of Islamic banks across the world. The term '*murabaha*' refers to a particular kind of sale. Unlike ordinary sales, the seller in *murabaha* transactions discloses the real cost of the object offered for sale to the buyer and adds a certain profit above the cost price. Thus, *murabaha* is known as a mark-up sale. The mark-up may be a lump sum amount or may be based on a percentage. In *murabaha* transactions, the buyer can make the payment at spot or at a subsequent date agreed upon by the parties. Islamic banks should not charge differently if the payment is made spot or any time in the future.

There is a serious debate as to whether *murabaha* or mark-up transaction really complies with Islamic principle. The debate stems from the fact that the mark-up or the extra charge above the cost price is pre-fixed which is akin to conventional bank lending. Since the profit earned from *murabaha* is certain and pre-fixed, some Islamic economists criticize that *murabaha* is simply a conventional banking product in the guise of the Islamic name.

In a traditional *murabaha* transaction the buyer (customer) usually asks a seller (bank) to buy a particular product which the former promises to buy from the latter at a certain mark-up price. *Shari'ah* scholars consider this an invitation to do business together (Kettell, 2011). Upon the request from a prospective buyer, the seller (bank) locates the product according to the specification and possesses the legal title of the product. The bank then sells this product finally to the customer at a mark-up price. In this commercial transaction of Islamic banks, profits are made from sales. Whereas 'profits on loans' are unlawful, 'profits on sales' are allowed. Thus, *murabaha*, even if it is sometimes ambiguous whether it is falling into the PLS scheme, is considered a *Shari'ah*-compliant product.

However, *murabaha* transactions should satisfy certain conditions to be a *Shari'ah*-compliant product. Salient among them are as follows. The subject which is to be sold should exist at the time of sale which implies that transactions for any goods to be produced in the future are not permissible. Moreover, the bank must own the subject and take constructive (title) or actual possession of the good before selling it to the customer. The sale transaction must be instant and absolute and the subject of sale must be a property of value which means that money cannot be exchanged for money; exchange should be either commodity for commodity or commodity for money. In addition, the delivery of the sold commodity to the buyer must be certain and should not depend on a contingency or chance.

Hasan (2014) contends that the *murabaha* contract does not defy the *Shari'ah* norms. However, Islamic scholars sometimes question this mode of contract because of its overuse. Although *murabaha* is a *Shari'ah*-compliant transaction, it contributes less to the purpose for which PLS-based 'participatory' finance is designed and instructed. For instance, *musharaka* and *mudaraba* create real economic value through creating a joint venture for a certain specific purpose or a project whereas *murabaha* mostly takes ownership of an existing asset and hence contributes less to the value addition in an economy compared to *mudaraba* and *musharaka* contracts. This proposition, however, does not sufficiently consider the possibility that *murabaha* would contribute to economic value addition by helping the manufacturers buy the raw materials for their products.

Also, there are other issues which are at the centre of debate. For instance, how to decide mark-up amount or percentage? How high or low should it be?

Charging less or more may hurt the business of Islamic banks as in most cases they are competing with conventional banks. Presumably, Islamic bank managers are concerned about (i) the cost of fund and (ii) the expected margin of profits.

Tawarruq: *Tawarruq* is a reverse *murabaha*. In this contract, the buyer buys an asset from a seller (usually from a bank) at a cost-plus basis on a deferred payment system (*murabaha* contract). The buyer then sells the same asset to a third party (a bank usually manages the sale) on a cash basis. Thus, *tawaruuq* is called reverse *murabaha*. The buyer basically borrows the cash needed to make the initial purchase. Later, when he secures the cash from the second transaction, the buyer pays the original seller the instalment or lump sum payment he owes. This sort of transaction is somewhat controversial because the intention of the commodity purchases isn't for the buyer's use or ownership. Some scholars believe that the transaction isn't *Shari'ah*-compliant.

Bai bithman ajil: *Bai bithman ajil* (BBA) is also a popular product of Islamic banks particularly for long-term needs of clients. BBA, whereby the payment is on deferred terms and *musharakah mutanaqisah* or diminishing partnership (DP), dominates home financing contracts in Malaysia. For BBA contracts, before the bank can sell the asset (a house) from the customer, the bank has to either purchase the asset from the customer (*bay' al-'inah*) or enter into a novation agreement with the customer and the developer. Under the DP, the bank and the customer jointly own the asset and the bank will allow customers to buy out the bank's share in the asset progressively. In some countries such as Bangladesh and Pakistan, BBA is known as *bai muajjal*. Under this contract the seller earns a profit margin on his purchase price and allows the buyer to pay the price of the commodity at a future date in a lump sum or in instalments. He has to mention expressly the cost of the commodity. The margin of profit is mutually agreed upon. BBA is valid if the due date of payment is fixed in an unambiguous manner and can be fixed either with reference to a particular date or by specifying a period, but it cannot be fixed with reference to a future event the exact date of which is unknown or is uncertain.

3. *Murabaha* concentration of Islamic banks

As mentioned previously in the chapter, there are some products which are equity-like 'participatory' financing while some products are 'debt-like' financing. It is practically difficult to collect segregated data on financing and investing patterns of Islamic banks due to differences in reporting style. As a consequence, existing literature cannot provide convincing aggregate data compiled from a sizable number of banks. Here we have attempted to collect data pertaining to financing pattern of Islamic banks in various countries.

First, we have examined the financing and investment pattern of Islamic banks of GCC countries going through their audited financial statements. As expected, the reporting style varies among banks. Some banks do not segregate data according to financing pattern or investment types such as *murabaha, mudaraba, musharaka, istisna, ijara* etc. We have checked almost all the retail Islamic banks of

GCC countries. Then we have examined financing types shown in the balance sheet of banks as well as income from different financing sources for the financial year 2015 and 2016. We offer only comparative analysis to avoid the currency conversion problem because almost all the banks use their local currency as reporting currency except a few banks which use international currency. We have tried to reduce the financing categories to widely practiced terms such as *mudaraba*, *musharaka*, *murabaha* (in few instances, *mutajara* is included in *murabaha*), and *ijara*. The rest are grouped as 'others' which includes BBA (*bai muajjal*), *tawarruq*, *bai salam*, *istisna*, *wakala*, and other Islamic financial products. Table 2.1 and Table 2.2 depict the overall picture.

It is evident from the data that Islamic banks in GCC countries are comfortable in dealing with *Shari'ah*-compliant products instead of *Shari'ah*-based products. Financing in *Shari'ah*-based products averaged only 5 percent of the total finance extended by GCC Islamic banks in 2015 which remained almost the same in 2016. Few among the sample banks did not report any amount in the *musharaka* and *mudaraba* categories either because they did not finance based on *musharaka* and *mudaraba* principles or the amount was too small to report separately.

Based on our reported data, Islamic banks of Bahrain seem to be the leader of *Shari'ah*-based financing in the GCC countries. Bank Al Salam tops the list having 37 percent share of PLS finance in 2016. Al Baraka Islamic Banks and Bahrain Islamic Banks rank second and third, respectively, in the list.

Among the debt-like finance, *murabaha* dominates the list. In 2016, the *murabaha* mode of financing averaged more than 55 percent of the total financing of Islamic banks in GCC countries. The maximum percentage of this particular category accounts for about 90 percent of the total finance in Khaleeji Commercial Banks. Al Rajhi Bank was the least provider of *murabaha* finance in 2016 (25.84 percent). *Murabaha* and *ijara* combined accounts for on average 87 percent of the total financing of these banks. There is however no apparent difference in 2015 and 2016.

We also report data of the income share of Islamic banking (in Table 2.2) in commensuration with the financing pattern reported in Table 2.1. The matching of data reported in both tables indicates the accuracy of the calculation. Income data shows that the share of *Shari'ah*-based income accounted for little more than 5 percent of total income of sample banks. In contrast, the share of *murabaha* accounts for 56 percent of banks' total income in 2016, a slight increase from 2015. As expected, *ijara* is the second major source of income for banks after *murabaha*. *Murabaha* and *ijara* combined 50 percent at the minimum and 100 percent at the maximum of the total income of the sample banks (see Table 2.2).

The concentration of debt-like financing of Islamic banks in GCC countries is not a stand-alone case but rather it is a common phenomenon of Islamic banks everywhere. We collect data from the literature to examine the financial structure of Islamic banks in four Muslim-dominant countries: Bangladesh, Pakistan, Indonesia, and Malaysia (see Tables 2.3 and 2.4). Like dual banking systems in other countries, Islamic finance contributes a significant portion to meet the total

Table 2.1 Lending (financing) structures of Islamic banks (as percentage of total financing)

Bank	2016				2015			
	Mudaraba and musharaka	Murabaha	Ijara	Others	Mudaraba and musharaka	Murabaha	Ijara	Others
KSA								
Bank Al Bilad	3.36	61.65	34.99	0.00	5.65	60.25	34.10	0.00
Al Rajhi Bank	0.00	25.84	73.96	0.20	0.00	23.23	76.61	0.17
UAE								
Abu Dhabi Islamic Bank	1.11	57.45	41.07	0.37	1.19	59.25	39.09	0.47
Sharjah Islamic Bank	0.82	29.79	63.43	5.96	0.86	34.36	60.85	3.93
Emirates Islamic Bank	0.21	59.41	31.79	8.59	0.42	61.56	30.79	7.24
Ajman Bank	0.00	42.33	57.22	0.46	0.00	43.93	55.67	0.40
Bahrain								
Khaleeji Commercial	2.65	89.49	0.00	7.86	7.10	83.35	0.00	9.55
Al Baraka Islamic Bank	22.51	42.85	19.84	14.81	14.24	49.65	24.59	11.52
Kuwait Finance House Bahrain	0.05	44.63	55.32	0.00	0.16	44.85	54.99	0.00
Ithmar Bank	5.61	79.05	0.00	15.34	4.05	80.45	0.00	15.51
Bahrain Islamic Bank	15.94	60.71	23.34	0.00	17.03	61.02	21.95	0.00
Al Salam Bank Bahrain	37.31	34.62	28.06	0.00	38.08	37.92	24.01	0.00
Kuwait								
Warba Bank	0.00	83.78	16.05	0.18	0.00	75.30	24.42	0.28
Kuwait International Bank	0.00	32.88	16.39	50.73*	0.00	33.74	17.00	49.25*
Qatar								
Qatar International Islamic Bank	0.76	68.47	21.83	8.95	1.00	71.84	19.20	7.96
Qatar Development Bank	0.00	54.67	44.26	1.07	0.00	61.21	37.35	1.44
Qatar Islamic Bank	0.59	62.46	19.53	17.42	0.64	63.41	19.23	16.72
Barwa Bank	0.00	68.92	22.69	8.39	0.00	71.64	16.39	11.97
Average	5.05	55.50	31.65	5.27	5.02	56.50	30.90	5.13
Minimum	0.00	25.84	0.00	0.00	0.00	23.23	0.00	0.00
Maximum	37.31	89.49	73.96	17.42	38.08	83.35	76.61	16.72

Source: authors' calculation based on the audited financial statements of banks

* Since *murabaha* and *wakala* are reported separately in the balance sheet, we have included *wakala* in 'others' category

Note: there are two banks in Oman. However neither of them segregates data according to financing or investment patterns

Table 2.2 Financing income of Islamic banks (as percentage of total financing income)

Bank	2016				2015			
	Mudaraba and musharaka	Murabaha	Ijara	Others	Mudaraba and musharaka	Murabaha	Ijara	Others
KSA								
Bank Al Bilad	4.15	65.80	30.05	0.00	5.70	58.60	35.70	0.00
Al Rajhi Bank	0.00	28.86	70.52	0.62	0.00	22.33	77.12	0.55
UAE								
Abu Dhabi Islamic Bank	1.10	58.99	39.71	0.19	1.09	59.90	38.80	0.20
Sharjah Islamic Bank	0.00	33.55	62.90	3.55	0.00	34.63	62.02	3.35
Noor Islamic Bank	0.00	72.25	14.98	12.77	0.00	72.99	17.30	9.70
Emirates Islamic Bank	0.24	56.01	28.57	15.19	0.29	59.26	29.92	10.53
Ajman Bank	7.61	44.17	47.54	0.68	9.39	44.72	44.14	1.75
Al Hilal Bank	5.30	76.59	17.80	0.31	4.03	79.22	16.47	0.29
Bahrain								
Bahrain Islamic Bank	18.24	58.32	23.44	0.00	20.31	59.56	20.13	0.00
Al Salam Bank Bahrain	35.16	33.13	25.82	5.89	30.68	26.06	23.73	19.53
Al Baraka Banking Group	9.25	79.44	9.95	1.37	7.90	80.79	9.84	1.47
Kuwait								
Kuwait International Bank	0.00	37.88	16.72	45.40	0.00	43.30	17.07	39.63
Qatar								
Qatar International Islamic Bank	1.09	72.96	23.56	2.39	1.37	72.98	24.22	1.43
Qatar Islamic Bank	0.57	57.21	19.11	23.11	0.70	50.60	20.83	27.87
Barwa Bank	0.00	60.96	22.68	16.36	0.00	59.74	15.53	24.73
Average	5.51	55.74	30.22	8.52	5.43	54.98	30.19	9.40
Minimum	0.00	28.86	9.95	0.00	0.00	22.33	9.84	0.00
Maximum	35.16	79.44	70.52	45.40	30.68	80.79	77.12	39.63

Table 2.3 Income from *murabaha* (in percentage) of different Islamic banks in Bangladesh and Indonesia

Bank	Year				
	2011	2012	2013	2014	2015
Bangladesh					
Islami Bank Bangladesh Ltd.	58.20 (4.13)	58.68 (3.78)	59.18 (4.18)	60.02 (2.98)	58.56 (2.64)
First Security Islami Bank Ltd.	75.22 (0.00)	75.22 (0.00)	73.60 (0.00)	75.05 (0.00)	73.31 (0.00)
Export Import Bank of Bangladesh Ltd.	19.79 (0.00)	19.77 (0.21)	18.57 (0.66)	16.67 (1.10)	14.01 (1.38)
Shahjalal Islami Bank Ltd.	15.63 (0.00)	17.10 (0.00)	15.97 (0.05)	11.63 (0.10)	9.44 (0.00)
Social Islami Bank Ltd.	6.03 (0.42)	4.63 (0.41)	3.49 (0.67)	1.80 (2.26)	1.27 (1.89)
Al-Arafah Islami Bank Ltd.	25.66 (0.00)	15.93 (0.00)	11.56 (0.00)	10.75 (0.00)	8.06 (0.00)
Union Bank Ltd.	NE	NE	24.16 (0.00)	64.07 (5.75)	63.70 (15.73)
Indonesia					
PT. Bank Syariah Mandiri	58.00 (32.00)	66.00 (26.00)	69.39 (22.95)	69.83 (20.11)	64.29 (21.01)
PT. Bank Muamalat Indonesia	47.00 (43.00)	48.00 (42.00)	46.32 (45.09)	44.66 (45.82)	43.15 (47.29)
PT. Bank Mega Syariah Indonesia	88.00 (2.00)	85.00 (0.00)	89.47 (0.20)	93.40 (0.34)	92.46 (0.56)
PT. Bank Rakyat Indonesia Syariah	59.00 (16.00)	66.00 (18.00)	65.39 (23.04)	65.04 (24.39)	60.27 (26.48)
PT. Bank Negara Indonesia Syariah	51.00 (13.00)	56.00 (13.00)	64.05 (12.92)	71.58 (11.62)	72.20 (12.69)
PT. Bank Central Asia Syariah	31.00 (14.00)	36.00 (27.00)	42.99 (50.84)	47.75 (46.99)	48.96 (45.86)

Source: Created by authors based on Suzuki, Uddin and Pramono (2018)

Note: figures in parentheses represent the income from profit-and-loss sharing *mudaraba* and *musharaka*. NE stands for 'not established'

Table 2.4 Income share of *murabaha* of Islamic banks in Malaysia and Pakistan (data in parenthesis shows income from PLS-based financing)

Bank	Year				
	2008	2009	2010	2011	2012
Malaysia					
Bank Islam Malaysia Berhad	55.26 (0.08)	69.08 (0.08)	59.66 (0.04)	59.66 (0.04)	59.10 (0.04)
Bank Muamalat Malaysia Berhad	41.57 (0.07)	36.47 (0.21)	40.46 (0.41)	41.67 (0.31)	49.43 (0.00)
Al Rajhi Banking and Investment Corporation (Malaysia) Berhad	99.88 (0.00)	99.90 (0.00)	99.91 (0.00)	99.90 (0.00)	99.93 (0.00)
Pakistan					
Al Baraka Bank Pakistan	72.06 (11.31)	78.92 (8.55)	55.89 (17.70)	56.90 (16.43)	48.05 (19.54)
Bank Islami Pakistan	35.34 (31.99)	30.89 (34.37)	40.41 (35.93)	31.00 (38.33)	27.03 (26.10)
Burj Bank Ltd. Pakistan	42.86 (38.57)	30.42 (45.12)	51.91 (34.01)	53.68 (34.64)	29.88 (26.98)
Dubai Islamic Bank Pakistan Ltd.	13.96 (6.45)	11.59 (6.82)	13.01 (1.58)	11.81 (1.38)	13.72 (1.62)
Meezan Bank Pakistan	35.70 (19.70)	35.63 (17.23)	33.28 (12.15)	27.00 (10.93)	21.36 (0.07)

Source: adapted from Suzuki *et al.* (2017)

financing needs in these four countries. The existing financing pattern of Islamic banks in the sample countries clearly exhibits the concentration of *murabaha* financing. For instance, major income of Islamic banks in Bangladesh comes from the asset-based financing. Only one of the reported banks has been engaged in profit-and-loss sharing modes although the percentage is insignificant (less than 5 percent during the period under study). This phenomenon reflects a pure dominance of *murabaha* financing.

Contrasting to the scenario in Bangladesh, Islamic banks in Indonesia and Pakistan engage with the PLS mode at a larger extent. However, the dominance of the *murabaha* mode is still prevalent in both countries, as it reflects in the percentage of income in most of the reported banks under each case. Thus, the lending patterns of the Islamic banks in each of the countries can be linked to their respective performance indicators. However, a point to note is that Islamic banks in Indonesia and Malaysia contribute to *musharaka* modes of investment which is seriously skewed towards real estate financing (diminishing *musharaka*) and cannot be considered pure 'participatory' PLS investment.

The financing pattern of Islamic banks in Malaysia deviates from that of Indonesia and Pakistan but conforms to the financing pattern of Bangladesh. For instance, Islamic banks in Malaysia are significantly engaged in sales-based transactions, especially *murabaha* and *bai bithaman ajil* even though Malaysia is recognized as one of the pioneering countries where the development of Islamic finance and banking has been prevalent since 1983. The country has placed itself in a position to be considered an Islamic financial hub in the international financial market.

Not only that the *murabaha* concentration is universal for Islamic banks but also there is no sign of change in this trend. Referring to Aggarwal and Yousef (2000) we have shown that *murabaha* and *ijara* constituted about 52 percent of the total financing of Islamic banks in 1994 compared to *musharaka* and *mudaraba* which combined 20 percent. Also, Yousef (2004) shows that mark-up financing of Islamic banks constituted 86 percent in the Middle East, 70 percent in East Asia, and 92 percent in South Asia. Our analysis of data proves that there is no apparent change of *murabaha* concentration in the last 25 years or so. In some countries however the concentration has intensified further.

4. Critic on the naïve critics of *murabaha* concentration

Because of excessive concentration on *murabaha* mode of finance, Islamic banking and finance has received enormous criticism in this particular regard. However, critics are neither specific about the rational of this concentration nor do they offer a thorough analysis of its remedies. Obviously, some criticisms which aim at clarifying the theological foundation of Islamic banks (Choudhury, 2007; Kuran, 1996; El-Gamal, 2006) deserve more attention. Kuran (1996) argues that the question of Islamic financing is not about whether it can increase productivity or economic performance but rather Muslim attempts to adopt Islamic financial models in their economic lives as a means of protecting their cultural identity which underlies their moral sentiment. Kuran further argues that Islamic finance is a costly alternative to conventional banking. Historical roots of Islamic finance, on which Kuran recourses for this conclusion, may prove him correct. But, over the years Islamic financial institutions have come out of this moral tradition and successfully competed in terms of productivity and performance with the conventional banks. Rapid expansion of Islamic banking and finance does not endorse the 'moral view' that the clients and customers of Islamic banks are driven merely by moral sentiment rather than economic rationales. Productive efficiency and financial stability of Islamic banks are widely documented in the existing literature (see for example, Khan and Mirakhor, 1987; Siddiqui, 2001; Beck *et al.*, 2013; Miah and Sharmeen, 2015). The embedded benefits of efficiency and stability may offset the cost disadvantage of *Shari'ah*-compliance model even if repetitive transactions are required for a single contract, as it currently practiced.

Chong and Liu (2009) compare the changes in interest rate of Islamic banks in response to the changes in interest rate of conventional banks and find that changes in conventional deposit rates cause Islamic investment rates to change (not *vice versa*). Based on this evidence they conclude that Islamic deposits are not interest free, but are closely pegged to conventional deposits. This conclusion is flawed indeed.

The fact that the Islamic deposit rate follows the conventional deposit rate does not invalidate the proposition that Islamic deposits are based on profit-and-loss sharing (PLS). Although we should observe, in general, a non-stationary pattern of deposit rate pertaining to Islamic banks, there may have strategies to neutralize the fluctuation. Usually, Islamic banks offer '*hidah*' rate for *wadi'ah yad-dhomanah* (saving account) holders, and 'indicative profit rate' for *mudaraba* saving account holders. The point is whether or not the rate is legally predetermined and committed. The *hidah* rate and indicative profit rate are, in practice, quoted by Islamic banks, but legally not committed to pay. The deposit of Islamic banks is not interest free in a sense that they are not offering any return. At the same time, the deposit of Islamic banks is interest free in a sense that they do not have any legal obligation to pay any predetermined rate of deposit under the PLS agreement.

As argued before, most investments of Islamic banks take place in the form of cost-plus pricing. Islamic banks face a problem as to what should be proper magnitude of mark-up. If the mark-up is set too high, banks may suffer from lack of borrowers whereas too low rate would cause a negative impact on the profit of banks. Islamic banks can avoid the dilemma by improving the credit risk management (by engaging in the repeated transactions of the same type of asset-based financing) or by reducing the cost of fund. Since major funding source for banks is deposit, a strategy to reduce the cost of fund means to reduce the return on deposit which in turn, can be associated with decline in deposit of Islamic banks. This scenario entails that Islamic banks are forced by the competitive financial markets to pair their rates to conventional banks mechanized through profit equalization reserves (PER). In this sense, it is rational that the rate paid on Islamic banks deposit should have a positive relationship with the conventional banks.

However, the concentration of debt-like instrument including *murabaha* and *ijara* in the Islamic banking system is a proven fact. As a result, many scholars conclude that Islamic banks are not different from conventional banks. For instance, Ariff and Rosly (2011) argue that most of the products and services of Islamic banks *mimic* those of conventional banks and operate with interest in a disguised form. Similarly, Kuran (1996, p. 441) notes that although Islamic banks claim to be interest free in their operation, the deposit-taking and lending operations of these banks tend to be based on interest but Islamic banks disguise this fact through "the use of terms like 'markup' and 'commission' to designate what is tantamount to pure interest". In the same token, Khan (2010) notes that Islamic banks offer similar services to conventional banks except the fact that conventional banking terminology are replaced by Arabic terms.

Rosly and Bakar (2003) are also critical to the contemporary practices of Islamic banks. They judge Islamic banking through the lens of morality and argue that major Islamic banking products including *murabaha* and *ijara* resemble to interest-based financing and thus can be regarded as immoral. Hamoudi (2007) echoes the same critical tone and argues that the failures of Islamic finance which have led to the creation of a bizarre and highly artificial construct that does nothing to address the social concerns that are the central reason for the creation of Islamic banking and finance. Similarly, El-Gamal (2006) regards the existing practices of Islamic banks as '*Shari'ah* arbitrage' because, for El-Gamal, conventional lending practices are replicated in Islamically acceptable ways in the balance sheets of Islamic financial institutions. He further maintains that the Islamic finance industry has degenerated into one that is dominated by form over substance.

Although some of these criticisms are ill-founded or misdirected, the proposition to be endorsed universally for Islamic banking and finance is that debt-based instruments, despite gaining approval from *Shari'ah* scholars, should be kept as minimum as possible. At the same time, the number of equity-like contracts should be gradually increased if the overall social welfare objectives as envisioned in Islamic economics are to be realized.

We would feel it difficult to simply accept the perspective of Islamic 'perfectionist' economists concerning the '*murabaha*' concentration. Bakar (2016) gives a warning that Islamic economists advocate 'wealth distribution' while forgetting a much more important element, which is 'wealth creation'. We should cast doubt on the naïve conclusion reached by Islamic economists that equity-like 'participatory' financing be prioritized over debt-like financing upon the assumption that *mudaraba* and *musharaka* financing can be provided on a large scale without affecting the capital adequacy requirement. For instance, participatory financing of Islamic banks is risker than the debt-like financing which implies that an increase in this mode of finance is likely to increase risk-weighted assets at a higher percentage. This literally translates that Islamic banks which have substantial share in the participatory mode of investment would be required to maintain higher amount as statutory reserve. Since banks are not earning any return on statutory deposit but pay profit to depositors, the overall cost of banks tends to rise. Thus, under a regulatory environment in which Islamic and conventional banks have to maintain a fixed capital adequacy ratio, it is a rational move for Islamic banks not to dedicate too high of an amount to the participatory mode of finance.

Another question is: How feasible it is to achieve these socio-economic objectives through Islamic financing under the contemporary Islamic episte- mological foundation as well as financial set-up? The concurrent interpretation of Islamic epistemology does not convincingly clear an apparent paradox gener- ated by Islamic financing principles. For instance, Islam encourages PLS-based financing. At the same time it prohibits associated uncertainty (*gharar*). An attempt to increase PLS financing implies embracing fundamental uncertainty of entrepreneurs. Critics, however, have paid much less attention to this funda- mental issue than it really deserves. We offer a detailed discussion on this issue in Chapter 4.

Moreover, the existing financial set-up is unfriendly to the PLS-based financing. In *mudaraba*, banks work as fund providers (*rabb-ul-mal*) whereas entrepreneurs manage the business (*mudarib*). In this relation, *rabb-ul-mal* should fully trust the *mudarib* with the fund at the latter's disposal. As discussed earlier, the parties share profit as per the predetermined ratio. However, in the case of any loss, the *rabb- ul-mal* is the one who bears all the financial losses whereas the *mudarib* accepts the loss of his labors. A severe agency problem persists in this relation. How should a bank ensure that the *mudarib* will work up to the expectation for making a project successful even though he does not bear any financial losses? In addition, absence of a financial loss sharing provision may prompt entrepreneurs to accept higher risk believing in the premise that he may materialize good return if the project is successful but will lose merely his labor in the case of failure. Of course, a tighter screening and monitoring regime can reduce the likelihood of shirking and moral hazard. Although the relevance of screening and monitoring is equally important for commercial lending, risk-taking incentives are different. Debt covenants may provide more protection to financiers than a simple *mudaraba/musharaka* con- tract as it stands today. Thus, debt-like contract instead of participatory financing is a rational choice for Islamic banks.

In the two-stage *mudaraba* contract, as mentioned earlier, banks work as inter- mediary between the entrepreneurs and the depositors. If there is any loss in the project undertaken by an entrepreneur, he will pass the financial loss to the bank which in turn transfers the loss to the depositors. Assume that an entrepreneur which is a legal entity (public limited company) or an already well-off entrepre- neur requests funds from Islamic banks under *mudaraba* contract for a new project. How far is it Islamically logical that a loss suffered by a well-off entrepreneur will be passed on to many small savers (*rabb-ul-mal*)? Such a project would socially and religiously not be so suitable. This is another hurdle for participatory financing.

The origin of these anomalies and contradictions can be attributed to the inabil- ity of Islamic epistemology in decoding properly the scripture of Islam (Qur'an). El-Gamal argues:

> most Quranic legal verses tend to be general in nature. . . . In the economic realm, the Quran orders believers to fulfill their contractual obligations. . . .

However, the Quran does not state clearly which contracts are valid, and thus must be kept, and which are invalidated and voided.

(2006, p. 27)

Legal content of the Qur'anic verses should be obtained through Prophetic Sunna, as well as juristic analyses. Classical Islamic jurisprudence should be properly analyzed to derive an explanation for resolving these issues. Only then we can expect the penetration of participatory Islamic finance.

5. Conclusion

In this chapter we have attempted to briefly describe the salient products of Islamic banks. While *mudaraba* and *musharaka* are equity-like PLS contracts, Islamic banks have shown their reluctance to these particular modes of financing. Although the existing literature concludes based on some anecdotal facts that Islamic banks' financing is seriously skewed towards debt-like contracts such as *murabaha* and *ijara*, the literature provides less persuasive data supporting this claim. The reason can be attributed to the difference in the reporting style of Islamic banks. We have attempted to provide some empirical data on this issue from the Islamic banks of GCC countries; although the same reporting problem persists, we have been able to collect data from a sizable number of banks. Analysis of the data shows that financing of the sample Islamic banks is heavily concentrated on debt-like finance. More than nine-tenths of the total financing of Islamic banks are expanded in the form of *murabaha* and *ijara*. Accordingly, major income of these banks comes from these two financing sources. Furthermore, there is no change of this trend over the years.

Criticism against the concentration of debt-like financing has spawned recently. Some scholars have argued that the contemporary practice of Islamic banks is nothing but the surface change in which conventional banking terms are merely replaced by Arabic words. While the criticism against *murabaha* remains valid, the blanket assertion that Islamic banks are not really Islamic is invalid. The debt-like finance including *murabaha*, *ijara*, and *istisna* are not truly *Shari'ah*-based products but they are *Shari'ah*-compliant and Islamic.

Now the question is: Does the debt-like finance really uphold the spirit of Islamic finance? There is no simple answer for that. Among many purposes of Islamic finance, increase in efficiency and equity are at the core of classical Islamic jurisprudence. Because Islamic finance arranges multiple sales and purchase contracts for a single transaction which are subject to brokerage commissions and fees, the Islamic banking model is believed to be costlier than the conventional model. However, Islamic banks may have offset these adversaries through attaining internal efficiency and greater financial stability. Second, the criticism that debt-like finance does not contribute to the creation of economic value may not be necessarily true because Islamic banks through *murabaha* contracts help manufacturers and traders to acquire production equipment and inputs for their production process and hence create economic value.

Also, we like to say that the debt-like finance is ironically the logical consequence of the existing financial set-up under which Islamic banks operate. For instance, Islamic banks can capture a sizable amount of rent from expanding debt-like financing. This provides them with the less compelling evidence to engage in the participatory mode of financing including *mudaraba* and *musharaka*.

The solution to this problem, as many economists argue, hinges on the revival of substance-oriented Islamic jurisprudence. In addition, mechanisms are to be devised *ex ante* as safeguards against agency problems embedded in participatory finance. In practice, the current mode of PLS provides an idea of the difficulty of assuming equity-like 'participatory' financing. It is impractical to expect the acceleration of participatory financing without preserving much higher security margins to cover further PLS. *Shari'ah* scholars, the regulatory authorities, and other professionals need to design an appropriate financial architecture which can create socially acceptable levels of margin opportunities for Islamic banks, so that participatory financing may deal with fundamental uncertainty which should be socially diversified and absorbed under the concept of PLS.

Note

1 Opinions differ among four Imams of Islam in respect to distribution of profit. For instance, Imam Malik and Imam Shafi'i opine that profit of *musharaka* is to be shared according to the proportion of investment while Imam Ahmad ibn Hanbali views that it is the agreement between the partners not the investment that should dictate the profit ratio. Iman Abu Hanifah, on the other hand, argues that under normal circumstances, profit can be shared according to a pre-agreed ratio. However, the profit-sharing ratio of a sleeping partner cannot be more than the ratio of his investment. But in the case of loss, all the Muslim jurists are unanimous on the point that each partner shall suffer the loss exactly according to the ratio of his investment.

3 An inquiry into the scope of 'acceptable' *gharar*

Mohammad Hashim Kamali, Yasushi Suzuki and Mohammad Dulal Miah

1. Introduction

Avoiding *gharar* is one of the main principles of Islamic finance. The literal meaning of the word *gharar* is fraud (*al-khida'*), but in transactions the word has often been used to mean risk, uncertainty, and hazard. In a contract of sale the word *gharar* often refers to uncertainty, and the ignorance of one or both parties of the substance or attributes of the object of sale, or of doubt over this object's existence at the time of contract (Kamali, 2000, p. 84). *Gharar* is, however, a broad concept and may carry different shades of meanings in different kinds of transactions. In the Islamic mode of investment and financial intermediation, *gharar* is perceived in two dimensions; one refers to the lack of clarity in the terms and essence of the contract, the other refers to the uncertainty in the object of the contract (Ayub, 2007, pp. 59–60; El-Gamal, 2006, p. 58).

Complete contracting is intrinsically impossible. Therefore, some measure of uncertainty is always present in contracts. El-Gamal (2006, p. 58) notes that "jurists distinguished between major or excessive *gharar*, which invalidates contracts, and minor *gharar*, which is tolerated as a necessary evil." Also, the uncertainty in the object of the contract cannot be avoided in any business. "The problem, however, was that the extent of uncertainty making any transaction *haram* had not been clearly defined" (Ayub, 2007, p. 58). Ayub (2007) refers to *gharar-e-kathir* and *gharar qalil* (too much and nominal uncertainty) and agrees that only those transactions that involve too much or excessive uncertainty in respect to the subject matter should be prohibited. Al-Saati (2003) suggests that the *Hadith* (which prohibits *gharar*) does not intend to prohibit all *gharar*, but intends to prohibit *gharar* which can cause dispute and cannot be tolerated. Kamali (2000) insists that should there be a public good (*hajjat al-nas*) for it, *gharar*, even if excessive, will be ignored. This is because satisfying the people's need takes priority by virtue of the Qur'anic principle of removal of hardship (*raf' al-haraj*). Of course, depending on its scale and magnitude, *gharar* may render a contract totally null and void, or it may constitute a cause for indemnity and compensation (Kamali, 2000). This chapter aims to review, from a *trans-disciplinary* perspective, the scope of acceptable *gharar* which is still controversial in the academic debate. We follow the liberal position insisting that commercial transactions (*muamalat*) and contracts are permissible unless there is a clear injunction to the contrary of the *Shari'ah* norm.[1] Muslim jurists have held that the injunction which overrules the basic presumption of permissibility (*Ibahah*) must be decisive both in meaning and transmission (Kamali, 2000, p. 66). Upon the liberal view, we look at the first dimension of *gharar* – incompleteness of contracting from the viewpoint of New Institutional Economics, and the second dimension of *gharar* – uncertainty in the object of contracting from a post-Keynesian perspective. Drawing upon these economic perspectives, this chapter aims to propose a trans-disciplinary theoretical framework of making a contribution to the Islamic legal debate on the scope of acceptable *gharar*.

2. Incomplete contracting

The first dimension of *gharar* is related to incompleteness of contracting. In the Islamic mode of investment and financial intermediation, *jahl* – ignorance or non-clarity about the parties or their rights and obligations, the goods or the price – is considered a part of *gharar* (Ayub, 2007, p. 61). One should not undertake anything or any act blindly without sufficient knowledge, or risk oneself in adventure without knowing the outcome or the consequences (Ayub, 2007, p. 61). Kamali (2000) emphasizes that *gharar* can be summarized as occurring in four main ways. These are on account of uncertainty and risk pertaining to the existence of the subject matter of a sale, or its availability, uncertainty about the quantities involved and, lastly, uncertainty about time of completion and delivery (Kamali, 2000, p. 93).

The New Institutional Economics (NIE) and Transaction Cost Economics (TCE) have greatly contributed to building up a theoretical framework of how the incompleteness of contracting increase the 'transaction cost' of monitoring, resulting in the economic inefficiency (for instance, Arrow, 1974; North, 1981; North, 1990; North, 2005; Williamson, 1985). In their theoretical framework the transaction cost is defined as *the economic equivalent of friction in physical systems*. In the framework by Oliver Williamson, a Nobel laureate in economics, incomplete contracting often brings risks of 'opportunism'. In general, opportunism in terms of pursuing self-interest with guile involves subtle forms of deceit and refers to the incomplete or distorted disclosure of information, especially to calculated efforts to mislead, distort, disguise, obfuscate, or otherwise confuse (Williamson, 1985, p. 47). On the other hand, the TCE tells us that 'trust' may, not always but fairly often, play the role of *lubricant* for making the economic system run smoothly (Arrow, 1974, p. 23). In other words, risks of Williamsonian opportunism can be reduced by mutual trust. Trust is referred to as "attitudes and behaviour which indicate that each person is willing to rely on the other to act fairly and to take into account the other's welfare", as 'solidarity', and as "a belief in future harmonious affirmative cooperation". "Contract negotiations and performance will likely take place more effectively if trust is present and is generated by the process" (Cohen and Knetsch, 1992, p. 442). One of the invaluable insights of Kenneth Arrow, a Nobel laureate in economics, is to point out that trust has a large and measurable economic value and has an important bearing on economic organization. "Ethical elements enter in some measure into every contract; without them, no market could function. There is an element of trust in every transaction; typically, one object of value changes hands before the other one does" (Arrow, 1974, p. 24).

In the Islamic mode of investment, *Shari'ah* is considered the cornerstone of Islamic financial products and services. In theory, if all the concerned parties in the mode share a common belief in future harmonious affirmative cooperation (mutual trust) with *Shari'ah* compliance, the transaction cost of drafting and contracting would be very low, because it would be enough to insert a 'general clause' of promising to sincerely negotiate against any future event for mutual benefits. Arrow insists that the efficacy of alternative modes of contracting and monitoring would vary among cultures because of differences in trust. To some extent, cultural factors are related to the degree of trust relations. However, we would say that the degree of trust even in a particular culture or society could rather vary.

> Most of us operate in some middle realm where we admit social claims, sometimes forget about them for long stretches of time as we go about our daily private role, sometimes rise to an occasion, sometimes fall miserably short, as we assert our individuality in contexts that are not totally appropriate.
>
> (Arrow, 1974, p. 16)

Operationalizing trust, no matter how it is defined, has proved inordinately difficult (Williamson, 1985, p. 406).

From the Williamsonian opportunism perspective, we may say that the cooperative mode of economic organization, where trust and good intentions are generously imputed to the membership, has its weakness in being endowed with few organizational responses to the debilitating effects of opportunism. "Such organizations are easily invaded and exploited by agents who do not possess those qualities" (Williamson, 1985, pp. 64–65). Transactions that are subject to *ex post* opportunism will benefit if appropriate safeguards can be devised *ex ante* (Williamson, 1985, p. 48). We should note that, in other words, if safeguards are not sufficiently devised *ex ante*, opportunism would possibly emerge as a troublesome source of behavioural uncertainty in economic transactions. In our view, the first dimension of the prohibition of *gharar* in a context of encouraging the parties to pay best efforts to clarify the terms and essences of contracts in Islamic finance can be understood as an effective institutional setting for minimizing the occurrence of *ex post* opportunism.

3. Uncertainty from a post-Keynesian perspective

The second dimension of *gharar* is related to the fundamental uncertainty associated with investment and financial intermediation. As economies become more complex, it makes the screening and monitoring activities of investors and bank managers much more difficult. Fundamental uncertainty needs to be emphasized as a primary driver of this increase in complexity. Since the consequences of actions extend into the future, accurate forecasting is essential for making objectively rational choices. But in the real world, most choices take place under the condition of uncertainty. Keynes defined what he meant by 'uncertain knowledge':

> By uncertain knowledge, let me explain, I do not mean merely to distinguish what is known for certain from what is only probable. The game of roulette is not subject, in this sense, to uncertainty; nor is the prospect of a Victory bond being drawn. Or again, the expectation of life is only slightly uncertain. Even the weather is only moderately uncertain. The sense in which I am using the term is that in which the prospect of a European war is uncertain, or the price of copper and the rate of interest twenty years hence, or the obsolescence of a new invention, or the position of private wealth owners in the social system in 1970 [note: over 30 years later from the point in time of his writing]. About these matters there is no scientific basis on which to form any calculable probability whatever. We simply do not know. Nevertheless, the necessity for action and for decision compels us as practical men to do our best to overlook this awkward fact and to behave exactly as we should if we had behind us a good Benthamite calculation of a series of prospective advantages and disadvantages, each multiplied by its appropriate probability waiting to be summed.
>
> (Keynes, 1937, pp. 213–214)

The fundamental implication of Keynes's uncertainty is that all economically meaningful behaviour derives from agents' efforts to protect themselves from uncertainty (Dymski, 1993).

Frank Knight drew a famous distinction between 'measurable uncertainty' or 'risk', which may be represented by numerical probabilities and 'un-measurable uncertainty', which cannot (Knight, 1921). Numerical probabilities are in turn based on the possibility of repeated observation of an event that allows the calculation of a statistical probability for that event. In contrast, many events in the economic domain are not of this type. There is no repeated observation that can give us an objective probability for the success of an innovative process. Here, the risk involved is a subjective judgement, and this can vary across persons making the judgement based on their experience and knowledge of subtle and unquantifiable aspects of a situation. The formulation of subjective probability judgements is what Knight described as decision-making under uncertainty.

Knightian uncertainty, the same as Keynesian uncertainty, emerges when: (a) stochastic variation is not governed by stable probability distributions; (b) agents lack costless information providing insight into the true state of affairs in the economy; (c) agents cannot always determine the extent to which their own actions are responsible for the outcomes they experience; (d) it is impossible to preclude the possibility of systemic risk, because the economy has no parameters (see Dymski, 1993). Subjective probability can be distinguished from statistical or objective probability in the sense that uncertainty cannot be reduced to measurable risks.

Uncertainty may be more or less ignored or, alternatively, subjective probabilities may be applied, together with a risk premium to cover unspecified adverse events. Since there is no precise economic theory of how decisions are made under uncertainty, agents tend to observe each other's responses and do not deviate widely from the norm regarding which factors should be taken into account and how much weight should be assigned to them. But, "when the crowd is wrong *ex-post*, there is the making of a financial crisis" (Davis, 1995, p. 135).

Uncertainty makes the decision processes complex and volatile. Volatility stemming from lenders' (or investors') uncertainty, in particular, in terms of subjective probability in credit risk management, is a crucial factor contributing to the systemic fragility of financial markets. Uncertainty often encourages agents to adopt *rules of thumb* because standardization and coordination may be more effective than individual prediction (Simon, 1996, p. 42). However, such standardized *rules of thumb* can themselves become constraints on our decision-making: if they acquire the status of norms, they can reduce us to mere engines of procedural rationality. In international banking and credit operations, a codified assessment of credit risk in purely quantitative statistical terms (i.e. the quantification of credit risk upon the statistical expected default frequency or EDF provided by rating agencies) is now a widespread practice. The codified *rule of thumb* encourages lenders to measure expected credit losses mathematically and to maintain a capital buffer against unexpected credit losses. An important example of this paradoxical response to uncertainty is the gradual adoption of the Basel guidelines in international credit markets. Ironically, the convergence to standardized credit risk modelling creates a misleading homogenization of information flows and can contribute to undermine financial stability by amplifying herd behaviour in investment as was observed in the process of leading to the 2007–2008 US subprime loan crisis.

Although Islamic banks and financial institutions were not always immune to the subsequent 2008–2009 global crisis, they were to a considerable extent sheltered from the crisis. "Islamic finance institutions were better placed to weather the storm, receiving increasing interest from not only the Muslim community but also non-Muslim population around the world" (SESRIC, 2009, p. 3). SESRIC (2009) concludes that due to the prohibition of *gharar*, financing extended through the Islamic mode can expand only in line with the growth of the real economy and thereby help curb excessive credit expansion. "In this respect, the prohibition on *gharar* is often used to support the criticism of conventional financial practices such as short-selling, speculative trading, and derivatives" (SESRIC, 2009, pp. 5–6).

3.1 *Mudaraba*

In passing, we wish to refer to an Islamic financial form of '*mudaraba*'. *Mudaraba* is described as a special kind of *shirkah*[2] in which an investor or a group of investors provides capital to an agent or manager who has to trade with it; the profit is shared according to the pre-agreed proportion, while the loss has to be borne exclusively by the investor. The loss means a shortfall in the capital or investment of the financier. The loss of the agent (*mudarib*) is by way of expended time and effort, for which he will not be given any remuneration (Ayub, 2007). For the financier, in particular, the engagement in *mudaraba* is associated with higher risk and uncertainty. In the light of the principle of prohibition of *gharar*, how are the Islamic financial institutions allowed to be engaged in *mudaraba*?

Needless to say, though any ambiguity or ignorance regarding capital or ratio of profit makes the contract invalid, a number of sayings of the holy Prophet (pbuh) and reports by his Companions on the subject indicate that Islamic jurists are unanimous on the legitimacy of *mudaraba* (Ayub, 2007). The terms of the *mudaraba* contract offered by the Prophet's uncle Abbas were approved by the Prophet. Abu Musa, the governor of Kufa, wanted to remit public money to the Bayt al Mal. He gave the amount to Abdullah bin Umar and his brother, who traded with it. The Caliph's assembly treated it as an *ex post* factor *mudaraba* and took half of the profits earned by the two brothers, because the public money in their hands was not the loan. Caliph Umar also used to invest orphan's property on the basis of *mudaraba* (Ayub, 2007). Ayub (2007) points out that *mudaraba*, like other contracts, calls for lawful items of trade, failing which the contract will become void or voidable, as the case may be. Thus, a worker is not allowed to trade in wine or swine with the *mudaraba* capital. He suggests that the classical jurists generally restricted the use of *mudaraba* to the act of trade (buying/selling), but an overwhelming majority of contemporary jurists and scholars allow the use of *mudaraba* with a wider scope for use by Islamic banks as an alternative to interest-based financing.

While Islamic banks may hesitate to become *mudaraba* capital providers, there is little problem for them to assume as the *mudarib*. *Mudaraba* is a contract of fidelity and the *mudarib* is considered trustworthy with respect to the capital entrusted to him. He is not liable for the loss incurred in the normal course of business activities. As a corollary, he is liable for the property in his case as a result of the breach of trust, misconduct and negligence. A guarantee to return funds can be taken from him but can be enforced only in two situations: if he is negligent in the use of funds or if he breaches the stipulated conditions of *mudaraba*. Hence, his actions should be in consonance with the overall purpose of the contract and within the recognized and customary commercial practice (Ayub, 2007).

The issue is whether or not Islamic banks are allowed to assume as the financier of *mudaraba*. It is considered that the conversion of debt into a *mudaraba* is prohibited to safeguard against the abuse of usurious loan being camouflaged as a *mudaraba*, where, in essence, the financier would possibly ensure for himself not only the recovery of his debt but also an illegal return on his loan under the cover of his share in *mudaraba* profits (Ayub, 2007).

> *Mudaraba* business can be of two types: restricted and unrestricted *mudaraba*. If the finance provider specifies any particular business, the *mudarib* shall undertake business in that particular business only for items and conditions and the time set by the *rabbul-mal*. This is restricted *mudaraba*. But if the

Rabbul-mal has left it open for the *mudarib* to undertake any business he wishes, the *mudarib* shall be authorized \to invest the funds in any business he deems fit. This is called un-restricted *mudaraba*.

(Ayub, 2007: p. 324)

According to the majority of the traditional jurists,[3] a financier in *mudaraba* is not allowed to work for the joint business. He is not permitted to stipulate that he has a right to work with a *mudarib* and to be involved in selling and buying activities, or supplying and ordering. However, he has the right to oversee and ensure that the *mudarib* is doing his fiduciary duties honestly and efficiently (Ayub, 2007). In general, banks as depository corporations are expected to pay the best effort to protect general depositors' utility. In this context, it would make sense for banks to keep them away from the form of financing like *mudaraba*, at least, ostensibly associated with excess uncertainty, in which the financiers are allowed to retain only the limited scope of monitoring and controlling the borrowers including the *mudarib*. Should Islamic banks as depository corporation be discouraged to be engaged in *mudaraba* to comply with the principle of prohibition of *gharar*?

Now, we look at Keynes's concept of 'animal spirits' pointing out that while objective calculations of 'risk' were not possible for investments, he also rejected the idea that investments or stock markets were entirely based on mass irrational psychology. The bridge between the two was his concept of 'animal spirits'. Apparently, Keynes distinguished *enterprise* from *speculation*. "It is safe to say that enterprise which depends on hopes stretching into the future benefits the community as whole" (Keynes, 1936, p. 162).

But individual initiative will only be adequate when reasonable calculation is supplemented and supported by animal spirits, so that the thought of ultimate loss which often overtakes pioneers, as experience undoubtedly tell us and them, is put aside as healthy man puts aside the expectation of death.

(Keynes, 1936, p. 162)

Stock markets and investments more generally required 'animal spirits' in individual initiatives that supplemented and supported reasonable calculations of risk. If prevailing animal spirits were such that no investor could afford to absorb 'down-side risks' for a firm, it would not be able to raise capital. The existence of a large and diversified base of investors with a broad range of animal spirits was therefore essential for financing the entire range of economic activities in a growing and changing economy. As long as the base as a whole keeps the strength and capacity to absorb many different types of risks and uncertainty, the financial market backed by such a base of investors can be dynamic and powerful. However, if the market becomes exposed to risks and uncertainty beyond its capacity, the propensity to periodic financial disaster would be rapidly increased.

If I may be allowed to appropriate the term *speculation* for the activity of forecasting the psychology of the market, and the term *enterprise* for the activity of forecasting the prospective yield of assets over their whole life, it is by no means always the case that speculation predominates over enterprise. . . . Speculators may do no harm as bubbles on a steady stream of enterprises. But the position is serious when enterprise becomes the bubble on a whirlpool of speculation. When the capital development of a country becomes a by-product of the activities of a casino, the job is likely to be ill-done.

(Keynes, 1936, pp. 158–159)

Keynes treated the animal spirit in enterprise affirmatively, but that in speculation cautiously. On the other hand, it appears that the 'animal spirit' against major (excessive) uncertainty irrespective of enterprise or speculation is prohibited in the conservative Islamic mode of investment and financial intermediation. Table 3.1 shows the comparison how the Post-Keynesian and the Islamic mode of investment would look at animal spirits against minor/major uncertainties associated with *enterprise* and *speculation*, respectively.

El-Gamal (2006) suggests that if the commutative contract containing excessive *gharar* meets a need that cannot be met otherwise, the contract would not be deemed invalid based on that *gharar*.

A canonical example is *salam* (prepaid forward sale), wherein the object of sale does not exist at contract inception, giving rise to excessive *gharar*. However, since that contract allows financing of agricultural and industrial activities that cannot be financed otherwise, it is allowed despite that *gharar*.

(El-Gamal, 2006, p. 59)

Basically, Islamic principles of economics focus on clarity and lack of ambiguity, just and fair treatment for all and care for the rights of others (Ayub, 2007, p. 12). So far as these principles are necessarily ethical, incubating small- and middle-sized enterprises in agricultural and industrial sectors would be acceptable to an extent in which the associated major uncertainty can be shared and absorbed in the community through an adequate profit–loss sharing agreement.

Table 3.1 Comparison of the post-Keynesian view and the Islamic mode of investment of looking at animal spirits against uncertainties in enterprise and speculation

	Animal spirits in enterprise		*Animal spirits in speculation*	
	Minor uncertainty	*Major uncertainty*	*Minor uncertainty*	*Major uncertainty*
Post-Keynesian view	Positive	Positive	Acceptable	Cautious (or negative)
Islamic mode of investment	Acceptable	Cautious (or acceptable)	Acceptable	Negative

Ayub mentions:

> For a more efficient economy, we must promote systems in which people work in productive pursuits rather than unproductive ones. Change the system to relate it with real sector activities and all those clever dealers who earn huge profits out of thin air could become doctors, industrialists, business people and teachers instead!
>
> (n.d., p. 2)

Engagement in enterprise rather than speculation seems to be preferably considered in the Islamic mode of investment. *Ijtihad* (independent reasoning) is the main vehicle by which the *Shari'ah* can be adjusted so as to accommodate social change, and it relies, to a large extent, on the proper understanding and application of *ta'lil* (ratiocination) (Kamali, 2000). In accordance with the context of *ijtihad*, acceptable scope of *mudaraba* as the financier to be engaged in enterprise should entail further arguments.

4. Towards a trans-disciplinary framework

The perspectives mentioned previously in the chapter by El-Gamal (2006) and Ayub (2007) are to be supported by the liberal view in Islamic commercial law of generally characterizing the *Shari'ah* as the legal system of pragmatism and convenience (Kamali, 2000, p. 70).

> With regard to new transactions, there is in principle no need to search for supportive evidence in the views and precedents of the early jurists, for it is essentially incorrect to extend and apply a medieval juristic opinion to a form of trade that did not exist in medieval times. The correct approach in such instances would be to attempt independent *ijtihad* in light of the basic guidelines of the Qur'an and *Sunnah*.
>
> (Kamali, 2000, p. 70)

Kamali (2000) points out that the *madhahib* have differed regarding the scope of the parties' liberty with respect to such stipulations. The *Hanbalis* have given it the widest scope, and their contribution to the freedom of stipulation in contracts is widely acknowledged to be the most outstanding of the rich legacy of the juristic scholarship of the *madhahib*. The *Hanafi* and *Shafii* schools have taken an intermediate position on the subject, but both seem close to the *Zahiri* stance than to the *Hanbali* regarding the freedom of contract. They have departed from some of the rigidities of the *Zahiri* school by recourse to analogical reasoning, juristic preference, the consideration of public interest and custom. Consequently, they have validated certain types of stipulations and additions to nominate contracts on these grounds. But the *Hanafis* and *Shafiis* nevertheless remain fairly distant from the considerably more liberal position taken by their *Hanbali* counterparts on the freedom of contract. Although the *Maliki* school has not embraced the *Hanbali* view of the freedom of contract, in comparison with the other *madhahib*, they are closer to the *Hanbali* position. The *Malikis* have achieved this mainly through the application of their doctrine of unrestricted public interest (Kamali, 2000, pp. 75–76).

We should note the position of the *Shari'ah* in the area of *mu'amalat*, especially with regard to illicit gain (*riba*), hoarding and risk-taking (*gharar*), which are predicated on the prevention of conflicts, exploitation and injustice among people. There are not, in other words, founded on devotional (*ta'abbudi*) principles but on rational causes. This is an important *Shari'ah* principle that is sometimes neglected by those who maintain that the intellect and human reason have no place in the *Shari'ah*. Many problems in the fields of Islamic economics, banking and finance arise from this inability to understand the proper role of reason in the *Shari'ah* (Kamali, 2000, p. 78). He points out the differences between *ibadat* and *mu'amalat*, where the basic norm in the former is submission and devotion without expatiation in effective causes, but the law concerning *mu'amalat* is generally founded on their rational, effective cause and benefit. This means that the law in this area is open to rational analysis, enquiry and evaluation (Kamali, 2000, p. 78).

From the liberal position, Islamic financial institutions (IFI) are not necessarily discouraged to share the associated risk and uncertainty with the small- and medium-sized firms in the agricultural and industrial sector, so far as their *enterprise* is based on the Islamic principles of economics. On the other hand, many scholars point out the divergence between theory and practice, for instance, the excessive use of *murabaha* ('*murabaha* syndrome'[4]), which gives a fixed rate of return to the banks (Ayub, 2007, p. 446), and the financial disintermediation towards small-scale enterprises (Visser, 2009, p. 139). Unless the portfolio preference of a vast majority of depositors particularly in developing countries is not so risk-averse, it makes sense that even Islamic banks that specialize in small-scale credit tend to restrict themselves to *murabaha* and *bai'salam* finance (Visser, 2009, p. 139).

Hyman Minsky, a post-Keynesian economist with a reputation among monetary theorists for being particularly pessimistic (Kindleberger, 2000, p. 13), contributed in great deal to modelling the fragility of the monetary system and its propensity to periodic disaster. According to Minsky, if a business unit's cash flow commitments on debts are such that over some period the cash receipts are expected to exceed the cash payments by a significant margin, the unit is said to be engaged in 'hedge' financing. Then, a 'speculative' financing unit has cash flow payments that exceed the cash inflows expected during some of the periods. However, the present value of the cash flow expected to accrue to the firm from owned assets exceeds the present value of contractual cash payments. Since a speculative financing unit has a positive net worth, the borrower may be able to refinance its position. Finally, a 'ponzi' financing unit is a speculative financing unit for which the interest portion of its cash payment commitments exceeds its net income cash receipts, that is, business units engaged in ponzi finance have a negative net worth in computation of present values (Minsky, 1977, p. 143).

The risk-averse fund should not be invested in risky ventures. "However, in the case of single trade transactions or where satisfactory documentation is available, Islamic banks should use *musharaka*, as this will give them higher returns" (Ayub, 2007, p. 446). How do the IFI, successfully or reluctantly, screen and monitor the small-scale *murabaha* transaction and the *musharaka* or *mudaraba* equity-like engagement while responding to fundamental uncertainty? Lenders' screening and monitoring is the basis of their assessment of the extent to which expected cash inflows will cover cash payment commitments. Minsky called the excess 'margins of safety'. We should ask how the IFI evaluate the 'margin of safety' in the Hyman Minsky's term, to prevent from undertaking the excess credit risk. Minsky emphasized that the business units that engage in speculative or ponzi finance, even in hedge finance, are vulnerable to the events that reduce the cash flows from assets. Therefore, screening and monitoring of borrowers' cash flow projection is critical for credit appraisal. However, monitoring is always intrinsically imperfect because monitoring agents are always exposed to fundamental uncertainty.

5. Linkage between theory and practice – concluding comments

Suzuki (2013) conducted an interview with a director and bank managers of *Bank Syariah Mandiri*, the largest Islamic bank in Indonesia, reporting his impression that they perceived the prohibition of *gharar* in the context of avoiding incompleteness of contract or avoiding the transaction having gambling elements (*maisir*), rather than in the context of being cautious for the major risk and uncertainty associated with business and enterprise. Under the economic situation where the demand for asset-based consumers financing was strong, the bank did not have to challenge the *major* uncertainty associated with animal spirits in enterprise as mentioned in Table 3.1. The bank was engaged in the *musharaka* financing only in the case that it was hard to apply the *murabaha* scheme, such as the case of the bridge finance for the working capital demand in the construction period of a construction project. In the construction period, the cost for construction including the labour cost for construction was not yet fixed and it was intrinsically difficult to pledge the object building under the construction. The object building can be pledged as collateral after the construction (Suzuki, 2013).

In general, the credit strategy of the IFI is quite conservative resulting in the portfolio selection of the repeated and asset-based financing. The IFI are not allowed to impose penalties from the debtors that have fallen into arrears (Holy Qur'an 2: 280) and are not allowed to use the credit derivatives and hedging instruments to mitigate the credit risk. Under the prohibition of *gharar* in a sense of avoiding the major risk and uncertainty to share with, Islamic finance struggles with the limited scope for penalty clauses under *Shari'ah* law (Visser, 2009, p. 139). It makes sense that Islamic banks would rather not be involved in long-term financing under the current legal framework, except the secured financing like housing loans. Understandably, even Islamic banks that relatively specialized in small-scale credit tend to restrict themselves to the secured *murabaha* mainly for financing the purchase of specific goods.

Ayub (n.d.) mentions that study of the behaviour of the derivatives market reveals that it has the potential to cause a serious breakdown in the financial system. "The degrees of leverage that are afforded by option contracts can be so high that large unpredictable market moves in underlying prices may one day lead to the insolvency of a major financial institution" (Ayub, n.d., p. 2). According to him, even if *arbun* (down payment; a non-refundable deposit paid by a buyer retaining a right to confirm or cancel the sale) is accepted as valid transaction, most of the derivatives current in the market would still be unacceptable from *Shari'ah* angle due to involvement to *gharar* (Ayub, n.d.).

Kamali (2000) insists that the role that custom has played in the development of the *Shari'ah* is manifested in the acknowledgement that a great deal of what is known in the name of *ijma* (general consensus), *maslahah* (public good) and *fatwa* (juristic opinion) often originates in the customs and living experience of the community. A ruling of *fiqh*, a *fatwa* or *ijtihad* which originates in *urf* is particularly liable to change when there is a change in its underlying *urf*, and hence the legal maxim of *fiqh* that the 'change of rules is undeniable with the change of time'. Ratiocination in the Qur'an means that the laws of *Shari'ah* outside *ibadat* are not imposed for their own sake but in order to realize certain benefits (Kamali, 2000, pp. 80–82). For instance, as for the sales at the market price (*Bay'bi-Sir' al-Suq*), he suggests that in view of the considerable progress that has been made in market techniques for price determination and forecasting, more refined and reliable methods are now available to inject a certain degree of objectivity and professionalism in the determination of market prices. The concern that market prices may be liable to manipulation and distortion is no longer prominent. If the parties wish to agree on the prevailing market price within a particular time frame, there is no fear of excessive uncertainty or *gharar*, and the agreement should be seen as a manifestation of the individual freedom of contract of the parties to determine the terms of their contractual agreement (Kamali, 2000, p. 96).

This chapter has attempted to draw the wisdom of the prohibition of *gharar* through the lens of Institutional and Post-Keynesian Economics. We looked at one dimension of the prohibition of *gharar* which focuses on clarity and lack of ambiguity, just and fair treatment for all and care for the rights of others. We also looked at the other dimension which is related to the fundamental uncertainty associated with investment and financial intermediation. The lens of Institutional and Post-Keynesian Economics is useful to clarify two dimensions of *gharar*, respectively. Under the prohibition of *gharar* (also the profit–loss sharing) framework, it may have created a dilemma of the so-called *murabaha* syndrome leading to the financial disintermediation (particularly the dry-up of long-term funds) in hampering the potentials in agricultural and industrial sectors. Long-term growth may suffer as a result. In our view, based on the best effort to avoid the incompleteness of contract, it might be acceptable, to an extent in which the associated major uncertainty in *enterprise* can be shared and absorbed in the community through an adequate profit–loss sharing agreement, to incubate small and medium enterprises in agricultural and industrial sectors.

It is generally agreed that sufficient knowledge of the substance of an object of sale to an extent that precludes the possibility of disputes between the parties, is essential for the validity of a sale. As for the knowledge of attributes, the Hanafis maintain that this is not a prerequisite for validity but for enforceability (*luzum*) (Kamali, 2000, p. 89). How Islamic financial institutions will tackle the *murabaha* syndrome while improving the financial intermediation to the agricultural and industrial potentials should entail further arguments, we recommend, upon the liberal position insisting that commercial transactions (*muamalat*) and contracts are permissible unless there is a clear injunction to the contrary of the *Shari'ah* norm.

Notes

1 This position is precisely the opposite with regard to devotional matters (*ibadat*), because the basic presumption here is that they are forbidden unless there is a clear text to validate them (Kamali, 2000, p. 66).
2 The term *mudaraba* is interchangeably used with *qirad* and *muqaradah*. It is presumed that while the latter two originated in *Hajiz*, *mudaraba* was of Iraqi origin. Subsequently, the difference appears to have been perpetuated by the legal schools, the Malikis and Shafi'es adopting the terms of '*qirad*' and '*muqaradah*' and the Hanafis using the term '*mudaraba*' (Ayub, 2007).
3 Ayub (2007) point out that it is only according to *Hanbali* jurists and, to some extent, *Hanafi* jurists that the owner is allowed to work for the business with the *mudarib*. The reason for disapproval by the majority classical position is understandable if the basic idea that a person enters into a *mudaraba* contract because he lacks business skill is presumed to exist. But if the financier also has skill and has contracted *mudaraba* simply because he cannot do the entire work single-handedly, the rationale behind prohibiting him to work is not understandable.
4 Bank Indonesia (2009) shows the changes in the asset (credit) portfolio in the Indonesian Islamic banks. We observe that the share of *murabaha* operation, secured trading or asset-backed financing with relatively low credit risk, has been dominant (58.9 percent in 2008, 56.3 percent in 2009, respectively). The similar situation is observed in Malaysia. According to Annual Reports by Bank Negara Malaysia, in the asset portfolio in the Malaysian Islamic banks, the share of *murabaha* and *murabaha*-related operation (*bai bithaman ajil*) was 48.2 percent in December 2008, 48.3 percent in December 2010; the share of operating lease and lease-to-purchase financing (*ijarah* and *ijarah thumma al-bai*) was 33.1 percent in December 2008, 29.8 percent in December 2010, respectively. In parallel, it is worth noting that the share of *musharaka* in the Malaysian IFI was only 1.1 percent in December 2008, 2.5 percent in December 2010.

Part II

Issues in Islamic equity finance and microfinance

4 Altruism and reciprocity in Islamic equity fund

New Institutional and philosophical speculations

Yasushi Suzuki and Mohammad Dulal Miah

1. Introduction

Venture capital (VC) is considered a significant source of financing for early stage, innovative, and high-growth start-up companies (Elsiefy, 2013). Successful venture capital companies would help poverty alleviation by increasing employment and contribute to sustainable economic growth through capital accumulation to further innovations (See Gompers and Lerner (1999a) for detail discussion on the various roles of VC). Despite its widespread importance of financing the start-ups, traditional mode of VC suffers from numerous shortcomings including agency problems (Cumming, 2005), moral hazard (Bergemann and Hege, 1997), and asymmetry of information (Trester, 1998). These problems can be minimized if a precise and specific contract can be drawn *ex ante*. However, writing such a contract is infeasible due to the presence of high transaction costs. This leaves an enormous room for a partner in the VC to behave opportunistically (Broughman, 2010). If so, prospective financiers might find it discouraging to finance VC in the absence of sensible mechanism devised *ex ante* to tackle these problems.

Islamic altruism and reciprocity may contribute to setting up Islamic VC. Based on the best effort to avoid the incompleteness of contract, it might be acceptable, to such an extent that the associated uncertainty in *enterprise* can be shared and absorbed in the community through an adequate profit–loss sharing agreement, to incubate small- and medium-sized enterprises in the innovative sector (see Chapter 3 in this book and Suzuki, 2013). Çizakça (2011, p. 270) raises three financial institutions such as *waqf* of stocks, Islamic venture capital, and microfinance; a model of combining these institutions in its structure can play an important role in eradicating poverty, enhancing entrepreneurial spirits, and building up human capital in Islamic countries. In particular, he is of the opinion that venture capital (VC) is going to be the rising star of Islamic finance because it is a *Shari'ah-based* instrument and though risky, embodies huge profit potential. Despite these competitive advantages and huge potential, Islamic VC is not yet well developed in practice. The question is why?

This chapter aims to answer this question. In so doing, it examines the cultural advantages of Islamic altruism and reciprocity as important institutions which may contribute to setting up Islamic VC. The chapter further analyzes the feasibility of

Islamic venture capital shedding an analytical light on the tradition of New Institutional Economics (NIE) and Transaction Cost Economics (TCE). One of the salient contributions by NIE is to support the proposition that effective contracting depends upon 'institutions' in terms of 'rules that constrain economic behavior', including informal or intangible institutions such as religions, traditions and customary practices. Although there should not be an overemphasis on the cultural factors, this chapter argues that the unique institutional structure, which creates Islamic altruism and reciprocity, may enhance the supply of Islamic VC, but simultaneously, it may cause opportunistic behavior unless appropriate safeguards can be devised *ex ante*, consequently leading to the drain of the capital for future innovations. The structure of the chapter is as follows: Section 2 describes the theoretical contributions of the NIE and TCE, particularly the institutions of trust and *opportunism*. Section 3 applies some of these contributions to the analysis of general altruism and reciprocity embedded in Islamic principles. Section 4 points out cultural advantages and limitations of organizing Islamic equity finance which is followed by a brief conclusion.

2. Opportunism and trust in the NIE framework

The New Institutional Economics has been concerned principally with two basic issues of societies: economics of property rights and transaction costs (Williamson, 2000). The second issue is the concern of this chapter. Transaction Cost Economics employs two important human behavioral assumptions. The first set of assumption pertains to human 'bounded rationality' due to Herbert Simon who convincingly argues that human beings are *intendedly* rational but only *limitedly* so (Simon, 1961, p. xxiv). Simon (1993, p. 156) points out "they (human beings) would be unable to make the computations required for optimal choice even if they had perfect knowledge." In practice, human beings are *boundedly* rational partly because of information problems but mainly because of the complexity of computing the best strategies (Simon, 1996). For Simon, even if zero transaction cost facilitates the accumulation of all relevant information *ex ante* it is still possible to inaccurately model any contractual relation between contracting parties because the human brain possesses limited capacity to process and analyze information. Thus, bounded rationality is a critical foundation of contractual relation. The second behavioral assumption with which the theory is concerned is embedded in actors' 'opportunism'. For Williamson (1979, p. 234) "opportunism is a variety of self-interest seeking but extends simple self-interest seeking to include self-interest seeking with guile." Or simply, it is a kind of selfishness which is a vice whereas self-interest is a virtue.

The rational pursuit of self-interest is what makes the Adam Smith's invisible hands work in reality. The tendency of self-interest, an essential characteristic of one's well-being, is therefore, prerequisite for the market to function. In contrast, selfishness tends to make people exclusively concerned about them without caring for others. Selfish individuals may act in such a manner that imposes adverse effects on others (Hunt, 1990). Thus, opportunism can be considered a subset of selfishness. However, the assumption about human opportunism does not necessarily entail that everyone is perniciously self-interest seeker. Rather, the presence of a few opportunistic individuals means economic exchanges should be structured to protect against potential opportunism because it is difficult to differentiate between those who are less opportunistic and those who are not (Williamson, 1979).

Williamson (1985) analyzes the impact of bounded rationality and opportunism on transaction costs. He argues that admitting human-bounded rationality in the presence of non-opportunistic behavior does not require an extensive contracting for transactions because contracting problems arising *ex post* due to bounded rationality can be overcome since parties have agreed to cooperate (being non-opportunistic) and disclose all the relevant information generated once the contingencies occur. Williamson (1985, p. 20) argues, "rather than contemplate all conceivable bridge crossing in advance, which is a very ambitious undertaking, only actual bridge crossing choices are addressed as event unfolds." On the other hand, problems arising from opportunism require writing a comprehensive contract *ex ante* even if we assume unlimited cognitive power of the human brain. From this view, Williamson (1979, p. 234) postulates "opportunism is a central concept in the study of transaction costs."

Transaction cost can be defined as "the economic equivalent of *friction* in physical systems" (Williamson, 1985) or the cost of "running economic systems" (Arrow, 1974). Transaction costs, in general, include *ex ante* costs such as (i) finding the right partners, (ii) negotiating prices, (iii) drafting and writing appropriate contracts, (iv) *ex post* costs of monitoring, (v) cost of enforcing contracts, and (vi) cost of resolving disputing and contesting terms. The magnitude of transaction costs is determined by a number of different variables including the technology trading partners are dealing with, the distribution of bargaining power between them, the presence or absence of shared cultures that induce trust and self-enforcement and so on. In this sense, the level of transaction costs involved with contractual relation is determined by the existing set of institutions. In the context of NIE an 'institution' can be defined as rules that constrain economic activities and behaviors. Institutions consist of both formal rules such as laws and regulations, and informal institutions including customs, traditions, norms, and religions (North, 1990). These institutions are devised to reduce and limit the uncertainty of human cooperation, to give a steady structure for everyday life. While the formal institutions can be changed quite often informal institutions are changed very infrequently (North, 1990). As a result, informal institutions occupy the primary focus of institutional analysis.

Among various elements of informal institutions, 'trust' is one but key and essential element having a greater impact on transaction costs. Fukuyama (1995) stresses that contracting for goods or services with people one does not know well or trust is prohibitively costly. Trust has been defined as "attitudes and behavior which indicate that each person is willing to rely on the other to act fairly and to take into account the other's welfare", as 'solidarity', and as "a belief in future harmonious affirmative cooperation" (Cohen and Knetsch, 1992, p. 442).

Furthermore, "contract negotiations and performance will take place more effectively if trust is present and is generated by the process" (Cohen and Knetsch, 1992, p. 442). Fukuyama (1995), referring to what the sociologist James Coleman has called 'social capital', argues that the ability of people to work together for common purposes in groups and organizations and their ability to associate with each other depends on the degree to which communities share norms and values and are able to subordinate individual interests to those of larger groups. Fukuyama (1995, p. 10) further states "out of such shared values comes trust." One of the invaluable insights of Francis Fukuyama and Kenneth Arrow is to point out that trust has a large and measurable economic value and has an important bearing on economic organization. Arrow (1974, p. 24) notes "ethical elements enter in some measure into every contract; without them, no market could function. There is an element of trust in every transaction; typically, one object of value changes hands before the other one does."

In general, opportunism in terms of pursuing self-interest with guile involves subtle forms of deceit and refers to the incomplete or distorted disclosure of information, especially to calculated efforts to mislead, distort, disguise, obfuscate, or otherwise confuse (Williamson, 1985, p. 47). Moreover, risks of this opportunism can be reduced by mutual trust. While transaction cost is defined as the economic equivalent of *friction* in physical systems, we assume that trust may, not always but fairly often, play the role of *lubricant* for making the economic system run smoothly (Arrow, 1974, p. 23). However, operationalizing trust, no matter how it is defined, has proved inordinately difficult which results inadequate and limited empirical analysis of the variable (Williamson, 1985, p. 406). Arrow insists that the efficacy of alternative modes of contracting and monitoring would vary among cultures because of differences in trust. Cultural factors are strongly related to the degree of trust. Fukuyama (1995, p. 25) states "community depends on trust, and trust in turn is culturally determined." However, we would say that the degree of trust even in a particular culture or society could rather vary. Arrow (1974, p. 16) argues,

> most of us operate in some middle realm where we admit social claims, sometimes forget about them for long stretches of time as we go about our daily private role, sometimes rise to an occasion, sometimes fall miserably short, as we assert our individuality in contexts that are not totally appropriate.

Trust makes people altruist. Although the relationship between trust and altruism is intricate they are interconnected in the sense that both are greatly shaped by a common factor, culture. Fukuyama (1995) indicates that religion is a primordial source of culture. Thus, the association between religion (as cause) and altruism (as effect) is mediated through trust. Although the relationship can be bidirectional, the causal direction that religion affects altruism is more pronounced in the literature than the other way around (see for example, Soroglou, 2013). Zhao (2012) finds from his experimental research that religious people behave more altruistically to in-group members than non-religious people. One reason is that religious belief enhances within-group interpersonal trust. With greater trust, the chances of altruistic behavior within the group increases. This is however, not universal. Soroglou (2013) explains two dimensions of religion affecting altruism. The first dimension is referred to 'coalition dimension' which emphasizes the 'in-group' vs. 'out-group' barriers. Altruism from this perspective can be viewed as merely confined to those people who belong to the same community or share the same normative beliefs and practices. In contrast, the 'spiritual dimension' of religion connects altruistic behavior to divinity or spiritualism. This sort of altruism tends to achieve universal welfare. In this sense, altruism derived from religious faith and belief can be extended universally even sometimes going beyond the religion's boundary.

In the Simonian view, altruistic behavior shall only be encouraged if the docility of the individual can enhance the fitness of the group as a whole even if the individual's personal fitness declines. This view reflects an ultimate benefits actors receive from being altruistic, "individuals who are *docile* therefore have a great advantage in fitness over those who are not docile" (Simon, 1996, p. 45). Such a concept of altruism is purely based on the condition that the fitness loss to individual for being altruist is less than the gain to society. This perception echoes with the assumption of *homo economicus* or rational choice theory (self-interest behavior). Soroglou (2013) differentiates between behavioral altruism (self-interested) and genuine altruism (other-regarded). The former is preoccupied by the concept that altruism can be a strategic way of advancing an altruist's own interest, maybe in the form of boosting his own reputation, expecting social approval, triggering reciprocal returns from the receiver, or avoiding shame (Soroglou, 2013). Genuine altruism, on the other hand, can be defined as a behavior which purely orients to others' well-being even at the loss of the giver's. Such a genuine altruism can be influenced by strong self-determination or heightened self-esteem. Elster (2006) suggests that many charitable endeavors are performed for the inner audience. Bringing religion in the context, inner audience can be translated as a response for a divine or spiritual call. Altruism in this pursuit helps people behave altruistically even if no one knows about their philanthropy. Islam as religion provides various spiritual but pragmatic commands towards this direction.

3. Altruism and reciprocity in Islam

Green (2005) traces the origin of 'altruism' to August Comte who coined the term in the nineteenth century from the Latin word '*alter*' which means 'other' or 'care for others'. From this perspective, Green (2005) defines altruism as an intentional action which is undertaken for the welfare of others without expecting any benefits or in some cases the actor might suffer a loss. Homerin (2005) translates the Arabic word *al-ghayriah* from the word *ghayr*, meaning 'others'. However, the Qur'anic meaning of *ghayr* tends to indicate 'others' in general although it includes the intention of favoring 'others' than the self. Homerin (2005) further argues that the closet of 'altruism' in the Arabic word can be found in the mediaeval Sufi term '*ithar*' which means "preferring the other to the self" (Homerin,

2005, p. 84). *Ithar* is used in the Qur'an to mean charity (Yusoff, 2014). Likewise, scholars endorse charity to indicate altruistic behaviors of agents (Khalil, 2004). Hammond (1975, p. 115) specifies the concept: "altruism can be invoked to explain any charitable behavior we may observe. But it is not quite obvious that altruism must be invoked to explain all charitable behavior." For Hammond (1975), other than pure altruism, some charities are driven by egoism – a condition in which the altruist believes that his current altruistic actions would return in the future while he is in need. Or in the view of Fong (2007) the former is unconditional altruism while the latter is reciprocal altruism. All these views conform to our earlier discussion of behavioral altruism (egoism or reciprocal) and genuine altruism (unconditional). In light of this discussion it is safe to equate altruism to charity in the context of Islam. Undoubtedly, the Qur'an encourages people to be altruist "and they give food, in spite of their love for it to poor, the orphan, and the captive" (Qur'an, 76:8–9).

Charity in Islam can take many forms. For instance, Islam not only proposes *zakat* (almsgiving) as an obligation for well-off Muslims but also makes it one of the basic five pillars of Islam. Giving *zakat* can be considered an act of genuine altruism because the actor can expect no worldly return in exchange of paying *zakat*. But rather, failure to discharge this altruistic duty entails someone to be divinely punished. Other than compulsory almsgiving, Islam strongly encourages different voluntary charities one of which is *awaqaf* or perpetual charity. Hassan (2010) defines *awaqaf* as a perpetual charity which is to hold certain property and preserving it for the confined benefit of certain philanthropic purposes. Hassan (2010) further argues that *awaqaf* is widely practiced by both the Muslims and non-Muslims worldwide. This proves that altruism in Islam is pervasive and genuine. While Simon views docility as a means of enhancing group fitness to survive under the condition of human-bounded rationality (behavioral altruism), altruism in Islam is concerned with fulfilling the socioeconomic objectives of 'social justice' in accordance with the objectives of *Shari'ah*. It is a sort of moral and religious obligation for individuals to be altruist without thinking about worldly return (unconditional altruism). As such, Islamic altruism is broader in scope and application. It is mentioned in the Qur'an (4: 36) "show kindness to parents, and the kindred, and orphans, and to needy, and to the neighbor who is a kinsman and the neighbor who is a stranger, the companion by your side, and the wayfarer."

This verse clearly nullifies the confinement of the purpose of Islamic altruism merely to an increase in 'group well-off' or 'group fitness'. Rather, it encourages unconditional charity towards those who are really in need; sometimes prioritizing others' needs over self in the pursuit of *ithar*. The 'altruism' of the *Medinan* Muslims, praised by Allah in the Qur'an, was so great in its scope and impact:

> And (in this wealth there is also a share) for those (the Helpers) who had settled in the city (of Madinah) and had embraced the Faith before these (Refugees arrived there). They love those who migrated to them for refuge and (who) even though poverty be their own lot, found no desire in their hearts for that which is given to them (Refugees) but they gave them (Refugees)

preference over themselves. And (bear in mind that) those saved from the covetousness of their souls are the ones to achieve the goal.

(Qur'an, 59:9)[1]

The strength of Islamic altruism can be derived from the basic concept of ownership over wealth. In the Muslim society, there is the powerful concept of Allah's ownership of all wealth. Human beings are mere 'trustees' of this wealth (Qur'an, 3:180 and 57:10). It is summarized by Naqvi (2003:105) that the individual's right to spend his wealth is limited in several ways: (a) he must spend it according to Divine wishes (Qur'an, 57:10), (b) he cannot hoard it, especially when there are urgent social needs to be met (Qur'an, 3:180), (c) he must give it to the poor not as charity but as a matter of the latter's acknowledged right in his wealth (Qur'an, 70:24–25), and (d) he must spend wealth only in moderation because being spendthrift is both a social waste and a cardinal sin (Qur'an, 17:26–27). Attaching the concept of ownership of the poor to the wealth of the rich bestows upon *ithar*, another superior dimension missing in the economic and social analysis of altruism.

Many scholars including Mawdudi (2011) and Naqvi (2003) point out that the Islamic right of the poor to receive their share in the wealth of the rich strengthens altruism significantly in running efficiently and equitably an essentially individualistic economy, and it minimizes the free-riding and assurance problems. The Holy Qur'an unambiguously states that the poor have a due share in the wealth of the rich. Naqvi (2003, p. 107) further notes that "even the Rawlsian Difference Principle, which explicitly stipulates helping the poor on a priority basis, does not include in the rich man's wealth the right of those who cannot participate in market exchange." As such, he argues "Western theological systems are generally ambiguous about recognizing the poor's right."

While Islam praises and encourages altruistic behavior, it also makes provisions for punishment if somebody behaves opportunistically. For instance, the Prophet (PBUH) said:

> There are four characteristics, whoever has all of them is a true hypocrite, and whoever has one of them has one of the qualities of a hypocrite until he gives up: when he is trusted, he betrays; when he speaks, he lies; when he makes a promise, he breaks it; and when he disputes, he resorts to slander.
>
> (Saheeh al-Bukhari, Saheeh Muslim)

This implies that in Islam there is no scope for opportunism or breaking of trust. Also, in case of any dispute *ex post*, partners should resolve it according to their best wisdom with faith and morality. Any deviation from this state will turn them into a hypocrite. The punishment for hypocrites is mentioned in the Qur'an: "Allah has promised the hypocrites – men and women – and the disbelievers the fire of hell; therein shall they abide. It will suffice them. Allah has cursed them and for them is the lasting torment" (Qur'an 9: 68).

In Islam, the purpose of encouraging altruistic activities (mandatory and voluntary) on the one hand and provisioning punishment in the case of opportunism on the other aims at achieving social equality through eradicating poverty. Some scholars show that the difference in income between the rich and poor is less in Muslim countries than in non-Muslim countries. Based on available data from 1990–2006, Fisher (2011) shows that the average score of Gini co-efficient in Muslim countries is 38.0 whereas the score for non-Muslim countries is 41.1 and the difference is statistically significant. Moreover, the variation of inequality is higher in non-Muslim countries (Gini co-efficient ranges between 25 and 74) than in Muslim countries (Gini co-efficient ranges between 25 and 50). In explaining the reason for class equality in Muslim countries, Fisher points out that besides obligatory almsgiving, it is the social justice that occupies the pride of place in Muslim moral thinking. Muslim society is concerned about Islamic altruism as a driver for realizing this social justice.

Reciprocity, in one way or another, is embedded in altruism. Behavioral or reciprocal altruism is motivated by actors' strong expectation of receiving the return in worldly matter whereas genuine altruism is driven by expectation of receiving spiritual or divine reward. Regardless of the motives of actors, both unconditional altruists and strong reciprocators may support redistribution of wealth to the poor (Bowles, 2012). Bowles further raises a crucial issue regarding strong reciprocity:

> Altruism is a widely discussed and important motive for assistance to the poor. But strong reciprocity provides a quite different perspective: Strong reciprocators wish to help those who try to make it on their own but who, for reasons beyond their own control, cannot, and they wish to punish, or withhold assistance from, those who are able but unwilling to work hard or who violate other social norms.
>
> (2012, pp. 145–146)

Bowles refers 'strong reciprocity' to a propensity to cooperate and share with others similarly disposed, even at personal cost, and a willingness to punish those who violate cooperative and other social norms, even when punishing is personally costly and cannot be expected to result in net personal gains in the future (Bowles, 2012). He refers to a report in which the majority of the respondents (81 percent) favor public funding for child care if the mother is a widow who is trying to support three children, while only a few (only 15 percent) favor public funding when the mother has never married and is not interested in working. Bowles is concerned about strong reciprocity as a driving force of making people willingly help the poor, but withdraw the support when they perceive that the poor may cheat or not try hard enough to be self-sufficient and morally upstanding. Bowles also refers to 'genuine altruism' in the standard biological sense of the term, which is what motivates actors to help others in situations where the actor would increase her payoffs by not helping (Bowles, 2012, p. 131). Similarly, Segal and Sobel (2007) argue that a reciprocal individual responds to actions he perceives to be kind in a kind manner, and to actions he perceives to be hostile in a hostile manner. Thus, the preferences of actors in altruistic performance will be influenced by the behavior of the receivers. The question is: how far the well-intention of one measured by heavenly achievement is known to others?

In the tradition of Western political philosophy, altruism itself depends on recognition of the reality of the other persons, and on the equivalent capacity to regard oneself as merely one individual among many (Nagel, 1970, p. 3). In contrast, Islamic altruism appears to depend on reciprocity backed by mutual belief in the omnipotence and omniscience of the absolute power. As mentioned earlier, the Qur'an unambiguously states that the poor have a due share in the wealth of the rich. This unique institutional structure which creates Islamic altruism and reciprocity may help the supply of the fund for those entrepreneurs who face difficulties in fund-raising. But it is impossible for the altruist to know that the receivers are staying up to the spirit of divine principles. In this circumstance, a simple doubt about the possible opportunistic behavior of entrepreneurs can seriously inhibit the altruism towards the entrepreneurs. From the 'opportunism' perspective, we may say that the cooperative mode of economic organization, where trust and good intentions are generously imputed to the membership, has its weakness in being endowed with few organizational responses to the debilitating effects of opportunism. For Williamson (1985, pp. 64–65) "such organizations are easily invaded and exploited by agents who do not possess those qualities." Transactions that are subject to *ex post* opportunism will benefit if appropriate safeguards are devised *ex ante* (Williamson, 1985). We should note that, in other words, if safeguards are not sufficiently devised *ex ante*, opportunism would possibly emerge as a troublesome source of behavioral uncertainty in economic transactions.

4. Implication for Islamic venture capital

Basically, venture capital is identical to equity finance as well as *mudaraba/musharaka* financing. It is very close to equity-like PLS-based Islamic finance structures, notably *mudaraba* and *musharaka*,[2] although these have to be adapted to create the flexibility required by venture capitalists (Durrani, 2006). Çizakça (2011) summarizes the Islamicity of VC. First, VC is identical to *mudaraba* and is a part of the Prophet's *sunnah*. Second, unlike a loan or a credit transaction, there is neither interest nor collateral in a venture capital transaction. Finance is simply provided in return for shares which is a form of equity finance. Third, the entire system is based upon equity finance. There are no loans involved and hence there is no question of *riba*. If a third-party guarantees as insurance in order to encourage public participation, only the principal is guaranteed by the state. Fourth, venture capital is a profit-and-loss sharing system. Profit-and-loss sharing takes place in accordance with Islamic rules. Profit in a venture capital company is shared according to mutual agreement. This mutual agreement is expressed in the amount of shares the venture capital company obtains from the entrepreneur. Loss goes entirely to the venture capitalist or financier. This is without any doubt *mudaraba*. Fifth, a venture capital company is established just like a classical Islamic *shirkat*, that is, a partnership for limited duration, usually for 10 years. Last but not least, risks are truly shared and the venture capitalist does not demand collateral from the entrepreneur.

As we mentioned earlier, Çizakça (2011) is of the opinion that VC is going to be the rising star of Islamic finance because VC is a *Shari'ah-based* instrument and, though risky, embodies huge profit potential. He refers to a dimension of culture as an important factor encouraging entrepreneurship. He mentions that Islam assigns the highest social status to an honest merchant struggling to earn and enlarge its assets legitimately. It is believed in Islam that such merchants or entrepreneurs will be exalted and shall join the ranks of the martyrs in the life hereafter. This proves that enormous social importance is attached to entrepreneurship (Çizakça, 2011; Elsiefy, 2013). In parallel, the role of *waqf* is emphasized as an important contributor to organizing Islamic venture capital: *waqf* is considered retention of a property for the benefit of a charitable or humanitarian objective, or for a specified group of people such as members of the donor's family. The global *waqf* will focus on three basic activities: ongoing charity (*sadaqa jariyah*), education, and family *waqfs* (Çizakça, 2011). Ongoing charity can be interpreted as a strategy for poverty alleviation.[3]

Islamic altruism strengthened by the Islamic right of the poor to receive their share in the wealth of the rich may also contribute to organizing Islamic VC. Successful VC companies would help alleviate poverty by increasing employment and contribute to sustainable economic growth through capital accumulation to further innovations. The concept of venture capital here is different from the tradition of what we call social entrepreneurship even though both can be oriented towards poverty alleviation. For instance, a social enterprise is a business with the primary objective of the development of society and community rather than being driven by the need to maximize profit for shareholders and owners. In the case of venture capital, social utility is created by achieving self-fulfilling objectives. As such, economic value creation appears to be the primary objective for VC while social value creation is the supreme purpose of social enterprises (Seelos and Mair, 2005). Islamic altruism and reciprocity towards entrepreneurs may, in theory, contribute to setting up Islamic VC. However, in reality, Islamic VC is not yet well developed in Islamic economies. Figure 4.1 summarizes the discussion in this section and links to the reasons.

Though data to empirically prove the above claim is seriously limited, anecdotal facts and reference from Islamic banks' financing patterns can prove that Islamic equity/participatory financing is tremendously drained. For instance, Suzuki and Uddin (2014) analyze the performance of Bangladeshi Islamic banks compared to their conventional counterparts for the period 2008 to 2012. They find that the majority of Islamic banks' income is derived from the asset-based *murabaha*, whereas the income from equity-like *mudaraba* and *mushāraka* is very negligible. Only three banks are involved in this mode of financing whereas the remaining banks are totally reluctant to engage with the profit-and-loss sharing modes. They examine and compare the ratio of interest paid to depositors against interest received from borrowers between conventional and Islamic banks on a non-risk-adjusted basis. Based on the analysis they point out that the

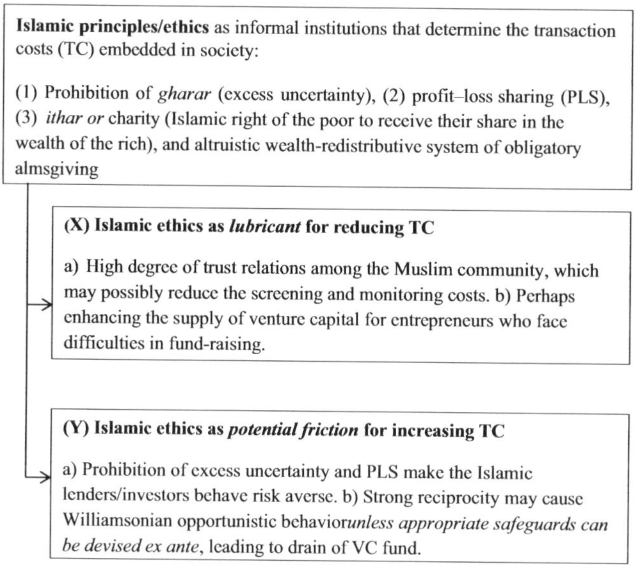

Islamic principles/ethics as informal institutions that determine the transaction costs (TC) embedded in society:

(1) Prohibition of *gharar* (excess uncertainty), (2) profit–loss sharing (PLS), (3) *ithar or* charity (Islamic right of the poor to receive their share in the wealth of the rich), and altruistic wealth-redistributive system of obligatory almsgiving

(X) Islamic ethics as *lubricant* for reducing TC

a) High degree of trust relations among the Muslim community, which may possibly reduce the screening and monitoring costs. b) Perhaps enhancing the supply of venture capital for entrepreneurs who face difficulties in fund-raising.

(Y) Islamic ethics as *potential friction* for increasing TC

a) Prohibition of excess uncertainty and PLS make the Islamic lenders/investors behave risk averse. b) Strong reciprocity may cause Williamsonian opportunistic behavior *unless appropriate safeguards can be devised ex ante*, leading to drain of VC fund.

Figure 4.1 NIE (TCE) framework explaining anomaly of Islamic venture capital

riba-free banking exercised by the Islamic banking windows/branches of these banks associated with a lower ratio than the *riba*-based banking in conventional branches. To be specific, for six of the reported banks the ratio has remained consistently lower during the whole period. It reveals the probability of prevailing higher profit opportunity under the asset-based financing in the Islamic banking sector, particularly under the dominant *murabaha*. In the case of Pakistan, *murabaha* and *ijara* comprise 82 percent of total financing whereas the share of *muḍāraba* and *mushāraka* in total financing stands at merely 4 percent (IFSB, 2014). In the context of MENA, Ali (2011) shows that the proportion of *murabaha* in total financing is 75 percent. Countries like Kuwait, UAE, and Yemen show a very negligible share of equity-based financing. The notable portion of the *mushārakah* mode of financing is contributed by Saudi Arabia, Lebanon, and Bahrain but the portion remains below 8 percent of the total financing in all these countries. The scenario of equity financing is almost similar for Islamic banks in all other countries.

Elsiefy (2013) raises several challenges Islamic equity finance or venture capital currently faces, including (a) the lack of transparency and uniform legal framework which creates substantial obstacles for foreign ownership and representation in the target investee company, also the lack of the legal structure that respects the intellectual property rights and patents. (b) There are no specific laws and courts to judge fast in cases of dispute like in VCs or traditional Islamic *muḍāraba* schemes. (c) The lack of know-how and education among investors about VC investment and its returns and risks. (d) The lack of educational programs that train young people on how to develop their ideas and become entrepreneurs. (e) The lack of the support and backing from the government in terms of tax incentives etc. While we acknowledge the lack of the 'formal' institutions hindering the sound development of Islamic VC, we should also note the unique feature of the Muslims' 'informal' constraints which make them hesitate to invest in Islamic VC.

It is worth noting Naqvi's arguments which are suggestive of answering this question. Naqvi (2003, p. 111) points out:

> it is motivationally rational for a person to sacrifice his selfish interests because (a) 'success' is measured, as Islam does, in terms of one's distance from greed and avarice; or (b) making a sacrifice in this world enhances the expected reward in this world as well in the hereafter.

He points out that public policy is required to assure the altruistic individual (one who is not inclined to free-ride) that his contribution will not go to waste and that others in society will not be allowed by the government to withhold their contributions. Naqvi further notes:

> An excess insistence on altruism can create a permanent tension between what a Muslim society is required to do and what eventually gets done in practice. Indeed, *there is a real danger that if moral perfection is demanded at all times, then the entire social system will become dysfunctional for want of the required supply of altruism.* Thus, in general, appropriate public policy must keep a balance between self-interest behavior and moral imperative because the principles of altruism and exchange are both mutually supportive as well as antithetical.
>
> (2003, p. 131)

From the Muslim perspective, there is no agency problem between the absolute existence as the principal and its followers (including fund providers, venture capitalists, and capital recipients) as the agent, because the followers retain their firm belief in the omnipotence and omniscience of the absolute existence. It is mentioned earlier that Islamic altruism appears to depend on reciprocity backed by mutual belief (among the followers) in the omnipotence and omniscience of the absolute power. At the individual level, the prospect of accountability on the Day of Judgment would bring positive behavioral changes. However, the current-life problem in equity finance is stemming from the structure that nobody knows the judgment of others. In other words, nobody on earth precisely knows which person among the others would not be allowed to enter into the Kingdom of God on the Day. The implication of this proposition is that the expected positive effect of Islamic principles as lubricant for reducing relevant transaction costs (X in Figure 4.1) is currently being cancelled out by the negative effect as friction (Y) embedded in the industry of Islamic equity finance (X - Y < 0). This is because, first, the prohibition of excess uncertainty and PLS makes the Islamic lenders or investors risk-averse (the *murabaha* syndrome). Second, strong reciprocity may cause Williamsonian opportunistic behavior of actors leading the drain of the fund for VC firms.

The shortage of funding for Islamic microfinance provides a support to this hypothesis. There is a growing tendency to view *zakat* as a source of funding for microfinance because it appears to be ideally suited to support Islamic microfinance as a poverty alleviation strategy (Karim *et al*, 2008; Yumna and Clarke, 2011). Yumna and Clarke (2011) however point out that although *zakat* is compulsory charity in Islam to fight poverty, the awareness among Muslims of paying *zakat* is not so high. They report that BAZNAS, the largest *zakat* institution in Indonesia, only collected US$ 2.6 million in 2010, where the national potency of *zakat* on household income reached US$ 61 trillion. This data tells that the *zakat* fund would not be reliable as a source of funding. Besides, an institutional analysis tells us that an excess reliance on charity may possibly cause moral hazard or opportunistic behavior in the agent involved with the microfinance industry. Unless appropriate safeguards and rules for protecting the right of the principal can be devised *ex ante*, it makes sense that the potential moral hazard or opportunistic behavior in the agent (particularly capital recipients) would make the principal (particularly fund providers) hesitate to share risks in enterprise if he/she is not an unconditional altruist.

Islamic financiers have traditionally used contractual obligations to counter agency problems. However, in theory and in practice, the Muslim principal (particularly fund providers) is exposed to higher agency risk because the fund providers have the divine obligation to share risks in enterprise under the PLS scheme as well as to share a portion of incomes with the poor or the entrepreneurs who face difficulties in fund-raising. This altruistic or reciprocal behavior is always monitored by the absolute existence yet appropriate rules of protecting the right of the principal (or of punishing the agent when its opportunistic behavior is revealed) should be installed.

It is obvious that the survival of an entrepreneur depends on a lot of important elements such as congenial business environment, the entrepreneur's personal characteristics, business acumen etc. However, when it comes to the question of encouraging and protecting venture capitalists as well as ultimate investors, it is essential to ensure that the capitalist does not perceive a material threat to be cheated. This feeling can come from many sources but most importantly it can stem from financiers feeling that entrepreneurs exert less than optimum effort, show carelessness or lack of enthusiasm and sincerity, and other such problems peculiar to traditional agency relation. Although, in the perspective of Islamic altruism, venture financiers count on the divine rewards for helping financially constrained entrepreneurs, nobody knows about the others' devotion to the life hereafter. Thus, it is crucial to devise some *ex ante* tangible measures to safeguard venture financiers as well as ultimate investors. These measures can include raising awareness through spiritual quotient among entrepreneurs about the worldly benefits (availability of finance) and divine rewards for being honest and trustworthy. Also, some regulations congruent with Islamic principles can be put forth for resolving any dispute *ex post*. For so doing, the availability of scholars qualified to render a decision (*fatwa*) is to be ensured. Given the scarcity of such scholars, training for young but promising scholars by the initiatives of the state can be arranged. Moreover, a trustee board can be formed to insure against any potential fraudulent or cheating activities by the entrepreneurs. Such arrangement is not purely an insurance against the financial loss stemming from the normal course of business but a safeguard for financiers against possible agency problems. Of course, it might appear irrelevant installing a safeguard for an activity which is considered charity purely driven by altruistic behavior. This question characterizes the current reality of charitable activities in the Muslim world. First, the amount of realized *zakat* is too negligible to count compared to the estimated amount. This can be attributed to the problems of strong reciprocity. If wealthy individuals who are suffering from a strong sense of reciprocity can be motivated through instituting the means to invest in venture financing outlined in this section, the amount of charity will definitely be increased.

The same applies to banks and non-bank financial institutions that wish to divert some funds from mark-up *murabaha* financing to pure profit-and-loss sharing transactions. Elsiefy (2014) notes that the partnership contracts are not suitable for the banking business model because they do not fit with it. Given the low level of development of private enterprises and high unemployment in many Muslim countries, there is a greater scope for venture capital firms to flourish. However, some changes in the legal and regulatory environment need to be implemented because the existing guidelines to promote Islamic VC (for instance, the Guidelines and Best Practices on Islamic Venture Capital issued by Malaysian Securities Commission) mainly address the VC companies and fund managers in the light of *Shari'ah* compliance and do not introduce any incentive and protection guideline for fund providers. Many consulting and law firms engaged in Islamic finance insist that the legal and regulatory framework for Islamic VC should be developed. For instance, Azmi & Associates, one of the largest Kuala Lumpur-based law firms, proposes that the establishment of a legal and regulatory framework or the appropriate guidelines to regulate the industry is still one of the critical constraints for thriving Islamic financial activities. In this regard, an effective and active *Shari'ah* advisory board is a critical requirement. Second, the legal framework must be strong and internationally competitive so that it can cover the delicate issues related to modern technology. Third, the state can provide some support in the form of training to high-caliber individuals and management teams with expertise in investment strategies for developing professional skills so that they can stay up to the expectation of the financiers. For instance, entrepreneurs' tendency to engage with activities which are prohibited by Islamic *Shari'ah* will discourage prospective financiers. Thus, potential entrepreneurs who possess business skills and capacity can be equipped with *Shari'ah* knowledge through training so that they do not engage in activities prohibited in Islam. Moreover, the support and backing from the government in terms of incentives like tax holidays and tax exemptions are to be systemized. Unless these tangibles guidelines are devised and put into practice the unique structure which institutionalizes Islamic altruism and reciprocity would rather drain the supply of the fund for VC, though a better system for enhancing equity finance can only be constructively adapted through a process of trial and error.

5. Concluding comments

Bounded rationality is human innate nature. Also, opportunism in the human behavior is a reality. Resultantly, transaction costs of writing a precise and specific contract are significant. Societies have devised various institutions – formal or informal – to tackle the adverse effect of these features of economic agents. Trust has therefore transformed into a social lubricant. Islam as a religion not only encourages followers to maintain trust and reciprocity but also strictly prohibits any opportunistic behavior. From this perspective, this chapter has attempted to analyze altruism and reciprocity as important institutions prevailed in Islam and how these institutions can contribute in developing Islamic venture capital. In so doing, the chapter has described the nature and causes of opportunism and its associated transaction costs through the lens of NIE. Also, the role and importance of trust as an informal institution have been examined.

Citing some Qur'anic verses and *Hadith* as well as reviewing the existing literature on Islamic finance, we have shown that the provision of trust and reciprocity is persuasively pronounced in Islam. According to Islamic conventions, the poor are considered to have a share of the wealth of the rich and poverty in society is seen as a problem which calls for strong attention by the rich. In this sense, it is a moral obligation for wealthy individuals to finance an entrepreneur who is having financial difficulty for materializing his entrepreneurial skill. This will bring the financier benefits in two ways: first, he/she is complying with the Islamic teachings in spending his/her wealth and can expect divine rewards; second, he/she can earn some profit from the venture in case of success which is *Shari'ah*-based. At the same time, Islam provides provision for severe punishment in belief, but the limited punishment in practice in case of any opportunistic behavior. The motivation of Islamic altruism on the one hand and the possibly reduced transaction costs of contracting on the other should make Islamic venture capital a lucrative investment opportunity for those who are blessed with wealth. However, Islamic venture capital has not been well developed.

In explaining this anomaly, we have argued that only very few countries enforce Islamic laws at the state level. In most cases, it is self-enforcing. In the absence of strict enforcement at the state level a voluntary compliance of Islamic laws depends on the actor's choice. People who truly believe in divine punishment might strictly follow self-enforced Islamic principles. In this case, a state of no opportunism can be expected. However, this self-enforced mechanism is not enough for motivating people to finance small entrepreneurs because this mechanism purely relies on the belief of divine punishment. It is impossible to know *ex ante* agents' cautiousness about the divine punishment and act thereupon. It can be known only as the facts are revealed *ex post* which is very late. This situation may create an uncertainty for capitalists about agents' behavior. People, no matter whether they are altruistic or not, have an innate tendency to avoid a situation in which there exists any possibility of being cheated. Financing purely based on good faith on the Day of Judgment sometimes creates such a dilemma. Given the availability of numerous alternatives to charity, financiers might shy away from financing VC projects. Second, investors who wish to accomplish charity but also expect little profit from VC financing might be reluctant to take risks involved with venture capital as long as there are other less-risky *Shari'ah*-based financial products available to invest.

Choudhury (2001) however offers some modification for existing Islamic financial instruments to be real *Shari'ah*-based products like venture capital. This possibility comes to the vision due mainly to the fact that venture capital as a pure Islamic financial investment is not yet pronounced or well formulated so that capitalists can understand the difference between VC and other *Shari'ah*-based schemes in terms of both compliance of Islamic principles and risk and return associated with them. An aggregate effect of the lack of formal institutions on the one hand and a clear understanding of the difference between traditional Islamic financial products and venture capital in terms of both *Shari'ah* compliance and risk-return possibilities on the other has turned Islamic financiers into 'risk-averse' actors. As a result, Islamic venture capital is still underdeveloped despite all these competitive advantages embedded in the system. To overcome these obstacles, a national financial system should devise some tangible provisions for installing financier/investor-friendly regulations consistent with Islamic principles.

Acknowledgement

This chapter is a revised and updated version of Suzuki and Miah (2016) 'Altruism, reciprocity and Islamic equity finance', *International Journal of Islamic and Middle Eastern Finance and Management*, Vol. 9 Issue: 2, pp. 205–221. We are grateful to Emerald Group Publishing Limited for its permission on the reproduction.

Notes

1 We refer to *The Holy Qur'an, Arabic Text and English Translation* (2010), 9th printing, Noor Foundation International Inc.
2 We should note the difference in them. The form of *mudarabah* is a trust-based financing, while that of *musharaka* is a participatory financing.
3 The subsequent Chapter 7 by Suzuki, Hasan and Pramono have a different view on this point. They consider that the major sources of funds for Islamic VC should be (1) the pool of funds created by ambitious investors who are ready to absorb risk and uncertainty and/or (2) the governmental initiatives upon its long-term strategy for incubating new frontiers of business. In their view, the primary mission of Islamic VC is to promote future innovation which would enhance the sustainability of our economy, rather than to directly promote poverty alleviation.

5 Anatomy of Islamic venture capital

Typology of Bahraini/Indonesian Islamic venture capital

Yasushi Suzuki, A. K. M. Kamrul Hasan and Sigit Pramono

1. Introduction

Venture capital (VC) is not a fresh topic in modern finance but Islamic venture capital (Islamic VC) is relatively new in the Islamic banking and finance literature. In this chapter we will discuss Islamic VC and its dilemma. VC cannot grow if there are no entrepreneurial activities or entrepreneurial spirit in society. Entrepreneurs have to build the confidence of venture capitalists in their projects through commitment. Open and free communication can be considered a catalyst in building a strong relationship between both of them (Shepherd and Zacharakis, 2001). This chapter begins with the discussion of basic differences between Islamic microfinance and Islamic VC. The rest of the chapter is structured as follows: the differences between Islamic microfinance and Islamic venture capital is discussed in Section 2. The evolution and relationship between entrepreneurship and VC is discussed in Section 3. The nature of venture capital is discussed in Section 4. The concept of Islamic VC, its evolution and the dilemmas are discussed in Section 5. Section 6 discusses two Islamic VC – Venture Capital Bank of Bahrain and PNM Ventura Syariah of Indonesia – as a case study to look at the performance and operations of Islamic VC. We aim to offer a theoretical framework for classifying different types of Islamic VC. At the end of this chapter we offer some inclusive recommendation for Islamic VC and raise some concerns for future research.

2. The differences between Islamic microfinance and Islamic venture capital

There is little doubt that Islamic microfinance aims to ultimately contribute to poverty alleviation among its beneficiaries. On the contrary Islamic VC focuses on entrepreneurship development through funding the start-ups. In Table 5.1 we attempt to clarify the basic differences between these two different streams of Islamic finance and then we discuss in detail all points.

We highlight the following eight dimensions to clarify the differences in nature between Islamic microfinance and Islamic VC. (1) The individual insolvent households/unbanked households are the main clients for microfinance institutions (MFI), while the innovators or new start-ups are the prime target for Islamic

Table 5.1 Differences between Islamic microfinance and VC

Elements	Islamic microfinance	Islamic venture capital
(1) Main clients	Individuals, microenterprises	Innovators, start-ups
(2) Nature of risk and return to be absorbed	Relatively high risk but not so high return to be expected	Much higher risk, associated with higher returns
(3) Size of each project (in terms of investing money)	Small	Large
(4) Objectives	Wealth distribution by empowering the poor	Wealth creation
(5) Instrument to control/solution mechanism	I. Group (mutual) monitoring II. Governmental or NGO initiatives for supporting the fund-raising by MFIs	I. Screening and monitoring by experts and professionals II. Ijtihad – of paying effort incubating new frontiers of business
(6) Ultimate goal/mission	Poverty alleviation by empowering the poor. Improving social justice	Incubate future innovation for the sustainability of our economy
(7) Required human capacity in the investee	Including the clients who had the limited access to primary education	Higher skill humans are required
(8) Sources of funds	I. Donation from rich Muslims/development partners (DP) II. Zakat (one kind of religious tax that is compulsory to pay by rich/solvent Muslims)	I. Pool of funds created by ambitious investors who are ready to absorb risk and uncertainty II. Government initiatives upon its long-term strategy for incubating new frontiers of business

VC. (2) In terms of the risk and return to be absorbed, microfinance, by nature, deals with relatively high risk, but expects not-so-high returns from their base of clients, while VC business, by nature, deals with much higher risk associated with higher returns if the investee is successful. (3) In general, the size of each microfinance project is small, while that of VC projects is large. (4) Islamic finance can contribute to both 'wealth distribution' and 'wealth creation'. In this categorization we may classify Islamic microfinance as a contributor to wealth distribution and Islamic venture capital as a contributor to wealth creation. (5) In microfinance, a mutual/reciprocal monitoring mechanism in grouping their client individuals and the regulatory framework of monitoring MFI plays a vital role to supervise the investment of Islamic microfinance. Islamic VC companies are expected to assign portfolio professionals of screening and monitoring upon the *Shari'ah* compliance. The professionals are expected to monitor and supervise the new and innovative investment proposal through the mind of *ijtihad* for making efforts at incubating new frontiers of business. (6) The mission of Islamic microfinance includes alleviating poverty by empowering the poor and contributing to social justice in wealth distribution. On the other hand, the mission of Islamic VC is to promote future innovation which would enhance the sustainability of our economy. (7) For MFI the clients' educational qualification/literacy is not necessarily a core criterion for screening and monitoring, while for the VC firm, the CEO and CFO's capacity with its leadership in planning and implementing their business model is a core criterion for screening and monitoring. (8) For running the Islamic MFI, the charitable and concessional funds donated by development partners, government and *zakat* organizations might be inevitable. In contrast, for running the Islamic VC, in general, the long-term fund provided by the individual and/or governmental active institutional investors (such as pension fund) who are ready to absorb various types of risk and uncertainty is contributing.

3. Evolution and relationship between entrepreneurship and venture capital

The word 'entrepreneur' is of French origin which means 'undertaker' in the sense of the one who undertakes to do something. J. B. Say, a well-known French economist in the early 1800s, characterized the entrepreneur as a person who seeks to shift economic resources from the areas of low to high productivity (Smith and Smith, 2000). Joseph Schumpeter used the term 'creative destruction' in describing the entrepreneurship (Schumpeter, 1942). Frank Knight (1921) referred to an entrepreneur as 'a manager of uncertainty'. Schumpeter (1934) viewed the entrepreneur as actively seeking out opportunities to innovate. Peter Drucker describes entrepreneurs as those who "create something new, something different; they change or transmute values" (Drucker, 1985, p. 22).

Drucker (1985, p. 28) mentioned that "the entrepreneur always searches for change, responds to it and exploits it as an opportunity." He mentioned seven sources for innovative opportunity: (1) the unexpected success, failure and outside event; (2) the incongruity between reality as it actually is and reality as it is assumed to be; (3) innovation based on process needs; (4) changes in industry structure or market structure; (5) demographics (population change); (6) change in perception, mode and meaning; and (7) new knowledge both scientific and non-scientific. Scott Shane in his book *General Theory of Entrepreneurship* mentions:

> The entrepreneurial process begins with the perception of opportunities, or situations in which resources can be combined at a potential profit. Alert individuals, called entrepreneurs, discover these opportunities, and develop ideas for how to pursue them, including the development of a product or service that will be provided to customers. These individuals then obtain the resources, design organizations or other modes of opportunity exploitation, and develop a strategy to exploit the opportunity.
>
> (2003, p. 10)

He also mentions two core attributes of successful individual entrepreneurs such as getting better information and being able to utilize the information in a better way. Some researchers advocate that governmental initiatives are helpful to explore entrepreneurial activity which leads to venturing. Culture, well-being (quality of life) of individuals and economic freedom are the three determinants of entrepreneurial activity (Kuckertz *et al.*, 2015). Block *et al.* (2017) find (after scrutinizing 102 empirical studies published in academic journals) that opportunities for innovative entrepreneurship are exploited from various sources and it is important to get assistance from more experienced or portfolio entrepreneurs when developing policies to stimulate innovative behavior among entrepreneurs. They argue that innovative entrepreneurship can emerge from four sources such as inventors, innovative and demanding users, employees and academics because these specific groups of individuals have frequent contact with knowledge and research-based opportunities and thus are more likely to be engaged in innovative entrepreneurship (Block *et al.*, 2017). Venkataraman and Shane (2000) theoretically describe entrepreneurship from the Schumpeterian concept to cognitive properties and conclude that exploits of entrepreneurial opportunities depend on the nature of the opportunity and individual differences in perceptions. They find from previous research that opportunity costs of pursuing entrepreneurial activities, costs of obtaining resources, previous employment or entrepreneurial experience influences the entrepreneurial opportunity exploitation of individuals (Venkataraman and Shane, 2000). They argue that discovering an entrepreneurial opportunity by an individual depends on information accumulation from the past and the cognitive ability to identify a more likely to be successful enterprise. Decisions to exploit the opportunity depend on the nature of the opportunity and willingness to exploit the opportunity by individuals (Venkataraman and Shane, 2000). Therefore, although entrepreneurship is an individual initiative, its exploitation, growth and dimension depend on various factors especially the surrounding arrangement to flourish the entrepreneurial activity.

Roche *et al.* (2008) conduct an empirical research on the Ireland technology cluster, Castanhar *et al.* (2008) on the Brazilian furniture industry, and Arikan (2008) on the New York Silicon Valley. Their findings that state support and VC play supplementary roles to boost the cluster development in their respective research region are almost the same. For example, Arikan (2008) mentions that the Lower Manhattan Revitalization Plan (LMRP) and New York Information Technology Center (NYITC) initiated by the New York City mayor in the 1990s and the venture capitalists provide risk capital to the newly emerging entrepreneurial ventures which make Silicon Valley a hub for the high-tech sector. Therefore, the role of government and, broadly speaking, state support are very essential for nurturing the entrepreneurship as well as venture capitalists. Porter (1990), in his book *The Competitive Advantage of Nation*, refers to the 'Diamond framework' consisting with four factors such as factor condition, demand condition, related and supporting industries, and firm strategy for enhancing a nation's competitiveness. While talking about related and supporting industries, he argues that the existence of internationally competitive industries within the nation shapes the nation's competitiveness. To build a competitive industries network, innovation is prerequisite. Chung *et al.* (2008) find the positive impact on policy intervention in the development of the Korean VC industry. Supapol *et al.* (2008) mention that Chinese state-owned institutions helped the individual-owned small business/new entrepreneurs.

Basically start-ups need 'equity finance' for diversifying the project risk. Usually, 'banks' as 'depository corporations' would hesitate to undertake the project risk (project finance in terms of non- or limited-recourse finance) by start-ups. Banks would prefer to consider the corporate risk (corporate finance); however, in the case of the start-ups which do not have the track record in operations, banks would face the difficulty of judging their corporate risk. Under this situation, the venture capitalists are expected to share the project risk of start-ups or entrepreneurs. To some extent the governmental initiatives such as fund allocation, tax exemption for VC firms and developing the capital market are necessary as the incentives for venture capitalists. The budget allocation for higher education is also another important governmental initiative for incubating skilled and innovative entrepreneurs in society. Silicon Valley in the US is considered the birth place of VC of the States. Silicon Valley is developed through a community initiative for incubating entrepreneurs and venture capitalists. Silicon Valley's inception and growing-up stages can be divided into several stages. In 1891 Stanford University was founded in the California area. In 1910, some individual investors arrived in the Bay Area and they basically dealt with critical electronics components of telephones, radios and televisions. In 1939, two Stanford graduates established Hewlett-Packard (HP) which is considered a milestone for Silicon Valley. Later on, semiconductor research and manufacturing companies landed in the Bay Area. In 1971 the term 'Silicon Valley' was popularized by electronics news. In the 1970s the private venture capital firm hugely gathered in Silicon Valley. As a result, a tremendous tech revolution occurred in the subsequent two decades in Silicon Valley and many innovative enterprises including Google, Facebook and Twitter were born at Silicon Valley (Bahrain Islamic Venture Capital Report, 2016).

4. Nature of venture capital

Venture capital investment screening, contracting and monitoring mechanisms are to be designed to minimize the moral hazard and adverse selection problem (Berger and Udell, 1998). Screening starts with a comprehensive due diligence about business, market etc. prior to investment which leads to designing an appropriate contract (Berger and Udell, 1998). Sahlman (1990) highlights the importance of contract design in minimizing agency costs. He argues that the role of venture capital in various stages of investment such as seed investment, start-ups, early development and expansion of rapid growth should be conducted with rigorous screening and legal structure, which would result in minimizing agency problems between venture capitalists and entrepreneurs; on the other hand there might arise agency problems between external investors who invest in VC firms and venture capitalists. He mentions that "there is inevitably a high degree of information asymmetry between the venture capitalists, who play an active role in the portfolio companies, and the limited partners, who cannot monitor the prospects of each individual investment as closely" (Sahlman, 1990, p. 493). To avoid this problem he stresses standardization of operating procedures and contracting by VC firms.

Amit *et al.* (1998) argue the importance of VC in alleviating information asymmetry and consequently potential moral hazard problems. While analyzing the Canadian venture capital firms' performance between 1991 and 1996, they find that the venture capitalists who enter in later-stage investment can overcome potential moral hazard problems as they enter in the business as an equity partner mitigating 'hidden information' or 'hidden action' problems possibly occurring in the relationship with the entrepreneurs. Amit *et al.* (1998) also argue that even though the VCs tend to specialize in those industries associated with higher risk and fundamental uncertainty, they would prefer the venture with less information asymmetries. In general, VCs would prefer the later-stage entrepreneurial firms than the early stage firms. On the other hand, through the accumulation of skills in screening and monitoring, VCs are expected to deal well with screening and monitoring entrepreneurial firms compared to other unspecialized investors (Amit *et al.*, 1998).

Well-screening and monitoring are possible by the evaluation of observable attributes of entrepreneurial ventures. These attributes include the tangible assets such as 'patent' (Hsu and Ziedenis, 2013; Conti *et al.*, 2013), 'prototype' (Audretsch *et al.*, 2012), 'business opportunity' (Kaplan *et al.*, 2009), 'prior knowledge' (Shane, 2000), 'human capital' (Hsu, 2007; Colombo and Grilli, 2010) and so on.

The importance of VCs is that they help entrepreneurial ventures to raise the funds which they cannot access from other sources, by way of alleviating information gaps for the sake of the investors to absorb the risk and uncertainty embedded in the ventures (Gompers and Lerner, 2001; Bertoni *et al.*, 2013). VCs not only provide capital but also monitor and support their portfolio companies (Gompers and Lerner, 1999b; Macmillan *et al.*, 1989). A positive impact of VCs with a higher patenting rate (Kortum and Lerner, 2000;) stimulating innovation (Hirukawa and Ueda, 2011) and company level (Chemmanur *et al.*, 2011; Hellmann and Puri, 2000), employment and sales growth (Bertoni *et al.*, 2011), speed of product to the market (Hellmann and Puri, 2000), professionalization (Hellmann and Puri, 2002) and VC's reputation have a positive impact on firm valuation (Hsu, 2004).

5. Islamic venture capital concept and dilemma

The provision of trust and reciprocity is clearly pronounced in Islam. In this context there must be a moral obligation for successful Muslim businessmen to incubate new entrepreneurs who are having financial difficulty in materializing their entrepreneurial skill (Suzuki and Miah, 2016). They also argue that "the motivation of Islamic altruism on the one hand and reduced transaction cost of contracting on the other should make Islamic VC a lucrative investment opportunity for those who are blessed with wealth" (p. 218). Well-raising and mobilizing Islamic venture capital through *mudaraba* and *musharaka* (M&M) depends on the cooperation and coordination among agents, firms and investment sectors (Choudhury, 2001). Choudhury (2001) advocates that through introducing extensive participation, such as Islamic venture capital, can reduce the pre-Islamic character of 'sleeping partnership' found in M&M instrument and it can be removed by increase in entitlement, empowerment and ownership in the extensively participatory enterprises. Hasan *et al.* (2011) mention two stages of Islamic venture capital evolution such as 'classical' and 'modern' Islamic venture capital. While the former one deals with M&M, the latter includes the contract based on the profit–loss sharing (PLS) and equity finance. In this section we will elaborate on the concept of venture capital from the Islamic point of view, the evolution of Islamic venture capital and the dilemmas in venture capital.

It is said that solutions based on the Islamic injunctions (collectively termed 'spiritual quotient') could serve to mitigate agency risks. However, as Suzuki and Miah (2016) point out, the Muslim principal (particularly fund providers) is exposed to higher agency risk unless appropriate rules of protecting the right of the principal (or of punishing the agent when its opportunistic behavior is revealed) are devised, because the Muslim fund providers have the divine obligation to share risks in enterprise under the profit–loss sharing (PLS) scheme as well as to share a portion of income with the poor or those entrepreneurs who face difficulties in fund-raising (see Chapter 4). Here we look at the dilemmas of Islamic venture capital which can broadly be categorized into two dimensions such as conceptual dilemmas and operational dilemmas.

5.1 *Conceptual dilemmas*

1   Exit route: Preferred stock is the most common tool used by VC firms as 'the form of investment' and the initial public offering (IPO) as an exit route.

Preferred stock is a lucrative instrument for venture capitalists. Preferred stock option in the context of '*gharar*' and '*riba*' is still controversial among *Shari'ah* scholars. Some *Shari'ah* scholars opine that preferred stock involves, in particular, *riba* as it is attached with the fixed dividend which is deemed the 'pre-determined' rate of returns to VC firms.

2   Moral hazard: The absence of standardization in *Shari'ah* compliance on venture capital may have created a moral hazard among the existing players and confusion for new entrants. Mentionable here is that four major *Madhabs* (*Shari'ah* schools of law) are commonly practiced in the Muslim countries and there exist some differences in opinions/interpretations among the four schools of *Shari'ah* scholars. For example, in Bahrain, Maliki Madhab is followed and AAOFI standards are strictly followed for Islamic financial institutions, while in Malaysia Muslims practice the Shafi'i school of laws. In general, the Shafi'i school offers a more flexible opinion than the Maliki and Hanafi schools which are influential in Middle Eastern Muslim countries like KSA and Bahrain, and South Asian countries like Bangladesh and Pakistan. We see that the differences in legal opinions (*fatwa*) give different incentives to venture capitalists. On the other hand, too much flexibility in the interpretation of *Shari'ah* principles may cause potential moral hazard problems in the VC business. The VC industry faces the difficulty of seeking a delicate balance in incubating new ventures while avoiding potential moral hazard problems.

5.2 *Operational dilemmas*

1   Lack of experts, professionals and academicians: 'Islamic banking' started to receive more attention among academics starting in the 1960s. But the financing mode of venture capital and microfinance collected less attention in Muslim-majority countries even in the late 1990s. A limited number of even academic research has been done over Islamic venture capital so far. Insufficient accumulation of skill and knowledge in Islamic venture capital may have failed to incubate the experts/professionals who are expected to screen and monitor the innovative venture seeds. Simultaneously, the failure to incubate the experts/professionals of screening and monitoring may have failed to accumulate the skill and knowledge in Islamic venture capital, consequently trapping Islamic VC in a 'vicious circle'.

2   Weak governance in *Shari'ah* boards: There exist potential conflicts of interest as well as "a huge paradox" (Bakar, 2016) between *Shari'ah* scholars and the other stakeholders under the situation that the *Shari'ah* board members are appointed and remunerated by the financial institutions (Chapter 9 in this book discusses this issue). Besides, we should note that while we could expect the role of the *Shari'ah* Advisory Council at the national level as the monitor of standardizing the operations of the internal *Shari'ah* board at individual Islamic 'banks'; on the other hand, the monitoring mechanism at the national and central level over the operations of *Shari'ah* boards in Islamic 'VC firms'

is in general underdeveloped, though the regulatory framework varies in each Muslim country, as is argued in the next list. This weak governance structure may give an ill incentive for the *Shari'ah* board members in Islamic VC firms to become too flexible or too conservative.

Now we look at some aspects of Bahraini, Malaysian, Bangladeshi and Indonesian VC law to reflect the regulatory guidelines of these countries.

1   *Bahrain Islamic VC law:* Central Bank of Bahrain (CBB) is the prime regulator of the country's capital market. In September 2017, CBB published the first *Shari'ah* Governance Module (SBG) for Islamic banks which will be effective beginning 30 June 2018. According to the module, all Bahraini Islamic Bank licensees must have a *Shari'ah* Supervisory Board (SSB) consisting of at least three scholars specialized in *fiqh-al-muamalat* and for the first time an Independent External *Shari'ah* Compliance Audit (IESCA) has been made mandatory for all Islamic banks.

2   *Malaysian Islamic VC law*: Securities Commission, Malaysia issued 'Guidelines on the Registration of Venture Capital and Private Equity Corporations and Management Corporations' in March 2015 for venture capital registration and the Islamic VC should also register under the same guidelines. For Islamic VC there is a clause (no. 5.01) in the guidelines regarding the appointment of a *Shari'ah* advisor, which is that:

> an applicant who wishes to undertake Islamic VC or PE activities must appoint a *Shari'ah* adviser to provide *Shari'ah* expertise and guidance on all matters pertaining to the Islamic VC or PE activities and ensure that all aspects of the activities are in accordance with *Shari'ah* requirements, including resolutions issued by the *Shari'ah* Advisory Council (SAC) of the SC.
>
> (SCM, 2015)

3   *Bangladesh Islamic VC:* Bangladesh Securities and Exchange Commission (BSEC) is the chief regulator of the country's capital market. In June 2015, BSEC first issued the guidelines for venture capital and private equity which is known as Bangladesh Securities and Exchange Commission (Alternative Investment) Rules, 2015. Although the venture capital market is in a very early stage in Bangladesh, there is a provision in the rules to form an 'Islamic Fund'. According to the rules, a '*Shari'ah* council' is required in every Islamic fund.

4   *Indonesian Islamic VC:* VC firms in Indonesia are categorized as one form of non-bank financial institutions. The previous regulations related to VC firms in Indonesia included Minister of Finance Regulation Number 18/ PMK.010/2012 of 2012 concerning venture capital companies. Basically, this regulation was issued with regard to implementing the provisions of Articles 8 and 11 of Presidential Regulation No. 9 of 2009 concerning financing institutions. Since the establishment of the Indonesian Financial

Services Authority (FSA) at the beginning of 2013, the arrangement and supervision of venture capital firms in Indonesia were transferred under the FSA's authority. The FSA issued new regulations related to business licenses and establishment, business management, *Shari'ah* principles, and governance for venture capital firms (VC) and/or venture capital firms based on *Shari'ah* principles (Islamic VC) as FSA regulation No. 31/POJK.05/2014 of 2014, FSA regulation No. 34/POJK.05/2015 of 2015, and FSA regulation No. 35/POJK.05/2015 of 2015. According to article 2 of FSA regulation No. 34/POJK.05/2015, VC and Islamic VC take a legal form of a limited liability company (Perseroan Terbatas/PT), cooperative, or limited partnership (*Commanditaire Vennootschap*). Based on article 2 and 6 of FSA regulation No. 35/POJK.05/2015, VC and Islamic VC's main activities are specified: (1) placement in equity participation, (2) quasi-equity participation (investment in convertible bonds and/or *Sukuk*), (3) financing through the purchase of convertible bonds or *Sukuk* issued by a start-up company, and (4) business development or other financing activities and fee-based income under the approval of FSA. As of 31 December 2016, there are 62 conventional VC firms (in which 3 companies have Islamic windows) and 4 companies involved in full-fledged Islamic VC operations (FSA, 2016).

6. The case of Bahraini and Indonesian Islamic VC

6.1 *Venture Capital Bank of Bahrain*

Venture Capital Bank of Bahrain (hereafter VCBB) is the first full-fledged Islamic VC (offering only the Islamic mode of VC solutions) in the GCC, Middle Eastern and North African (MENA) region, which was established in 2005. We take VCBB as a type of Islamic VC because it has the longest track record in operating Islamic VC and diversifies its investment portfolio into the GCC region, Turkey, the UK and the US. Although VCBB is established in Bahrain, Bahraini nationals occupy only 7.99 percent share in the shareholding. The Annual Report 2015–2016 reports that the company's shareholding composition as of 30 June 2016 was shared by KSA, Kuwait, Qatar, and UAE nationals with its share of 57.71 percent, 23.66 percent, 7.78 percent and 3.29 percent, respectively. VCBB has the *Shari'ah* board which is composed of three Islamic studies and *fiqh* scholars. The financial performance of VCBB is presented in Figure 5.1.

In addition, the VCBB exposure industry-wise from 2007 to 2016 is shown in Table 5.2.

While considering the net profit of the bank it shows a steady trend since 2013 to 2015 and decline in 2016. However regarding the decline of profit in 2016 VCBB explained that the fair value of losses and impairment of provisions negatively affected the income statement. Moreover, VCBB experienced a negative profit in 2010 and 2011 due to fair value losses and impairment of real estate sector investment that occurred due partly to the Arab Spring. On the other hand, the bank has built a strong capital base through its 10-year journey. Its assets base

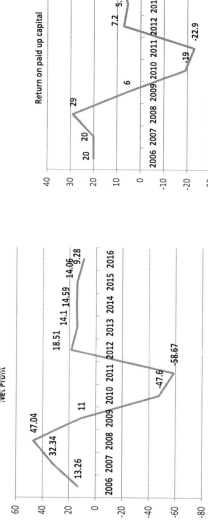

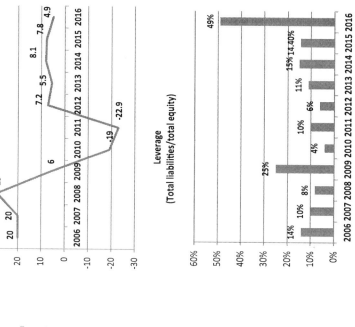

Figure 5.1 VCBB's net profit (US$ million), return on capital, total investment to total assets, and leverage from 2006 to 2016

Source: created by authors based on the annual reports of VCBB during 2007 and 2016

Table 5.2 VCBB's total asset concentration (industry sector-wise)

Industry sector	2007	2008	2009	2010	2011	2013 (for 18 months)	2014	2015	2016
Trading and manufacturing	4.8%	8.0%	7.5%	13.0%	18.8%	13.5%	15.0%	15.6%	11.2%
Banks and FIs	35.5%	15.8%	20.3%	18.4%	22.6%	17.7%	14.2%	7.7%	7.8%
Real estate sector	25.5%	48.4%	46.4%	33.3%	27.8%	26.3%	26.2%	27.2%	31.8%
Oil and gas	4.5%	6.2%	2.7%	4.1%	3.2%	5.9%	5.4%	5.1%	3.2%
Healthcare	0.0%	3.8%	3.5%	7.7%	7.7%	6.8%	8.1%	7.4%	5.7%
Technology	5.2%	2.9%	1.4%	1.1%	0.0%	1.7%	1.5%	1.2%	0.7%
Transportation/shipping	8.1%	6.1%	4.8%	8.0%	9.4%	8.5%	7.1%	7.5%	13.0%
Others	16.4%	8.7%	13.3%	14.4%	10.5%	19.7%	22.4%	28.4%	26.5%
Total	100%	100%	100%	100%	100%	100%	100%	100%	100%

Source: created by authors based on the annual reports of VCBB during 2007 and 2016

stood at US$ 334.3 million at 30 June 2016 compared to US$ 90.9 million at 30 June 2006, and shareholders' equity stood at US$ 224.3 million at the end of financial year 2016 vs. US$ 79.8 million at the end of financial year 2006. Leverage ratio and return on capital also show moderate trends over their life spans. This indicate that VC bank tries to strengthen its footstep first.

It has shown that, during its first five years of journey, VCBB concentrated on the real estate sector but the negative externality by the US subprime loan crisis and the subsequent Arab Spring in the MENA region and political unrest in Bahrain lost their profit base, then VCBB seemed to be forced to change its investment strategy. VCBB has started to build expertise in healthcare, oil and gas, and shipping to diversify its portfolio and to go beyond the MENA region (i.e. Turkey, the UK and the US) as a strategy to mitigate the geographical risk. This strategy seems to have proven well and VCBB maintains a steady profit margin since 2013. Also we should note that VCBB has reduced its investment on bank and financial institutions which may have partly contributed to the two-step loans to real estate projects.

Regarding the business model of VCBB we can say that VCBB was still looking for a suitable market niche to survive. It is observed from VCBB's last 10 years of investment policy that initially it focused on real estate sector. Later it concentrated on the retail and healthcare sectors in the MENA region and some real estate sectors in the UK to ensure guaranteed return at the end of the financial year and a safe investment exit strategy which reflects VCBB's risk-averse attitude. However, VCBB seems to have resumed its focus on the real estate sector. Meanwhile, it is reported that VCBB reshuffled its human resources as a cost reduction strategy during the period 2010 and 2011 and it focused on building its own human capital expertise to enter in a stable market like Turkey. However, although VCBB has committed to invest in new ventures, it is observed that VCBB has focused on later-stage enterprises which have a previous transaction record and track record of performance. We can say that the VCBB model can be considered a conservative form of venture capital that seeks reasonable returns while avoiding the genuine project risk embedded in new ventures.

6.2 PT PNM Ventura Syariah

Small- and medium-sized enterprises (SMEs) have been proven to contribute significantly to driving the real sector economy and absorbing many employees in the Indonesian economy. Based on *Statistic of Micro and Small and Medium Enterprises Year 2008–2009* (Ministry of Cooperative and Small and Medium Enterprise 2010), there were at least 52 million SMEs including microenterprises in 2009 which accounted for 99.99 percent of the number of business units in the economy. Furthermore, SMEs absorbed 96 million employees (97.3 percent of total employees) and contributed 58.27 percent of the Indonesian GDP (Ministry of Cooperative and Small and Medium Enterprises, 2010; Dewi and Kasri, 2011).

Nevertheless, there exist obstacles which hinder the improvement of the competitiveness of microenterprises and SMEs (MSMEs) in Indonesia. The MSMEs' limited access to finance and capital sources is raised as one of the major obstacles (Bank Indonesia 2016). To ease their funding constraint, a state-owned enterprise, namely PT Permodalan Nasional Madani (Persero or PNM), was established based on Government Decree of Republic Indonesia No. 38/99 dated 29 May 1999. PNM was expected to play its strategic roles in supporting MSMEs through training the management skills and facilitating their financial access. The following contributions are reported by PNM (2016): (1) conducting financing through a cooperative microfinance institution with more than 1,200 cooperatives and rural banks (Bank Perkreditan Rakyat/BPR); (2) conducting direct financing to the micro and small enterprises through the Micro Capital Services Unit (Unit Layanan Modal Mikro/ULaMM); and (3) developing the Mekaar unit (Membina Ekonomi Keluarga Sejahtera/Developing Prosperous Families' Economy) as a group-based empowerment service for underprivileged women of micro business practitioners.

In this chapter we are more concerned with how PNM have contributed to incubating new ventures. In 2000, PNM established a VC firm as its subsidiary known as PT PNM Venture Capital (99.99 percent of the shares are owned by PNM). Then, in 2002, PT PNM Venture Capital established PT PNM Ventura Syariah (99.995 percent of the shares are owned by PT PNM Venture Capital) as a VC firm which is operated under the *Shari'ah* principles.

Table 5.3 shows the comparison of total asset and total financing of the banking industry, venture capital companies (VCC), and PNM, respectively, in selected years. We can see the marginal magnitude of the fund from VCC and PNM compared to that of the banking industry.

Figures 5.2, 5.3, and 5.4 present the total asset, the total financing, and the total revenue of PNM, PNM Venture Capital (PNM-VC) and PNM Ventura Syariah (PNM-VS), respectively, in 2015 and 2016. These figures clearly show that the magnitude of the VC vehicles (PNM-VC and PNM-VS) in the PNM Group was still marginal. Besides, we can see that the size of PNM-VS was around half or one-third of that of PNM-VC.

Table 5.3 Comparison of total asset and total financing of the banking industry, Venture Capital Company and PNM in selected years (in trillion Rp)

YEAR	Total asset			Total financing		
	Banking	*Venture Capital Company (VCC)*	*PNM*	*Banking*	*Venture Capital Company (VCC)*	*PNM*
2010	3,055	3.0	3.3	2,810	3.0	1.6
2015	6,198	9.5	6.0	6,051	6.8	4.1
2016	6,844	12.0	7.7	6,680	8.8	5.4

Source: created by authors upon Financial Services Authority (2016a, 2016b, 2017a, 2017b) and Bank Indonesia (2016)

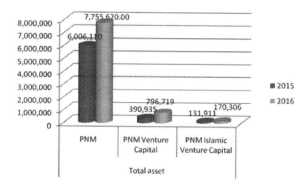

Figure 5.2 Comparison of total asset of PNM, PNM Venture Capital, and PNM Ventura Syariah in 2016 and 2015 (in million Rp)

Source: authors, constructed from annual reports of each company, respectively

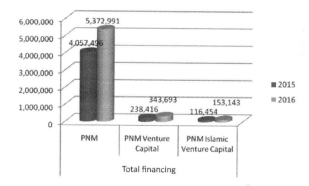

Figure 5.3 Comparison of total financing of PNM, PNM Venture Capital, and PNM Ventura Syariah in 2016 and 2015 (in million Rp)

Source: authors, constructed from annual reports of each company, respectively

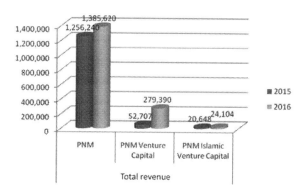

Figure 5.4 Comparison of total revenue of PNM, PNM Venture Capital, and PNM Ventura Syariah in 2016 and 2015 (in million Rp)

Source: authors, constructed from annual reports of each company, respectively

Table 5.4 presents the selected financial performance of PNM, PNM-VC and PNM-VS, respectively, in 2015 and 2016. We can see that the profitability (ROE and Profit Margin Ratio) of PNM-VS was in a lower level among the PNM group, though the Operating Ratio of PNM-VS suggested a better performance in efficiency.

We conducted interviews on 9 and 13 October 2017 with a senior officer and member of the *Shari'ah* Supervisory Board (SSB) of PNM-VS. The following interviewee's comments are suggestive; first, the interviewee considers that the limitation in funding is the main obstacle for PNM-VS to expand its business. According to the interviewee, the PNM group is, in general, exposed to the more severe competition for raising the necessary funds, even though the group has been financially supported by the government (as we recognized that in the period 1999–2014, PNM group was appointed as credit management of ex-Credit Program Liquidity of Bank Indonesia (Bantuan Likuiditas Bank Indonesia/BLBI)). The increase in the cost of fund forces the company to cut the cost of operating for improving the efficiency. Nevertheless, it is worth noting that currently, in order to have a lower cost of fund, management of PNM-VS has taken an initiative to perform a strategic alliance with Indonesian *Waqf* Board (Badan Wakaf Indonesia/BWI) in utilizing *waqf* funds as a financial source in financing Muslim entrepreneurs' business projects. Second, the interviewee realizes that PNM-VS is facing the difficulty of training the professionals in effectively managing the VC fund. As a result, the skills and knowledge of screening and incubating innovative start-ups have not yet been accumulated in PNM-VS. Third, the interviewee considers that PNM-VS is facing the difficulty of diversifying and socializing the risk embedded in the participatory mode of financing (for instance, *musharaka mutanaqisa* (diminishing *musharaka*) which is expected to be utilized for incubating innovators-entrepreneurs.

We are not sure how much of the VC fund would be necessary for meeting the demand by innovative start-ups and ventures in Indonesia. However, we should

Table 5.4 Comparison of selected financial performance of PNM, PNM Venture Capital, and PNM Ventura Syariah in 2016 and 2015

Financial performance	2015			2016		
	PNM	PNM Venture Capital	PNM Ventura Syariah	PNM	PNM Venture Capital	PNM Ventura Syariah
Return on equity (ROE)	3.79%	3.94%	1.67%	3.95%	9.51%	0.66%
Liquidity ratio	510.83 %	532.31 %	16,935.05%	618.00%	487.00%	17,444.18%
Profit margin ratio	8.93%	5.17 %	3.69%	6.31%	9.24%	1.33%
Operating ratio	67.29%	105.44 %	43.79%	77.05%	107.64%	44.87%

Source: authors, constructed from annual reports of each company, respectively

note that even though 15 years have already passed since its establishment in 2002, the size and performance of PNM-VS has been quite marginal. Perhaps the PNM group has been focusing on financing to MSMEs, rather than financing the start-ups and ventures. It seems that PNM-VS as an Islamic VC firm, despite being financially supported at least indirectly by the government, fails to accumulate the skill and knowledge necessary to incubate and support innovative ventures, consequently losing its *raison d'être* in the market.

6.2.1 Typology of VC firms

Based on the discussions in this chapter on historical trend of venture capital and two cases on Islamic venture capital, we wish to offer a theoretical framework for the typology of Islamic venture capital. In our model, we are mapping each domain of following four types, taking into account each strategy for challenging risks and expected return (see Figure 5.5). Each domain may be overlapped in practices.

1 *Typical VC in matured economies:* In the relationship between risk (with uncertainty) and returns, typical VC firms particularly in matured economies are expected to explore innovative venture seeds, challenging 'high risk' but expecting 'high return'-type profit opportunities. The domain of typical VC particularly in matured economies is drawn as in Figure 5.5.
2 *Commercial banks (including Islamic commercial banks):* In contrast, the basic preference of credit portfolio selection by commercial banks is quite conservative, mainly because they are responsible as depository corporations for ensuring the returns to the depositors.

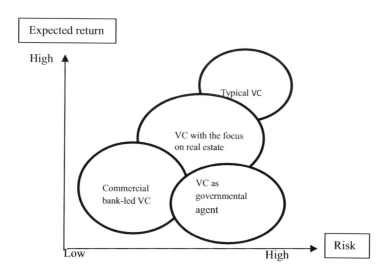

Figure 5.5 Typology of Islamic financial institutions including Islamic venture capital firms

3   *VC with the focus on real estate projects.* Due partly to the lack of skill and knowledge in screening and monitoring innovative seeds or the weak demand for incubating high-end industries in pre-matured economies, this type of Islamic VC may prefer a conventional strategy to seek relatively higher returns upon the mortgage over the real estate projects by mitigating the project risk. VCBB can be categorized into this type.

4   *VC with governmental support.* This type of VC plays the role as 'agent' for facilitating governmental funds (policy lending) for the purpose of incubating innovative SMEs which have the limited access to the credit/loan markets. PNM takes the role as the agent of mediating governmental funds. PNM itself does not necessarily seek higher returns.

7. Concluding remarks

In fact, Islamic venture capital is the newest wing of the Islamic finance industry. In this chapter we begin with the clarification of the difference between Islamic microfinance and Islamic venture capital. We reviewed the contemporary literature on venture capital and the historical background of Silicon Valley, then discussed about the dilemmas facing Islamic VC firms. In addition, we discussed about two different types of Islamic VC firms.

We should note that the role and strategy of Islamic VC firms are not identical. In the case of Bahraini Islamic VC firm (VCBB), their strategy is, by nature, considered still conservative for focusing on the real estate projects backed by the mortgage, though VCBB is now diversifying their credit portfolio and mitigating the geographical risk, as well as accumulating the skill and knowledge of screening and monitoring innovative start-ups. In the case of Indonesian Islamic VC, PNM-VS is expected to play the role as 'agent' for facilitating governmental funds (policy lending) for the purpose of incubating innovative (or sick) SMEs which have the limited access to the credit/loan market by commercial banks. However, it seems that PNM-VS as an Islamic VC firm, even though it has been financially supported, at least, indirectly by the government, has failed to accumulate the skill and knowledge necessary to incubate and support innovative ventures, consequently losing its *raison d'être* in the market.

As mentioned earlier, VC cannot grow if there are no entrepreneurial activities or entrepreneurial spirit in society. Entrepreneurs have to build up the degree of confidence of venture capitalists in their projects through commitment, and open and free communication can be considered a catalyst in building a strong relationship between both of them. This leads us to ask: How are Islamic VC firms ready to build up the degree of confidence in entrepreneurs? It might be a bit too early to judge it. However, we are afraid that what Islamic VC firms particularly in the stage of developing can do for contributing to entrepreneurial activities in society would be very limited.

6 *Sukuk* environment and challenges in Bangladesh and Malaysia (with the supplement of the Japan-*sukuk* case)

S. M. Sohrab Uddin, Nahid Afroz and Yasushi Suzuki

1. Introduction

Sukuk (Islamic bond) is an alternative financing instrument that represents undivided ownership of an underlying asset, specific project or investment activities based upon the principles of Islamic *Shari'ah* (Islamic law). The main concept of *Sukuk* stands on the Islamic principle of prohibition of *riba* (interest). Before the origination of *Sukuk*, the Muslim community used to have a few choices for investment in interest-free instruments. They either had to invest their funds in real assets or in *Shari'ah*-compliant stock market securities (Tariq and Dar, 2007; cited in Ahmed *et al.*, 2015). The income from such investment was highly risky and irregular in nature and accordingly Muslims required some low-risk fixed income from their investment. The issuance of the first *Sukuk* in Malaysia in the 1980s has been able to meet the demand of the Muslim community. The net outstanding amount of world *Sukuk* stood at $349.1 billion in 2016, a 576 percent growth in 10 years (Bank Negara Malaysia and Surahanjaya Sekuriti, 2009; Surahanjaya Sekurity, 2017a). Such an upsurge indicates the potential of the *Sukuk* industry for attracting investors around the world.

A number of countries are joining the list of *Sukuk* issuers every year. Starting in 1980, Malaysia has continued to be the market leader in the *Sukuk* industry for almost three decades. The successful position of Malaysia is grounded on its planned infrastructure. In addition, the combined effort of the government of Malaysia, Bank Negara Malaysia (central bank of the country), Surahanjaya Sekurity (Securities Commission Malaysia), and National *Shari'ah* Board is the strength of the *Sukuk* industry in Malaysia. On the other hand, Bangladesh started its voyage in this industry in 2004. However, the absence of required infrastructure and the mechanism for Islamic securities have been causing hindrance to further issue of *Sukuk* securities. The success of Islamic banking in Bangladesh, currently one-fifth of the banking sector as a whole indicates that there exists high potential for further acceleration of *Sukuk* instruments.

Even though a significant number of studies are conducted on *Sukuk*, very few of them concentrate on cross-country comparison. At this backdrop, this chapter aims at examining the *Sukuk* environment and challenges in Bangladesh and Malaysia by analyzing the *Sukuk* instruments available in both countries, by identifying the areas in which the *Sukuk* market of Bangladesh is different from that of Malaysia, by portraying the potential of Bangladesh for *Sukuk* issuance to a greater extent, and by highlighting the obstacles of the *Sukuk* market in Bangladesh.

The latter part of the chapter is divided into six sections. Section 2 focuses on the literature review. Section 3 offers an overview of existing *Sukuk* instruments of Bangladesh and Malaysia. Section 4 highlights the purposes for investment in *Sukuk* instruments in both countries. Section 5 provides a summary of the legal and regulatory framework for *Sukuk* in Bangladesh and Malaysia. Section 6 introduces the potential for further acceleration of the *Sukuk* industry in Bangladesh. In parallel, Japan is an evolving case showing how a form of financial praxis originally based in the identity and ethical concerns of Islam has acquired new appeal and is thereby expanding into regions of the global economy that is lacking large Muslim populations (Morrison, 2013). Section 7 aims to review the J-*sukuk* issuance scheme and the tax measures regarding J-*sukuk*, and to draw the dilemmas and challenges in J-*sukuk*. The last section concludes the paper with some policy recommendations.

2. Literature review

Sukuk represents certificates of equal value characterized by undivided claims on the income of underlying *Shari'ah*-compliant assets or investment activities or projects. According to Islamic Financial Services Board (IFSB), *Sakk* (singular form of *Sukuk*) as understood in its contemporary form[1] means Islamic bonds or certificates with "a proportional undivided ownership right in tangible assets or a pool of predominantly tangible assets or a business venture". These assets or business activities must comply with *Shari'ah* principles. In addition, Accounting and Auditing Organization of Islamic Financial Institutions (AAOIFI) describes *Sukuk* as "certificates of equal value representing undivided shares in ownership of tangible assets, usufruct and services or in ownership of the asset of a particular project or a special investment activity" (AAOIFI, 2003, p. 299).

The term *Sukuk* has come into existence to replace conventional debt instruments. However, many scholars mark *Sukuk* as a combination of conventional stock (equity) and bond (debt). Similar to bonds, *Sukuk* has a fixed term to maturity, regular income, and a final payment at the end of maturity. Again, the profit-sharing nature and uncertainty in amount of profit resembles some features of stock. These resemblances to conventional securities emphasize the necessity to distinguish *Sukuk* from other instruments. A *Sukuk* must meet three criteria to be *Shari'ah* compliant: must represent ownership (not a claim of indebtedness), payments should come from after-tax income (not payable in case of loss, unless stated otherwise), and the payment at the end of maturity should reflect the market value of the underlying asset (not the original amount of investment) (Godlewski *et al.*, 2013). Basically, *Sukuk* is a debt instrument. However, longer tenors, perpetual bonds, and 'hybrid capital' issues allowing a mix of debt and equity are all now commonplace among *Sukuk* instruments (HSBC Bank Malaysia Berhad, 2015). We should note that a type of *Sukuk* has a 'hybrid' characteristic of debt and equity.

As an emerging area, literature on *Sukuk* studies is yet to assume a mature shape. Zulkhibiri (2015, pp. 247–248) describes this situation as an "underdeveloped state of research". He argues that absence of historical, related, and consistent data along with the insignificant number of journals attributed to Islamic finance are the principal reasons for such a situation.

The existing literature on *Sukuk* can be divided into three categories. The first category intends to introduce *Sukuk* and its securitization process. This category focuses on the ways in which *Sukuk* complies with the *Shari'ah* law and the opinions of scholars on this subject. Other studies in the same category focus on the areas in which *Sukuk* differs from conventional debt instruments. Godlewski *et al.* (2013) show that stock market investors react differently to announcements of *Sukuk* and conventional bonds. Using multivariate analysis and event studies, they find the stock market is neutral to announcements of conventional bond issues while it shows negative reactions to announcements of *Sukuk* issues. Nagano (2016) has performed comparative analysis to identify the difference between *Sukuk* issuers and conventional debt and equity issuers. Based on firm-based micro-level data, he provides empirical evidence to the fact that low financial constraints and undervalued stock in pre-issuance periods stimulate the *Sukuk* issuance. Klein and Weil (2016) have examined the factors inducing firms to choose *Sukuk* instead of conventional bonds. According to them, information asymmetry and moral hazard have significant impact on the selection of *Sukuk* issuance.

The second category focuses on the standardization, pricing, rating, and innovation on the structuring of *Sukuk*. Wilson (2008) reveals the necessity of special purpose vehicles (SPV) in the issuance and management of *Sukuk*. He suggests gross domestic product (GDP) growth rate as an alternative pricing benchmark for sovereign *Sukuk*, instead of benchmarks such as the London interbank offer rate (LIBOR). Ahmed *et al.* (2015) extend the study of Wilson (2008) with a discussion on pricing mechanisms and credit rating in Malaysia. Wedderburn-Day (2010) addresses the impact of changing opinions of *Shari'ah* scholars and the financial crisis of 2007 on the issuance of *Sukuk*. According to his findings, the existing *Sukuk* market was adversely affected by both phenomena whereas the sovereign *Sukuk* market remained impassive to these factors.

The final category concentrates on globalization of *Sukuk*, the *Sukuk* environment in particular countries or regions, and comparison of various aspects of *Sukuk* across different countries. Grassa and Miniaoui (2017) analyze the issuers' choice between *Sukuk* and conventional bonds particularly in Gulf Cooperation Council (GCC) countries. They identify that issuers favor *Sukuk* over conventional bonds in case the issuance is of large size and tenure. They also give evidence to a positive correlation between quality of credit and issuance of conventional bonds and negative correlation between quality of credit and issuance of *Sukuk*. Kamarudin *et al.* (2014) focus on *Sukuk* defaulter profiles in Malaysia and prove that defaults and potential defaults are triggered by creditworthiness of the issuer rather than by faulty structure.

3. *Sukuk* instruments available in Bangladesh and Malaysia

The *Sukuk* market in Bangladesh is comprised of various Bangladesh Government Islamic Investment Bonds (BGIIB) issued under *mudaraba* (profit-and-loss sharing) principle. In 2004, these BGIIBs were issued for the first time with maturities of six months, one year, and two years. Later, the circulation of one-year and two-year bonds was suspended and the circulation of three-month BGIIB began on January 1, 2015 after making an amendment to the guidelines on BGIIB rules 2004. The net outstanding amount of BGIIB stood at BDT 85.14 billion in 2016 and increased by 34 times during the last five years (Bangladesh Bank, 2016). The Islamic capital market in Bangladesh also comprises *Shari'ah*-compliant *mudarabah* perpetual bonds issued by one of the Islamic banks in Bangladesh, namely Islami Bank Bangladesh Limited. However, there is argument on whether this Islamic bond should be considered *Sukuk*. Wilson (2008) argues that *Sukuk* has to be for a fixed tenure rather than perpetual. Nevertheless, Sarkar (2009) terms this perpetual bond as *Sukuk*. Due to such confusion, we keep this bond out of the discussion. Currently, a new issuance of corporate *Sukuk* of BDT 1 billion is in the pipeline as a result of an agreement reached between Pran-Foods Limited (PFL) and Green Delta Capital Limited in April 2016 (The Financial Express, 2016).

Islamic banks, financial institutions, and resident and non-resident Bangladeshis who have agreed to profit–loss sharing according to Islamic *Shari'ah* are eligible to purchase BGIIB. On a pre-specified date, banks and financial institutions directly and individual investors through banks or financial institutions in an open bid file their bid forms. The amount of each purchase should be in BDT 100,000 or multiples of BDT 100,000. Islamic banks purchase this instrument as part of their statutory liquidity ratio (SLR). As per Section VI of the Guidelines for Conducting Islamic Banking 2009, the excess liquidity of Islamic banks or Islamic branches/windows of conventional banks needs to be invested in BGIIB. In case of a liquidity crisis, Islamic banks may collect funds against liens of investment bonds. In effect, Islamic banks, *Shari'ah*-compliant financial institutions, or any other institution who have agreed to follow *Shari'ah* compliance in line with instructions from the government may borrow from special Islamic bond fund accounts for not more than 180 days against demand promissory (DP) notes. Table 6.1 offers a summary of BGIIB's performance during the last eight fiscal years and reflects a gradual pattern of progression over the years. The sale of these BGIIBs has increased by 7.5 times between 2009 and 2016. Interestingly, in fiscal year 2013, the sale of BGIIB experienced more than 240 percent growth from the previous year. This extraordinary change occurred due to liquidity mopping up needs of Bangladesh Bank for sterilization of its intervention in the foreign exchange market (Bangladesh Bank, 2016). Before 2013, a major portion of the fund collected from issuance of BGIIB was distributed to Islamic banks as loans.

Table 6.1 Sale, financing, and net outstanding amount of BGIIB

Particulars	2009	2010	2011	2012	2013	2014	2015	2016
Sale	16.4	23.4	25.3	31.48	107.13	121.34	135.84	122.94
Financing	12.1	15.4	22.8	31.26	67.78	24.37	25.40	37.80
Net outstanding	4.3	8.0	2.5	0.22	39.35	96.97	110.44	85.14

Source: constructed by authors based on Bangladesh Bank (various years)

Note: amounts are in billion BDT

Malaysia is the issuer of the first *Sukuk* security and the third largest bond market in Asia, and accounts for almost half of the new issuance of the global *Sukuk* market. Moreover, the first global *Sukuk* issuance also came out from the Malaysian government in 2002 (Jabeen and Javed, 2007). The Malaysian market has experienced exponential growth over the years and accounted for 52.6 percent of the world *Sukuk* outstanding (Bank Negara Malaysia, 2016). The Malaysian *Sukuk* market contains both government and corporate *Sukuk* securities. The top issuance comes from the financial services, government, power and utilities, and transportation sectors. Since its inception, the Islamic financial market in Malaysia has been continuing its operation side by side with the conventional debt market. However, the outstanding amount of *Sukuk* has gradually outstripped the outstanding amount of conventional debt securities. In addition, the government *Sukuk* securities market faces competition from the growing private sector. The corporate *Sukuk* market in Malaysia has captured 75 percent of the total *Sukuk* outstanding almost 10 years ago in 2008 (Bank Negara Malaysia and Surahanjaya Sekuriti, 2009). In 2016, the aggregate amount of 32 new corporate *Sukuk* issuances was RM 64.82 billion leading to a total corporate *Sukuk* outstanding of RM 393.45 billion (Surahanjaya Sekurity Malaysia, 2017a). The major government and corporate *Sukuk* securities are shown in Table 6.2.

Government *Sukuk* in Malaysia includes both short-term and long-term securities issued by the Malaysian government and Bank Negara Malaysia. These securities are of the highest class and act as the standard for evaluating and pricing of other securities. although the Malaysian securities market is getting more private market driven, government *Sukuk* issuance still accounts for 49 percent of total *Sukuk* issuance. GIIs are long-term dividend-bearing *Sukuk* instruments based on *Bai'Al-Inah* (sale with immediate repurchase) principle with maturities of 3, 5, 7, and 10 years. According to *Bai'Al-Inah*, the government will sell a particular asset and afterwards buy that back at purchase price plus a profit percentage. The commitment to pay the price agreed on in the tender process is securitized in the form of GII securities. The profits are payable semiannually and the nominal value of securities are payable at maturity. GIIs are issued through competitive auction and traded in the Islamic interbank money market. Unlike GII, MITBs are short-term *Sukuk* securities based on the *Bai'Al-Inah* principle with an original maturity of one year. Securities are issued through a closed auction on each Thursday and the actual issuance is made on Friday. MITBs are tradable in the secondary market

Table 6.2 List of major government and corporate *Sukuk* securities in Malaysia

Government Sukuk	Corporate Sukuk
Government Investment Issues (GII)	Khazanah
Malaysian Islamic Treasury Bill (MITB)	Sandat ABBA Cagamas (SAC) or
Sukuk Bank Negara Malaysia *Ijarah*	CAGABAIS
(SBNMI)	Sandat *Mudarabah* Cagamas (SMC)
Merdeka Savings Bonds (MSB)	Asset Backed Securities (ABS) on
Sukuk Simpanan Rakyat (SSR)	Islamic principle

Source: constructed by authors based on different reports published by Bank Negara Malaysia and Surahanjaya Sekurity Malaysia

on a yield basis based on remaining days to maturity. The funds collected by GII and MITB are used to finance the development projects and operational activities of the Malaysian government.

On the other hand, SBNMIs are issued by Bank Negara Malaysia on the *Al-Ijarah* (sale and lease back) concept. An SPV oversees the issuance of this *Sukuk*. MSB is a scrip-less *Shari'ah*-compliant instrument designed for older citizens (56 years and above) or any Malaysian citizen retired on medical grounds. Each investor must invest at least RM 1,000 to a maximum range of RM 50,000. The MSB instrument is distributed on a first-come-first-served basis with a monthly profit. Finally, SSR are scrip-less investment instruments issued on a first-come-first-served basis. Malaysian citizens of 21 years or above are eligible to make investments in this instrument in a range from RM 1,000 to RM 50,000 per investor. The profit on SSR is payable on a quarterly basis to holders' accounts through the agent bank.

The co-existence of the conventional bond market and *Sukuk* market in the Malaysian economy calls for open competition. The corporate *Sukuk* market in Malaysia is gradually wining the competition by snatching away the market share from its conventional counterpart. The recent statistics shows that corporate *Sukuk* issuance stands at 75.68 percent of total corporate bonds and *Sukuk* issuance, and *Sukuk* outstanding stands at 73.85 percent of total corporate bonds and *Sukuk* outstanding in 2016 (Surahanjaya Sekurity Malaysia, 2017a). The major corporate *Sukuk* securities include the *Khazanah* bond, which is a long-term zero-coupon bond based on the *Murabaha* principle and issued by *Khzanah* Nasional Berhad, the investment wing of the government. With maturity periods of 3, 5, 7, and 10 years, *Khazanah* bonds include bullet repayment of face value at maturity. SAC or CAGABAIS is a semiannual dividend-bearing *Sukuk* security based upon the principle of *Bai'Bithman Ajil* (deferred payment sale). SAC is used to support the purchase of Islamic housing loans and hire purchase contracts. Along with the semiannual dividend distribution provision, this security involves payment of par value with dividends due upon maturity. SMC is similar to CAGABAIS except that it is based upon the principle of the *Mudaraba*. It also supports the purchase of Islamic housing loans granted on the basis of *Bai'Bithman Ajil* and Islamic hire purchase under the principle of *Ijara Thumma Al-Bai* (lease to purchase). Along with the semiannual profit distribution at a pre-specified rate, this security involves

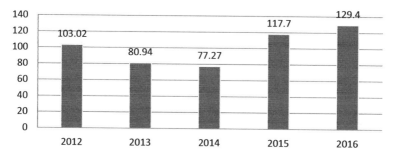

Figure 6.1 Malaysian *Sukuk* issuance

Source: constructed by the authors based on Bond Pricing Agency Malaysia (2015) and Ramli (2015)
Note: Amounts are in billion RM

payment of par value upon maturity unless there is any demission of value. Finally, ABS is a basic form of *Sukuk* security and is backed by house purchase.

A comparative picture of government and corporate *Sukuk* issuance during the period 2012–2016 is shown in Figure 6.1. Since Malaysia leads the *Sukuk* industry, its market walks in line with the global market or, in a more precise way, Malaysia draws the line of the global market. In 2012, the global *Sukuk* issuance reached its peak. Malaysian *Sukuk* issuance also experienced an upsurge in the same year contributing towards the major portion of this expansion. After a gradual decline, the *Sukuk* market in Malaysia has experienced recovery and 2016 was termed a record year.

4. Purposes for investment in *Sukuk* instruments in Bangladesh and Malaysia

BGIIB is issued as a means for Islamic banks and financial institutions to invest their excess funds for short terms. BGIIB also acts as part of the SLR requirement. The profit earned on this instrument falls far below the rate of other interest-bearing instruments and deposit rates (Sarkar, 2015). Thus, the sole reason for investment in the *Sukuk* instrument in Bangladesh is to fulfill the requirement of liquidity by investing in a *Shari'ah*-compliant instrument as per the guidelines of the central bank. However, the resident and non-resident Bangladeshi citizens eligible for investment in BGIIB may do so for religious cause, as profit potential is very low for the instrument.

The financial market in Malaysia is loaded with bundles of different *Sukuk* securities along with different classes of investors. These investors, both institutional and individual, choose *Sukuk* instruments for investing their surplus funds to serve a variety of purposes. The investors who choose government *Sukuk* prefer low-risk investments to high-risk volatile corporate *Sukuk* instruments. Among government and Bank Negara Malaysia issues, GII acts as a long-term source of investment. Individuals and investors with idle funds, pension funds, and Islamic institutions seeking long-term benefit with considerable low risk invest in GII.

On the other hand, MITB meets the need of financial institutions for short-term investment of surplus funds. MSB and SSR provide regular income to old and young investors respectively, acting as the social welfare arm of the Malaysian government. The investors of corporate *Sukuk* usually invest in them for earning a rate of profit higher than that of government instruments. Another class of *Sukuk* investors exists in the market place that invests in *Shari'ah*-compliant debt securities for strict religious purpose either as a personal standard or as compulsory institutional requirement for *Shari'ah* compliance.

5. Legal and regulatory framework for *Sukuk* in Bangladesh and Malaysia

Bangladesh Bank as the central bank of the country formulates regulations on issuance, pricing, distribution, and redemption of government *Sukuk*. It also maintains and utilizes funds collected from the investors of BGIIB by providing them as loans to Islamic banks and *Shari'ah*-compliant financial Institutions. Bangladesh Bank conducts issuance and dealings of BGIIB as per the guidelines on BGIIB Rules 2004 and the guidelines on BGIIB Amended Rules 2014. In addition, Section VI of the Guidelines for Conducting Islamic Banking is also applied by Bangladesh Bank to deal with the instructions on BGIIB from the perspective of liquidity management of Islamic banks. Any issuance of corporate *Sukuk* also requires the permission of the central bank. Table 6.3 provides a summary of basic aspects covered by the different guidelines.

Central *Shari'ah* Board for Islamic Banks of Bangladesh (CSBIB) is a non-profit research-oriented national body of Islamic banks and Islamic banking branches/windows of conventional banks registered under Bangladesh Bank. The board was formed on August 16, 2001 to ensure uniform guidelines for all Islamic banks and to provide *fatwa* (decision) and implementation of such decisions regarding *Shari'ah* compliance. *Shari'ah* scholars, Islamic economists, and members of the *Shari'ah* council of Islamic banks are the members of CSBIB. Currently the board has 65 members and 21 member organizations. The main objective of CSBIB is to advise the government, Bangladesh Bank, regulatory organizations, and member banks, and to supervise the work of Islamic banks in terms of *Shari'ah*. The board holds regular meetings and discussions, and acts under the supervision of Bangladesh Bank to formulate the guidelines in conducting Islamic banking in Bangladesh. Though the board primarily deals with Islamic banking, it plays an advisory role in case of the issuance and allotment of BGIIB. Figure 6.2 represents the *Sukuk* mechanism in Bangladesh.

Figure 6.3 exhibits the *Sukuk* mechanism in Malaysia. Bank Negara Malaysia is entrusted with the responsibility of supervision of issuance, registration, distribution, settlement, and redemption of government *Sukuk* securities under the Government Funding Act 1983. This act empowers the bank to raise funds on behalf of the government of Malaysia through *Shari'ah* compliance and National *Shari'ah* Advisory Council-approved instruments including GII and MITB. Bank Negara Malaysia performed its role as principal regulator of the *Sukuk* market until

Table 6.3 Basic aspects covered by the guidelines

BGIIB Rules 2004 (originated by issuing circular number FRTMD (PDS) 146/2004–16 by Bangladesh Bank on 15.09.2004)	• The guideline is applicable in cases of Islamic banks and financial institutions and persons or their representatives who will buy or hold this bond and Islamic banks and financial institutions and other institutions approved by the Bangladesh government and Bangladesh Bank, which will use the fund collected by issuance of this bond. • The issuance and payment will be conducted by the respective office of Bangladesh Bank. • A non-resident Bangladeshi who agrees to share profit-loss according to *Shari'ah* should collect this bond through a non-resident foreign currency deposit account (NFCD) in any Bangladeshi Bank opened in his name. • The eligible institutions and persons may transfer this bond among themselves and use it as collateral. In all cases, it should be recorded with the issue office. • The holder of an Islamic bond will receive profits at the end of a six-month, one-year and two-year maturity period at, respectively, 2 percent, 1.5 percent, and 1 percent less from the average realizable profit rate. At maturity, the face value (after adjustment of loss) and profit on BGIIB is paid from the issue office. • The proceeds from the bond fund are disbursed among Islamic banks and financial institutions for 180 days against collateral and the monthly profit on such a loan is equal to the profit rate on the *Mudaraba* deposit account of the respective Islamic bank.
BGIIB Amended Rules 2014 (originated by issuing circular number 08.036.014.00.003. 2004–128 by Ministry of Finance on 18.08.2014)	• The guideline has suspended the circulation of one-year and two-year bond and begun the circulation of a three-month Islamic bond. • The amended guideline extends the purview of holders and investors of BGIIB to Islamic banking branches of conventional banks. • The eligibility for participation in open bid is restricted to *Shari'ah*-compliant banks and financial institutions and Islamic banking branches of conventional banks. • Islamic bond is circulated through open bid on the basis of profit-sharing ratio (PSR) and Bangladesh Bank determines the rules of auction from time to time. • The government may also circulate Islamic bonds of different maturities on specific *Shari'ah*-approved sector or assets. • The fund of Islamic bonds is deployed only against demand promissory note issued by respective institutions. • The nominee clause is excluded in these rules and no mention has been made on the same in any other place of these rules.
Section VI of the Guidelines for Conducting Islamic Banking (issued by Bangladesh Bank in November 2009)	• Islamic bonds have to be the first source of investment of excess liquidity and first line of defense to face liquidity crisis of Islamic banks and Islamic banking branches of conventional banks. • In times of liquidity crisis, loans can be availed from Islamic bond funds against liens of Islamic bonds. • The Islamic banks and Islamic banking branches of conventional banks may borrow from Bangladesh Bank at a provisional rate on its respective *mudaraba* short notice accounts even if the bank has no surplus investment in BGIIB at that time.

Source: constructed by the authors based on respective guidelines

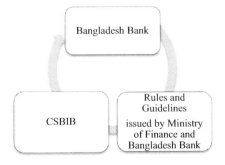

Figure 6.2 Sukuk mechanism in Bangladesh

Source: constructed by the authors

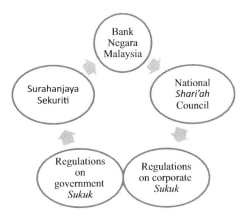

Figure 6.3 Sukuk mechanism in Malaysia

Source: constructed by the authors

2000, when the corporate *Sukuk* market came under the supervision of Surahan-jaya Sekuriti (Bank Negara Malaysia and Surahanjaya Sekuriti, 2009). The bank still plays its supportive role to ensure stability and growth of the *Sukuk* market as well as the overall financial structure of Malaysia. On the other hand, Surahanjaya Sekuriti acts to ensure a fair, efficient, secure, and transparent capital market from its origination on March 1, 1993 under the Securities Commission Act 1993. It is a self-funding and self-regulatory statutory body entrusted with the responsibility of regulating the capital market participants and ensuring proper conduct of market institutions and licensed persons through circulating a number of guidelines, regulations, and practice notes.

The National *Shari'ah* Advisory Council, the highest *Shari'ah* authority in Islamic finance in Malaysia, is an authoritative body of *Shari'ah* scholars, jurists, and market practitioners. Under the regulation and supervision of Bank Negara

Malaysia, the council started its operation in May 1997. It acts as the reference body and advisor of the central bank in matters relating to Islamic banking, *Takaful* (Islamic insurance), the Islamic financial business, and the Islamic development financial business. It also validates Islamic banking and *Takaful* products, and advises on any issuance of Islamic instruments for *Shari'ah* compliance. The ruling of it shall prevail over any contradictory ruling of any other *Shari'ah* body or committee in Malaysia. The court is also required to take the advice of the National *Shari'ah* Advisory Council in any issues relating to Islamic finance after the Central Bank of Malaysia Act 2009. The body of the council currently consists of ten members who are qualified individuals and experienced in matters of Islamic banking, finance, economics, and *Shari'ah* rulings on economic activities.

Bank Negara Malaysia is responsible for issuing guidelines and regulations on government *Sukuk* instruments dealing. Islamic banks, commercial banks, and investment banks registered and licensed under the central bank may deal with government securities. The trading of such securities falls under the purview of the Capital Markets and Services Act 2007. On the other hand, Surahanjaya Sekuriti has acted as the principal regulator of the corporate securities market since July 2000. Surahanjaya Sekuriti publishes guidelines on the issuance of Islamic securities, oversees trading, and performs joint investigations with Bank Negara Malaysia. The following guidelines, practice notes, and regulations of Surahanjaya Sekuriti displayed by Figure 6.4 deal with *Sukuk*.

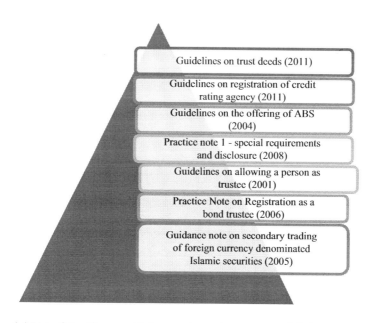

Figure 6.4 List of significant guidelines and practice notes on *Sukuk*

Source: constructed by the authors based on the information collected from Surahanjaya Sekuriti (2017b)

6. Potential for the *Sukuk* industry in Bangladesh

The underdeveloped financial market of Bangladesh presents huge potential for turning the wheel of financial innovation in any particular area. In addition, more than 80 percent Muslim population and continuous rise of Islamic banking make a suitable combination for issuance of Islamic securities in Bangladesh. The growing and highly competitive lease financing industry faces strong competition in raising required funds. These leasing companies currently operating in Bangladesh are also surrounded by only a few investment choices. The issuance of *Ijarah Sukuk* may present these financial institutions an avenue for investment for their funds. Furthermore, the non-bank financial institutions may launch *Ijara Sukuk* or *Mudaraba Sukuk* for raising sufficient funds. Government institutions may also raise their needed financing for large projects by issuing *Sukuk* instruments under the principle of *Bai'Bithman Ajil, Bai'Inah* or *Murabaha*. The private–public partnership of Bangladesh government presently accounts for $4,549 million of investment in 56 projects. The issuance of government *Sukuk* will enable the government to reduce dependence on high-cost foreign loans and protect the national economy from the burden of public debt.

7. In parallel: potential of the *Sukuk* industry in Japan

There has yet to be any *Sukuk* issued in Japan, despite the so-called J-*sukuk* issuance having been legally possible since April 2012. J-*sukuk* is defined as "a financial instrument which enables an issuer to raise capital from not only conventional investors but also from Islamic investors. It is legally not a bond itself, but it treated as if it were a bond for tax purposes" (FSA, 2012, p. 1). Japan is an evolving case showing how a form of financial praxis originally based in the identity and ethical concerns of Islam has acquired new appeal and is thereby expanding into regions of the global economy that are lacking large Muslim populations (Morrison, 2013). This section aims to review the J-*sukuk* issuance scheme and the tax measures regarding J-*sukuk*, and to draw the dilemmas and challenges in J-*sukuk*.

Financial Services Agency of Japan (FSA) describes the merits of Japanese companies' issuing of *Sukuk* as follows: (1) Because issuers can issue *Sukuk* and raise capital from Islamic investors, to whom they have never had access, they can diversify their financing measures. (2) By issuing *Sukuk* compliant with Islamic law, favorable attention to the issuers in the Islamic world is expected. Thus, the issuers are expected to gain favorable positions in marketing in the Islamic world (FSA, 2012). As is mentioned earlier, J-*sukuk* is defined as a financial instrument which is structured using a *quasi*-bond beneficial interest of a specified purpose trust prescribed in the Act on Securitization of Assets of Japan. A quasi-bond beneficial interest is an interest-receiving pre-fixed amount like interest on a bond. It is legally not a bond, but is treated as if it were a bond for tax purposes by the 2011 tax reform (FSA, 2012).

As an illustration, FSA (2012) explains *Ijara Sukuk* as an example of the J-*sukuk* issuance scheme: [I] At the time of the issuance of J-*sukuk*: (1) the issuer entrusts its owned real estate to the trustee of the special purpose trust; (2) the investors pay the issue price of J-*sukuk* to the issuer; (3) the issuer issues J-*sukuk* to the investors. [II] From the issuance until the redemption of J-*sukuk*: (4) the issuer leases the entrusted real estate from the trustee; (5) the issuer periodically pays rental fees to the trustee; (6) the trustee periodically pays distribution amounts funded by the rental fees to the investors. [III] At the time of the redemption (maturity) of J-*sukuk*: (7) the issuer purchases back the entrusted real estate from the trustee; (8) the issuer pays the purchase price of the real estate to the trustee; (9) the trustee pays the redemption amounts funded by the purchase price of the real estate to the investors.

In a case where real estate is entrusted on issuing J-*sukuk*, registration and license tax on the real estate transfer registration and real estate acquisition tax are not imposed. In addition, the repurchase of the real estate is neither subject to registration and license tax nor real estate acquisition tax, if the following requirements are mainly satisfied (FSA, 2012): (1) On entering into the specified purpose trust (SPT) agreement, the issuer grants an option to sell back the entrusted real estate to the trustee. (2) The issuer treats such real estate as its fixed asset for accounting purposes in between the effective time of the SPT agreement and its ending time (on-balance transaction). (3) The issuer continuously owns part of the principal of the beneficial interest of the SPT from the effective time of the SPT agreement. (4) The issuer leases the entrusted real estate. (5) The issuer repurchases such real estate at the ending time of the SPT agreement. (6) The redemption period of J-*sukuk* is within 20 years.

Besides, taxes on the distribution amounts by foreign investors (as well as domestic financial institutions) are being exempted. In order for the distribution amounts of J-*sukuk* to be treated as pay-through payments for tax purposes, it is necessary for J-*sukuk* to be publicly offered (with an aggregate issue price of 100 million yen or more) or subscribed by institutional investors only (FSA, 2012). The tax exemption for the distribution amounts of J-*sukuk* received by foreign investors will expire on March 31, 2019. Also, the exemption of registration and license tax on the repurchase of the real estate, along with the J-*sukuk* issuance scheme, will expire on March 31, 2019.

A *Samurai-sukuk* is considered a type of J-*sukuk* issued in Japan by a foreign government or foreign company. A Samurai-bond is a yen-denominated debt security issued in Japan by a foreign government or foreign company. One of the uses of J-*sukuk* is that foreign governments or foreign companies in the Islamic world use J-*sukuk* as financing measures in Japan. In this case, J-*sukuk* economically have the same function as Samurai-bonds have. To be specific, various schemes may be taken into consideration. For example, it is considered that a foreign government or foreign company in the Islamic world would entrust its own *Sukuk* (originated in its jurisdiction) to the trustee of the specified purpose trust and issue J-*sukuk* (FSA, 2012).

Interestingly, there has yet to be a *Sukuk* issued in Japan, despite J-*sukuk* issuance having been legally possible since April 2012. Bedi Gunter Lackmann, Nomura Institute of Capital Markets Research, raises possible reasons: (1) when using a basic scheme such as *Ijara*, the issuance amount is limited by the market value of the underlying assets; (2) not many companies own the *Shari'ah*-compliant assets needed to back a *Sukuk* issuance; (3) there is a lack of companies with the necessary expertise (legal, accounting, and *Shari'ah*-compliance assessment) to issue a *Sukuk* or to provide consulting services (in Japanese) on issuing *Sukuk*; (4) *Sukuk* have higher issuance costs than conventional bonds, and their issuance process takes longer (generally 12 to 20 weeks); and (5) domestic investors have no incentive to invest if *Sukuk* yield is not set higher than conventional bond yields because the dividends received from a J-*sukuk* get the same tax treatment as the interest on a bond, and thus issuers who want to raise yen funds with a *Sukuk* wind up being reliant on finding Islamic investors overseas with a desire to invest in a yen-denominated *Sukuk*. Thus issuing corporate *Sukuk* in Japan remains difficult for several reasons (Lackmann, 2015).

This entails further investigation and discussions. As for the yield, traditionally, Islamic finance in general and *Sukuk* in particular has been more expensive than conventional loans and bonds. But it is worth noting that the gap between the two, especially in the fixed income sector, such as *Sukuk* and bonds, has narrowed during the last few years and may, for now, disappear completely (Bakar, 2017, p. 69; IFSB, 2017). Bakar (2017) raises the case of Emirates Airline as an example. In January 2013, Emirates Airline issued a 12-year conventional amortizing bond of US$ 750 million at 300 basis points over a seven-year mid-swap. A few months after that, it issued a *Sukuk* of US$ 1 billion at a cheaper cost of fund. He points out that this reflected that the liquidity for *Sukuk* was deeper, having a wider investor base.[2]

> *Sukuk*'s rise is driven by the growing influence of consumers who want investment and savings products compliant with *Shari'ah* laws and principles. Interest is strong in the Gulf Cooperation Council member states and in growing economies such as Malaysia and Turkey. For those seeking finance, offering *Shari'ah*-compliant debt offers access to the large pool of capital in oil-rich countries in the Middle East and Southeast Asia.
>
> (HSBC Bank Malaysia Berhad, 2015, p. 1)

There has yet to be a *Sukuk* (J-*sukuk*) issued in Japan, though "Japan's Financial Services Agency is right to promote the growth of its *Shari'ah*-compliant finance sector" (HSBC Bank Malaysia Berhad, 2015, p. 1). In contrast, outside of Japan there have been *Sukuk* issues from Japanese corporations in recent years, although actual *Sukuk* issuances by Japanese corporations are still few. According to Lackmann (2015), Aean Credit Service (issued in 2007)[3] and UMW Toyota Capital's (issued in 2008)[4] intent in issuing *Sukuk* in Malaysia was likely in order to (1) diversify their funding methods, (2) obtain funding in local currency, (3) fund *Shari'ah*-compliant businesses, and (4) increase their acceptance by, and expand their customer base among, local Islamic consumers.

On the other hand, global financial institutions like Nomura Holdings (issued in 2010)[5] and The Bank of Tokyo-Mitsubishi UFJ (Malaysia) (issued in 2014)[6] are motivated to enter this market to (1) diversify their funding sources by region and currency, (2) raise funds aimed at providing *Shari'ah*-compliant financial services to the local market, (3) improve their franchise value and name recognition in the Islamic world, (4) gain access to investors in Southeast Asia and the Middle East, (5) assume the role of an arranger for future Japanese *Sukuk* issuances (a longer-term objective of accumulating expertise and helping other Japanese companies obtain funding through *Sukuk*), and (6) strengthen their relationships with governments seeking to develop Islamic financial markets and with major market players.

Japan's Financial Services Agency has given the green light for banks to move into Islamic financing. In spite of it, we have to ask: Why has J-*sukuk* been never materialized? There must be widespread sentiment that issuing *Sukuk* is (still) too complex, time consuming, and costly. We should continue to watch the dilemmas and challenges in J-*sukuk*.

8. Conclusion

Bangladesh started its journey in the *Sukuk* industry almost 13 years ago. In spite of the stellar growth of the Islamic banking sector, the country still trades on a single government *Sukuk* instrument. Nevertheless, Malaysia is considered the pioneer of the global *Sukuk* market, possessing both government and corporate *Sukuk* instruments. Keeping all these issues in mind, this chapter aimed at evaluating the *Sukuk* environment in both of these countries supplemented by the case of J-*sukuk*. It is evident from the findings that Malaysia and Bangladesh portray completely different pictures in terms of the existing *Sukuk* instruments available, the legal and regulatory framework, and the participation of different stakeholders of the industry. In spite of the high potential for growth, Bangladesh has failed to make any significant progress. The future of the industry largely depends on firm planning and co-ordination among regulatory authorities, Islamic banks, Islamic financial institutions, *Shari'ah* scholars, and other markets participants. Most importantly, the Malaysian success story can be the mantra for Bangladesh and Japan for achieving the pace of the growing global *Shari'ah*-compliant securities market. In addition, the Malaysian case may show the other two countries how they may board into the fastest growing train of *Sukuk* keeping their conventional capital market growth on track.

Notes

1 The name '*Sukuk*' is derived from the word of '*Sakk*' which means a legal instrument, deed, and check. In *lisan al-Arab*, the meaning of *Sakk* is 'to strike one's seal on a document' or 'imprint one's mark on a clay tablet'. However, the *Sukuk*, as understood in its contemporary form, lies in a decision of the Islamic Jurisprudence Council in February 1988 which provided that "any combination of assets (or the usufruct of such assets) can be represented in the form of written financial instrument which can be sold at a market price provided that the composition of the group of assets represented by the *Sukuk* consists of a majority of tangible assets."

The main function of *Sukuk* is to provide an alternative for conventional bonds, in other words, to provide the benefits associated with conventional bonds but in a *Shari'ah-compliant* manner (Abduh, 2016).

2 Although many reports and analyses tend to attribute the lower pricing of *Sukuk* to a bigger and wider investor base, Bakar (2017) also points out that this is not the case all the times. He refers to two Indonesian government *Sukuk* which were priced a few bps more than their conventional bonds. In the end, it is entirely dependent on market forces and market conditions. "A wider investor base will surely help but it will not guarantee that the sukuk issuance will always be cheaper when it is issued by the same issuer with the same rating and tenor" (Bakar, 2017, pp. 69–70).

3 The issued amount is 400 million ringgit through the *musharaka* scheme with a maturity of seven years. The underwriters are BTMU Malaysia, CIMB Investment Bank, and ASEAN Bankers Malaysia.

4 The issued amount is 1 billion ringgit through the *musharaka* scheme with a maturity of seven years. The underwriters are BTMU Malaysia and CIMB Investment Bank.

5 The issued amount is US\$ 100 million through the *ijarah* scheme with a maturity of two years. The underwriter is Kuwait Finance House (KFH, Malaysia). The yield is LIBOR + 1.6 percent.

6 The issued amount(s) are JPY 2.5 billion and US\$ 25 million through the *wakala* scheme with a maturity of one year. The underwriter is CIMB Investment Bank.

7 A comparative study between the Grameen and Islamic modes of microfinance in Bangladesh with reference to Islamic microfinance in Pakistan

Yasushi Suzuki, Helal Uddin and Mohammad Dulal Miah

1. Introduction

The importance of microcredit in our society cannot be ignored by any means. It creates self-employment opportunities (McKernan, 2002; Erhardt, 2017); increases income and consumption (Zeller, 2001); improves health, education, and women's empowerment etc. (Nader, 2008; Swain and Wallentin, 2009). Microfinance contributes to development at both the individual and national levels. For instance, Raihan *et al.* (2015) mention that microfinance has a positive effect on GDP. In general, it contributes to both micro and macro levels of the economy by creating new employment and empowerment. According to the United Nations (UN) General Assembly Report 2004, microcredit can contribute to the achievement of the Millennium Development Goals, in particular the goal of poverty reduction, gender equality, women's empowerment, and community development. To emphasize the importance of microfinance that has global importance and ramifications, the year 2005 was declared the 'Year of Microcredit' by the UN and in 2006 Professor Muhammad Yunus and Grameen Bank (GB) together won the Nobel Peace Prize.

The Grameen mode of microcredit mechanism (group lending) has been replicated in Bolivia, Chile, China, Ethiopia, Honduras, India, Malaysia, Mali, the Philippines, Sri Lanka, Tanzania, Thailand, the US, and Vietnam. Suzuki *et el.* (2011) have found that the Grameen mode of microcredit, without much modification, has been prevailing all over the world. Microfinance spreads quickly across the globe because few other tools promise to fight poverty as effectively as microfinance can do (Morduch, 2000). A good volume of research in the existing literature can be found which focuses on several dimensions of microfinance including its effects on the national economy. For example, Schuler et al. (1997), Pitt and Khandker (1996), Imai *et al.* (2010), Montgomery and Weiss (2011), Deloach and Lamanna (2011), Imai *et al.* (2012), and Mazumder and Lu (2015) find that the Grameen mode of microfinance has a positive impact on poverty eradication as well as employment creation.

Despite the marvelous growth of conventional microfinance having its sweeping impact on the development of the individual and national levels, a segment of the target population remains out of the touch of this magic wand. Specially, a large number of Muslim populations are reluctant to accept finance from conventional microcredit providers because these financiers deal with interest which is prohibited in Islam. Despite this setback involved with the conventional microfinance institute (MFI), mainstream Islamic financial institutions do not show adequate interest in catering to the financing needs of these marginal borrowers. In particular, the unprecedented growth of mainstream Islamic finance is unrivalled to the sluggish growth of Islamic microfinance. For instance, the Islamic financial market has been growing at a significant pace since its beginning in the 1970s. It was estimated that the annual growth rate hovered around 40.3 percent between 2004 and 2011. It is further predicted that the annual growth rate will be about 19.7 percent until 2018 (Suzuki and Miah, 2015).

The rise of the Muslim population on the one hand and the reluctance of mainstream Islamic financial institutions to support small and marginal borrowers on the other have created a huge gap between the demand and supply of Islamic microfinance. For instance, Islamic microfinance has a total estimated global outreach of only 380,000 customers served by 126 institutions in 14 countries, and accounts for only an estimated 1.5 percent of total microfinance outreach (CGAP, 2008). According to the Center of Islamic Banking and Economics Report 2014, the size of Islamic finance reached $2 trillion whereas the contribution by Islamic microfinance accounts for 1 percent in the total assets held by Islamic financial institutions. Despite huge potential for Islamic MFI, this model has failed to emerge.

Although the contemporary literature pays much attention to the conventional mode of microfinance, the domain of what Islamic MFI can learn from the success story of conventional MFI has largely remained unexplored. This research thus aims to fill this gap. In so doing, the research analyzes the factors hindering the growth of the Islamic microfinance industry *vis-à-vis* the success factors of conventional MFI in Bangladesh. In this regard, the research analyzes how Grameen Bank, the largest microfinance provider in Bangladesh, has overcome typical obstacles involved with microfinancing including asymmetry of information, moral hazard, and transaction costs. Then a detailed analysis of the Rural Development Scheme (RDS), the largest Islamic microfinance provider in Bangladesh, is offered along with identifying the critical hindrances restricting its growth. A comparative analysis of these two MFIs is helpful in the sense that they are working in the same macroeconomic environment but with different success trajectories. Thus, the differences between them can be attributed to their respective functions, strategies, and management systems.

The chapter has been structured as follows. Section 2 elaborates the obstacles hindering the growth of Islamic microfinance whereas Section 3 details the current practices of Islamic microfinance in Bangladesh. Section 4 compares and contrasts between Grameen Bank and the Rural Development Scheme. Section 5 analyzes the current state of Islamic microfinancing in Pakistan. This is followed by the conclusion and policy prescriptions.

2. Challenges to the growth of Islamic microfinance

The existing literature has identified several key obstacles that are hindering the expected growth of MFI. For example, Wulandari and Kassim (2016) identify the issues and challenges of Baitul Mal-wat Tamil (BTM) and find four types of challenges: sources of finance, collateral status, mode of financing, and the default cases faced by BTM. Rahman and Dean (2013) find that the low market penetration, the fragility of MFIs due to lack of funds and high administrative costs, and the expected role in alleviating poverty are the main reasons for its growth constraint. Ali (2015) highlights that most of the microfinance providers are managed not for profit but for social development. Also, a large number of MFI depends on donor, government, and individual funds to carry out their businesses. The current mechanism for channeling those funds, especially government and donor funds, has been proved inefficient. The cost of materializing donor funds is exorbitant if administrative costs are accounted for (Ahmed, 2009). It is difficult to say how much of initially allocated funds actually reach the poor. According to Yunus and Jolis (1999) only 10–25 percent of donor funds actually reach the borrower while the rest is spent on administration, overhead, and training purposes. Therefore, MFIs, in general, are facing a barrier to expanding their operation because of their limited resources. Suzuki and Miah (2015) conclude that there is a huge demand for Islamic microfinance across the globe. However, the supply side, especially the lack of loanable funds, has apparently failed to meet the needs of rising demand.

We can roughly categorize the obstacles towards the growth of MFI into four broader classes: (I) lack of loanable funds (Haque and Yamao, 2011; Riwajanti, 2015; Glaubitt *et al.*, 2008; Ahmed, 2009); (II) asymmetry of information between MFIs and their clients (Boateng and Agyei, 2013); (III) improper regulatory framework (for incubating the infant microcredit industry)/failure to incubate the managers (human resources) who would well-manage MFIs (Muhammad, 2010; Ahmed, 2009; Dogarawa, 2011; Mirghani *et al.*, 2011; Ashraf and Ibrahim, 2013); and (IV) insufficient infrastructure (transport, utility, and so on) as well as dominance of conventional MFIs (lack of scale efficiency in Islamic MFI) (Boateng and Agyei, 2013; Ali, 2015).

Though these explanations seem to have their own merit, we raise some critiques to these explanations. First, insufficiency of loanable funds might be one of the causes of the marginal outreach of microcredit. However, it would be naïve to simply assume that MFIs would increase the exposure to the micro-clients if the availability of loanable funds is increased. This is because their marginalized clients are not necessarily credible and their business is not always commercially viable. Second, we note that the asymmetry of information between MFIs and their clients is severe. The efforts of attenuating the asymmetry of information through initiating closer monitoring might accelerate the flow of more financial resources to their clients. However, this explanation also understates that the business of marginalized clients is always exposed to high risk and fundamental uncertainty. Closer monitoring does not necessarily guarantee the attenuation of risk and uncertainty associated with the business of clients. Third, failure to incubate the managers who would well-manage MFIs is agreeable. However, this explanation insufficiently explains how we can create an appropriate incentive for the managers to develop their skill and knowledge of credit risk management. Also, these explanations understate that the business by marginalized clients is always exposed to (not bankable) risk and uncertainty. It would amount to a risky strategy to expect too much for the MFI managers to tackle the 'not bankable' level's risk and uncertainty. Finally, the development of infrastructure would reduce the cost of screening and monitoring. However, this explanation also understates that the business by marginalized clients is always exposed to high risk and fundamental uncertainty. The lower transaction cost of monitoring does not necessarily reduce the risk and uncertainty associated with the business by marginalized clients.

This postulates that while these factors are important, the literature has paid much less attention to how the fundamental risk and uncertainty involved with marginalized borrowers can be adequately tackled for materializing the potential of Islamic microfinancing. In other words, mitigating these challenges may be the necessary conditions for incubating the Islamic microfinance industry but not sufficient on their own. Thus, we first evaluate the GB and RDS through the lens of these criteria, and second, we add the uncertainty dimension to evaluate the slow growth of Islamic microfinance.

3. Current practices of Islamic microfinance in Bangladesh

Among the 165 million population of Bangladesh, 36 percent live in the urban area and the remaining live in the rural and suburban areas. An estimation by the Asian Development Bank (ADB, 2017) shows that 31.5 percent of the total population live under the national poverty line (income $1.25 per day) and 73.5 percent of the total population live below $1.90 purchasing power parity per day. The majority of the population depend on agriculture whereas a tiny portion of them is employed in the service sector which contributes the lion share of the GDP. According to the available statistics, the service sector accounts for 56.3 percent of the GDP followed by industry (28.6 percent) and agriculture (15.1 percent).

Bangladesh is viewed as a synonym to microfinance. The concept of modern microfinance was born in Bangladesh by the introduction of Grameen Bank (GB). GB is a special type of bank owned by the borrowers whom it serves. Borrowers of the bank own 95 percent and the remaining 5 percent is owned by the government. It was initiated by professor Dr Muhammad Yunus, a professor of Economics at the Chittagong University, Bangladesh. GB provides small loans to the poor people who are excluded from formal financial institutes. The formal financial institutes provide loans backed by collateral assets but GB provides loans without any collateral. GB started its operation in the eastern part of Bangladesh with a fund of US$ 27; now its total asset is estimated to be US$ 2,803 million and its cumulative disbursement has amounted to BDT 1,531.24 billion as of 2017.

Table 7.1 Performance of Grameen Bank

Particulars	2011	2012	2013	2014	2015
Active borrowers (in millions)	6.58	6.71	6.74	7.03	7.18
Gross loan portfolio (BDT millions) [changes from the previous year: %]	75,294 [+13.48]	80,317 [+6.67]	84,381 [+5.06]	87,491 [+3.69]	96,422 [+10.21]
Branches	2,565	2,567	2,567	2,568	2,568
(a) Total assets (BDT billions)	140,441	158,952	178,937	200,961	220,885
(b) Net profit (BDT billions)	12597.56	27180.79	24424.90	8339.88	485.95
ROA [(b) / (a)] (%)	8.97%	17.10%	13.65%	4.15%	0.22%

Source: created by the authors upon GB, 2015

Now GB serves 81,392 villages through 2,568 branches which cover 97 percent of the total Bangladesh landscape (see Table 7.1).

The microfinance industry in Bangladesh is composed of NGOs, Grameen Bank, state-owned commercial banks, private commercial banks, and specialized programs of some ministries of Bangladesh government. As of June 2015, there were 659 NGO-MFIs in Bangladesh. To monitor and supervise this growing sector, the Government of Bangladesh (GoB) has established 'Microcredit Regulatory Authority Act 2006' by which a new independent authority 'Microcredit Regulatory Authority' (MRA) was established to stimulate and foster the sustainable development of the microfinance sector. According to MRA (2015), total loan disbursement was BDT 634 billion in 2015, the double of BDT 303.18 billion in 2011 (see Table 7.2). According to Bangladesh Bank (the central bank of Bangladesh) statistics, by the end of June 2016, there were 680 licensed MFIs and 191 provisional licensed MFIs serving over 26.3 million clients.

Despite its sharp growth in terms of outstanding loan and disbursement, this sector is far behind achieving its objective. According to ADB (2017) about 31.5 percent (50.37 million) of the Bangladeshi population still lives under the national poverty line. If it is assumed that all MFIs serve only the clients who live under the national poverty line there are still 24.07 million people living under the poverty line and are unbanked (BB, 2016). Suzuki and Miah (2016) mention that religious faith is one of the critical reasons for low microfinance outreach in Bangladesh.

Bangladesh is the world's third largest Muslim country and its official religion is Islam. Therefore, Muslim people hesitate to engage in any activities that are prohibited by their religion. Conventional microfinance engages with interest in both deposit and loan markets. The Muslim population in Bangladesh constitutes 90 percent of the total population and Islam plays a significant role in their social and economic lives. A portion of the Muslim population was not always

Table 7.2 Loan disbursement and outstanding trend in MF sector (amount in billion BDT)

Particular	2011	2012	2013	2014	2015
Loan outstanding	173.79	211.32	257.01	282.20	352.41
Loan disbursement	303.18	456.02	432.28	462.00	634.00

Source: MRA, 2015

satisfied with conventional microfinance services because they are involved in interest (*riba*). To serve this market niche, some MFIs came into being with some financial products which are compliant with Islamic *Shari'ah*. Even though some Islamic MFIs (currently seven Islamic MFIs are operating in Bangladesh) come to serve this niche market, their outreach is still very low. In fact, the Rural Development Scheme (RDS) being the market leader covers only 5 percent of total microfinance outreach.

Islami Bank Bangladesh Ltd. (IBBL) is the largest Islamic commercial bank in Bangladesh. It was established with an objective of establishing a balanced economic growth by ensuring balance between rural and urban markets. Commercial banks provide loans to their clients backed by collateral while there are many potential clients particularly in rural areas without collateral. IBBL as a commercial bank feels it is very difficult to provide loans to these potentially unbankable clients. To mitigate this dilemma, IBBL introduced a special scheme of microfinance in 1995 named 'Rural Development Scheme'. Basically RDS was introduced to fulfill the financial or investment needs in the agriculture and rural sectors which would create more employment opportunities and generate income that would reduce poverty.

RDS is the first scheme that facilitates Islamic microfinance in Bangladesh. The main funding sources of RDS are its clients' voluntary and forced deposits in addition to the fund allocated from IBBL. RDS imitates the GB mode of group lending. However, one of the salient features of this scheme is that RDS does not provide any funds directly to the client but sells the goods the client needs to get on a deferred payment condition. RDS does so to comply with *Shari'ah* principles. After eight weeks of observation by the group member as well as field officers on his/her regular attendance in center meetings, each member becomes eligible to apply for a loan. Upon receiving the application, the field officer and the investment committee thoroughly review the loan proposals. Before receiving the loan, each member must attend the training for skill development, environmental awareness, and entrepreneurship development to improve proper utilization of funds as well as efficient management and investment.

RDS provides loans in nine sectors with the maturity period ranging from one year to a maximum of three years and the investment from BDT 20,000 to a maximum of BDT 50,000. Initial investment starts with BDT 10,000 (US $125) and regular repayment increases the loan amount from BDT 2000 to BDT 5000 for every next time up to the ceiling of every sector (see Table 7.3). The rate of return of RDS investment is 12.5 percent and the timely repayment rebate is 2 percent.

Table 7.3 Purpose, period and ceiling of investment

Sl.	Sector of investment	Duration	Ceiling of investment (BDT)
1	Crop production	1 year	25,000/-
2	Nursery and commercial production of flowers and fruits	1 year	50,000/-
3	Agriculture implements	1 to 3 years	50,000/-
4	Livestocks	1 to 2 years	50,000/-
5	Poultry and duckery	1 year	35,000/-
6	Fisheries	1 to 2 years	50,000/-
7	Rural transport	1 year	20,000/-
8	Rural housing	1 to 5 years	50,000/-
9	Off-firm activities	1 year	50,000/-

Source: RDS website

Table 7.4 RDS performance from 2012–2016

Particular	2012	2013	2014	2015	2016
Villages	15,507	17104	18086	18615	19418
Centre	24,883	26887	27874	28822	28960
Members	733,520	836227	911470	947305	999140
Total savings (BDT mil)	3,323.15	4531.46	5727.15	6932.89	7952.64
Total outstanding inv. (BDT mil)	10,390.71	13730.92	17379.97	20798.82	24476.99
Recovery rate (%)	99.72	99.70	99.50	99.47	99.54

Source: IBBL 2016

Every member must maintain a *Mudaraba* Saving Account (MSA-RDS) in their individual name. The minimum compulsory deposit amount is BDT 20 per week. Out of 318 IBBL branches, 228 branches carry out RDS activities in 64 districts of the country and total loan outstanding has become BDT 24,476.99 million (see Table 7.4).

4. Comparison between Grameen Bank and the Rural Development Scheme

As we discussed in Section 2, the existing literature raises the following explanations of the slow-paced penetration of the Islamic microfinance industry: (I) lack of loanable 'microcredit' funds, (II) improper regulatory framework, (III) information asymmetry between MFIs and their clients, and (IV) failure to materialize the economies of scale. This section argues how well the GB has mitigated these obstacles and why the RDS has yet to address these challenges.

4.1 Lack of loanable 'microcredit' funds

The GB is one of the largest MFIs in the world. It started its operation in the eastern part of Bangladesh with an amount of US$ 27 which rose to US$ 2,803 million and its cumulative disbursement amounted to BDT 1,531,244.85 million by 2017. As for the RDS, total outreach is estimated to be BDT 47,757.25 million which is 35 times less than that of GB. If we have a closer look at the financial statements of GB and RDS, GB receives four concessional soft loans. The International Fund for Agricultural Development (IFAD) provided SDR equivalent of BDT 6,200,000 on 8 January 1990 at a 2 percent interest rate with a grace period of 2 years which is to be repaid within a maximum of 80 years. Norwegian Agency for International Development (NORAD) provided Norwegian Kroner 55,000,000 on 4 August 1986 at a 2 percent interest rate with a grace period of 10 years, repayable in 30 years. Swedish International Development Authority (SIDA) funded SEK 60,000,000 on 30 November 1986 at a 2 percent interest rate with a grace period of 10 years, repayable in 30 years. Dutch Grant Loan provided a loan to GB of DFL 2,000,000 equivalent of BDT 44,283,298 in 1986 at a 2 percent interest rate with a one-year grace period, repayable in 15 years. Japan International Co-operation Agency (JICA) provided GB with an amount of Yen 2,986,000,000 in March 1996 repayable in 30 years including a 10-year grace period. GB places fixed deposits amounting to BDT 93,917.20 million with 27 Bangladeshi conventional banks on an average 10 percent interest (Suzuki *et al.*, 2011), which provides GB with an opportunity to make smart deposit interest spread on an average of 8 percent upon its funding cost of around 2 percent from the concessional loans.

GB also keeps high spread margins on their loans and advances on an average 15.6 percent (Suzuki *et al.*, 2011). This opportunity to earn high interest incomes may have encouraged the GB to expand its business outreach in Bangladesh. Another funding source of GB is the deposit from non-members. The GB opens a depository scheme for non-members who can deposit their funds in GB. By the end of 2014, the total non-members' fund amounted to BDT 64,138 million. Recently GB also started to issue corporate bonds when it faces shortage of funds. These bonds are guaranteed by the Government of Bangladesh.

On the other hand, the funding of RDS depends solely on the budget allocation by IBBL, though some Islamic charity funds such as *zakat* and *waqf* are contributing to its funding. Only an independent organization is eligible to borrow from Islamic Development Bank (IDB) or other Islamic multinational financial institutions. Therefore, it is difficult for RDS which is solely subsidized by IBBL to diversify its funding sources. Besides, RDS is not allowed to receive any soft loan from the official development aid providers such as IFAD, NORAD, SIDA and JICA because of their involvement with interest which is strictly prohibited in Islam. Issuing *Sukuk* (Islamic bond) is one way by which RDS can raise their funds. But according to Bangladesh Security and Exchange Commission Act, for issuing any kind of stock, bond, or debenture, the issuer should be an independent organization. RDS is not a separate or independent organization from IBBL.

Therefore, it is not publishing its own annual report. As a result, RDS is not eligible for issuing any kind of bond in the Bangladeshi capital market.

4.2 Improper regulatory framework

Regulatory framework is the key to financial stability and development. A well-designed regulatory framework would help to incubate an infant industry. It provides the economic players in the industry with appropriate incentives and sanctions leading to its development and further innovation. A well-organized regulatory framework is necessary for microfinance industry for its development.

Rural Economics Program (the initial name of GB) worked to help the poor by providing small loans. Subsequently, it was converted to an independent bank called 'Grameen Bank' by the government ordinance on October 2, 1983, which is known as Grameen Bank Ordinance, 1983. This ordinance provides a full regulatory framework for GB. In 2013, the Bangladesh Parliament passed 'Grameen Bank Act' which replaces the Grameen Bank Ordinance, 1983, authorizing the government to make rules for any aspect for the smooth running of this institute.

For smoother operation of other microcredit organizations in Bangladesh, the government passed a microcredit act known as 'Microcredit Regulatory Authority Act 2006'. This law has been enacted in order to establish an authority and formulate rules and related matters for efficient regulation of microcredit programs ensuring transparency and accountability in the activities of microcredit organizations operating in Bangladesh. By this act, Microcredit Regulatory Authority (MRA) was born which is the prime authority of all microcredit organizations of Bangladesh. MRA is the regulatory authority that monitors and supervises microfinance operations. License from the Authority is mandatory to operate as microfinance provider in Bangladesh.

RDS is a unique microfinance organization in Bangladesh, operating directly neither under the Bangladesh Bank nor the MRA. RDS is a subsidiary of IBBL, that is, the only microfinance organization run by a commercial bank. RDS is also unique in the light of their operation because it has neither central body to monitor and supervise its operation nor does it have an independent or central *Shari'ah* board to ensure the compliance with *Shari'ah*. IBBL also faces some dilemmas when it plays its role as a monitoring and supervisory authority because the operation of a commercial bank is totally different from that of a microfinance organization.

4.3 Information asymmetry between MFIs and their clients

Asymmetric information problems or 'lemon' problems arise from the differences in information held between lenders and borrowers (Healy and Palepu, 2001). Boateng and Agyei (2013) and Ahmed (2002) suggest that information asymmetry is one of the reasons that would limit the growth of Islamic microfinance. Here, we are going to analyze how information asymmetries would restrain the growth of RDS and how well GB has overcome this particular problem.

Development of microfinance is one of the main innovations in the past 25 years (Servin *et al.*, 2012) which changed the concept of financial intermediation. GB shows that all the segment of the population is bankable including the poor households who were excluded from the formal financial market. Formal financial institutions excluded them because of their lack of collateral status. For the commercial banks, the collateral condition is essential for maintaining a certain level of the loan recovery. On the other hand, GB provides loans to the poor without any collateral and achieves a recovery rate of about 98 percent, a standard which the mainstream financial institutions find it difficult to achieve. The secret of this remarkable recovery rate is the 'group lending model' or what Besley and Coate (1995) call "joint liability".

Initially, GB made many trials and errors in their delivery and recovery method. After a considerable period of trial and error, GB has finally discovered that the formation of group lending method is crucial to the success of its operations (Yunus and Jolis, 1999). To be eligible for applying for a loan from GB, every borrower must become a member of a group. Every group consists of 5 members and 2 to 10 groups operate under one center. These groups are formed in a mechanized way such that every group member is jointly liable for any of the member's default. If any member in the group defaults the whole group is liable to repay the remaining amount. If not, GB's policy is not to extend any credit to any member of the group in the future (Suzuki *et al.*, 2011). This group lending model helps GB in two ways; first, it works as a sanction mechanism for the poor borrower; and second, it reduces information asymmetry and potential moral hazard. It is difficult for GB to monitor its borrowers because monitoring is costly and time-consuming because of information asymmetry. Also, it is difficult to screen good borrowers from bad borrowers. Wydick (2001) mentions that self-select membership helps mitigate potential adverse selection effects. Besley and Coate (1995) also identify that joint liability improves the willingness of loan repayment.

RDS has adopted the GB lending mechanism with some modification. They also provide small loans based on groups and if one member defaults the whole group will be liable to recover that loan and the default member is to be expelled from the group as well as restricted from further benefits provided by RDS as well as the IBBL[1] (Al-Mubarak, 2011). In such a circumstance, the whole group is not considered default and credit can be extended to other members of that group. The condition of RDS in dealing with default members is completely different from that of GB. Based on the profit–loss sharing (PLS), Islamic financial institutions are not allowed to penalize any defaulter or late payers (Parker, 2010). A survey was conducted by Hossain *et al.*, (2008) about RDS problems and prospects by taking an interview of 36 IBBL employees from different branches. Of the respondents, 78 percent have mentioned that monitoring of RDS clients is costly. RDS employees physically inspect at least two client locations every week to identify if the promised goods for which finance is sought have been actually purchased and are in possession of the client (Obaidullah, 2007).

4.4 Economies of scale

Infrastructure is the basic or fundamental feature of a system or organization that facilitates smooth operation. Every industry requires its basic infrastructure to grow. Different industries require different infrastructure and the same infrastructure can be used by different industries. As such, the microfinance industry requires some basic infrastructure for its smooth operation. The main infrastructure for the MFI is its communication facility. It can be a branch network, roads, communication skill etc.

In terms of branch network, GB has a total of 2,568 branches serving over 81,000 villages constituting about 97 percent of the country's landscape. This means that it covers almost the whole country. On the other hand, RDS is falling behind the GB because it is unable to establish its own branch network. But rather, it operates through the IBBL branches. RDS runs it operation through 252 IBBL branches that cover 19,418 villages constituting only 23 percent of the country. This is one of the major disadvantages for RDS which is presumably restricting the growth of Islamic microfinance in Bangladesh.

5. A glimpse of current practices of Pakistani Islamic microfinance

Pakistan is a Muslim-dominant country where Islamic microfinance has been struggling to grow responding to the emerging demand of the country. In this section, we attempt to reflect the current status of Islamic microfinance in Pakistan and what Islamic MFIs can offer or learn from similar institutes in other countries.

We should note that the state of financial inclusion in Pakistan, as a whole, still depicts a dismal picture. Only 16 percent of the adult population has access to the banking system and 23 percent of the population use formal financial services. The statistics are worse in the rural areas where only 14 percent of the adult population are banked. In the case of women, only 11 percent are banked. Pakistan continues to lag behind other Indian sub-continental countries. According to the Global Findex Database 2014 of World Bank, the share of formal savings reached only 3 percent in Pakistan (compared to 7 percent in Bangladesh) and the share of formal borrowings reached only 2 percent (compared to 10 percent in Bangladesh) (PMN, 2016).

Despite these setbacks, microfinance industry in Pakistan, as a whole, witnessed continuous growth and expansion in outreach in the year 2015 (see Table 7.5). Pakistan Microfinance Network [PMN] (2016) points out that the major development took place in the policy and regulatory fronts such as the launch of the National Financial Inclusion Strategy (NFIS) and the introduction of a regulatory framework for Non-Bank Microfinance Institutes (NBMFI) by the Securities and Exchange Commission of Pakistan (SECP) in 2015. In addition, results of the second Access to Finance Survey were launched. With the launch of NFIS, a roadmap for achievement of financial inclusion in the country has been laid out.

Table 7.5 Microfinance industry in Pakistan

	2012	2013	2014	2015	2016
Active borrowers (in millions)	2.0	2.4	2.8	3.6	4.2
Gross loan portfolio (PKR billions) [changes from the previous year: %]	33.1	46.6	61.1	90.2	132.0
	[+33.46]	[+40.78]	[+31.11]	[+47.62]	[+46.34]
Branches	1,460	1,606	1,747	2,754	2,367
(a) Total assets (PKR billions)	61.9	81.5	100.7	145.1	225.3
(b) Total revenue (PKR billions)	12.5	17.3	24.3	32.8	41.8
ROA [(b)/(a)] (%)	20.19	21.22	24.13	22.60	18.55

Source: created by the authors upon PMN (2016, 2017)

Now with the introduction of the rules and regulations for NBMFI a level playing field has been created in the industry which provides an opportunity for non-bank players to scale up their businesses. Despite sustained efforts having been put forth by the policymakers, regulators, and donors a lot more needs to be done for an enviable microfinance environment in Pakistan (PMN, 2016, p. 3).

Second, we should note how poorly Islamic MFI has contributed to the microfinance industry in Pakistan. Here we look at NRSP Microfinance Bank Limited ('NRSP Microfinance Bank'), headquartered in Bahawalpur which commenced its operation in March 2011 as a national-level microfinance provider. NRSP is one of the leading players of the microfinance sector in Pakistan. According to its website, the bank has endeavored to offer cutting-edge banking services to its customers with the launch of Islamic microfinance operations. Being the first Islamic micro-lending institution, the bank intends to cater to the greater demand of *Shari'ah*-compliant solutions and services to the microfinance industry of Pakistan. The bank builds on the experience of its parent institution, the National Rural Support Program (NRSP), to alleviate poverty and promote financial inclusion in the country. Its capital has been contributed by highly reputed organizations including the International Finance Corporation, Acumen, KFW, and the National Rural Support Program. Through a network of 108 branches across 32 districts, NRSP bank offers a range of financial services including deposits, micro-credit, and micro-insurance to the financially excluded individuals living in both urban and rural areas of Pakistan (see Table 7.6).

We observe that the share of Islamic advances provided by NRSP-MB is in increasing trend. However, the share of Islamic advances in the Microfinance Bank is still at a marginal level compared to that of conventional microcredit (see Table 7.7).

Third, we should note the limited effect of various microfinance industry initiatives by the government. According to PMN (2016), the Government of Pakistan (GoP) launched an interest-free microloan scheme ('Prime Minister Interest Free Loan Scheme') in 2014 to address the issues of poverty and rising unemployment in the country. Under the scheme, PKR 3.5 billion were allotted from the federal

Table 7.6 Performance in NRSP-MB

	2012	2013	2014	2015	2016
Active borrowers	126,717	171,718	194,489	258,444	325,521
Gross advances (PKR in billions)	3.06	4.85	5.19	9.09	13.27
Profit before taxation (PKR in millions)	148	338	286	650	960

Source: NRSP-MB (2016)

Table 7.7 Share of Islamic advances in NRSP-MB (percentage in parentheses)

Loan type	2015		2016	
	No. of loan outstanding	Amount outstanding Rupees (in millions)	No. of loan outstanding	Amount outstanding Rupees (in millions)
Microcredit	257,240 [99.53]	9,008.18 [99.15]	318,750 [97.91]	12,863.57 [96.93]
Islamic advances	1,204 [0.47]	77.33 [0.85]	6,771 [2,08]	407.47 [3.07]
Total	258,444 [100.0]	9,085.51 [100.0]	325,521 [100.0]	13,271.04 [100.0]

Source: NRSP-MB (2016, p. 48)

budget to facilitate the poor and destitute segments of the population for gearing up their livelihood. However, in order to safeguard the interests of the MFPs it was decided that the funds under this scheme would be routed through the national apex, PPAF, and would only be extended in Union Councils that have a low or no penetration of conventional microfinance. As of December 2015, PKR 2.25 billion have been disbursed under the scheme to approximately 110,000 beneficiaries, out of which 66,000 were female and 44,000 were male applicants. These interest-free loans are being made available to men and women from households with a score of up to 40 on the Poverty Score Card (PSC) and with little or no access to banks or microcredit institutions. Most of the loans have been utilized in the livestock sector, followed by business and trading, services, and agriculture.

As was observed, NRSP Microfinance Bank is focusing more on the conventional mode than the Islamic one. According to an ex-staff member of NRSP Microfinance Bank, in the case of transacting the Islamic mode of microcredit with the government, the borrower pays back only the principal amount without interest, then the government pays 16 percent profit margins to NRSP Microfinance Bank. Nevertheless, as reported in Table 7.7, the disbursement rate for the Islamic mode has been very low because the applicants cannot meet the NRSP Microfinance Bank's credit criteria.

Lastly, we should note that financing against gold-backed loans by Microfinance Banks (MFBs) have gained widespread popularity in the last few years in Pakistan. According to PMN (2016), it has allowed MFBs to move from traditional group lending to individual lending and also increase their loan sizes. PMN (2016) points out that this mode of financing drew its strength from the fact that gold and gold ornaments have been a traditional mode of savings among the masses which in times of emergency is liquidated often at a deep discount. Obtaining a loan against this gold without having to liquidate may provide a better alternative to potential borrowers. This product effectively transformed gold from a non-liquid asset into a liquid and earning asset. Pioneered by Tameer Microfinance Bank (TMFB), it was soon adopted by other MFBs. At this time up to five MFBs are dealing in this product and the percentage of the gross loan portfolio financed against gold ranges from 20 percent to 55 percent.

The issue is whether the loans were being utilized for consumption purposes rather than for productive ones (PMN, 2016). Also, the concern as to whether the loan amounts being determined based on the value of the gold or based on the repayment capacity of the client led to strengthening the belief that gold-backed loans were against the spirit of microfinance which promotes lending without physical collateral. It is reported that overall group lending methodology continues to dominate the industry. However, individual lending is gaining popularity (PMN, 2016). Presumably, financing against gold-backed loans may be related to the share of individual lending.

The direction of Islamic finance must be in conformity with the *maqasid al-shari'ah*, which has been defined as the "purpose and wisdom behind the enactment of all or most of the *Shari'ah* rulings" (Çizakça, 2011, p. 240). Simultaneously, Çizakça (2011) points out that *mudaraba/musharaka* investments demand a totally different management approach than ordinary banking. Whereas the former involves a style of management that requires a very personal and often hands-on approach, for the latter a hands-off approach would suffice. Indeed, conventional bankers as well as Islamic bankers with conventional banking backgrounds are trained to detach themselves from the business of the entrepreneurs they finance. By contract, *mudaraba/musharaka* investments demand a constant cooperation and support for the entrepreneur. Çizakça (2011, p. 246) argues that "Islamic bankers with a conventional mindset are simply not prepared for this sort of management." This leads us to ask: Can his claim be held for Islamic microfinance? Probably, Islamic bankers with a conventional mindset are simply not prepared for the MFI management, either. This may explain a cause of extremely low rate of Islamic advances in the Pakistani MFI and, on the contrary, higher portfolio of financing against gold-backed advances. Though this entails further investigations, the MFI bankers' mindset and the market for gold-backed advances might be raised as the factors which hinder the development of the Islamic microfinance industry in Pakistan.

6. Conclusion and recommendation

There is a huge demand for Islamic MFIs around the globe but the outreach is very marginal compared to the demand. This chapter has explored its reasons and possible remedies. In so doing, we have analyzed and compared Grameen Bank as a successful conventional MFI with IBBL-RDS as an emerging Islamic MFI in Bangladesh. We also have provided the current status of Islamic MFIs in Pakistan.

We have identified potential obstacles for MFIs mainly from four dimensions: lack of loanable 'microcredit' funds, improper regulatory framework, information asymmetry between MFIs and their clients, and the economies of scale. Our analysis suggests that GB has gained a competitive advantage in the microfinance industry which helps it overcome these obstacles successfully whereas RDS has been in a trap of these obstacles. We also have identified several structural problems facing RDS. First, RDS has the limitation in raising the loanable funds. The funding of RDS as the subsidy of IBBL depends solely on its parent company. Besides, it is structurally difficult for RDS to diversify its funding sources to tap Islamic multinational financial institutions (due to the lack of eligibility criteria) or multinational and bilateral donor agencies (facing the *Shari'ah*-compliant issue). Second, RDS is less recognized under the governmental policy for enhancing the microfinance compared to the GB which has been fully supported by the government. Third, under the current Islamic mode of profit–loss sharing (PLS), RDS is in a disadvantageous position to discipline its clients, even though RDS follows the same 'group lending' model developed by GB for mitigating potential moral hazard problems. Fourth, it is not easy for RDS to seek its scale efficiency to compete with GB which has gained the wider branch network in Bangladesh.

We further provide a glimpse of the current practices of Islamic MFIs in Pakistan. Here we have observed how poorly Islamic MFI has contributed to the microfinance industry in Pakistan. Even though this argument entails further investigations, this chapter has pointed out the limited effect of various microfinance industries initiated by the Pakistani government. Also we are concerned that financing against gold-backed loans by Microfinance Banks (MFBs) has gained widespread popularity in the last few years in Pakistan, which has allowed MFBs to move from traditional group lending to individual lending and also increase their loan size. We should watch the evolution of the Pakistani Islamic microfinance industry, too.

Before closing, we wish to draw some policy options for incubating and enhancing the Islamic microfinance industry:

- To develop and diversify the funding sources for Islamic MFIs, the role and scope of Islamic multinational financial institutions such as Islamic Development Bank (IDB) should be expanded to meet the demand of loanable funds by Islamic MFIs. Development of financial schemes (for instance, through the issuance of Islamic bonds) to get multinational and bilateral donor agencies engaged with the Islamic microfinance industry should be promoted.
- The current mode of PLS should be reviewed from the perspective of protecting the lenders' rights in the credit agreement and effectively disciplining the borrowers. Otherwise, commercially sustainable Islamic microfinance business is not feasible.

- The government has to consider the 'level playing field' for incubating Islamic MFIs by giving the opportunity (time) of learning the skill of monitoring microenterprises and of expanding their branch network for gaining the economies of scale. If fair competition between Islamic and conventional MFIs is ensured, MFIs are expected to bring growth-enhancing effects to society.

Note

1 According to Parker (2010), an Islamic financial institution is obliged to try to resolve defaults or late payments through refinancing or restructuring, and any imposition of late payment charges and fines should be a last resort and should consider the customers' financial capability and motives.

8 An impact assessment of Islamic Saving–Loan and Financing Cooperatives in Indonesia

Preliminary findings from the artificial neural networks technique

Yasushi Suzuki, Saiful Anwar, Sigit Pramono and Trisiladi Supriyanto

1. Introduction

Currently, the debate on the similarities between Islamic and conventional financial products has shifted to a more fundamental question – how does Islamic finance contribute to promoting welfare, building social-cohesion, and realizing social justice as an ultimate goal of Islamic economics? Abu Zaharah (1997) classifies the main objectives of Islamic laws into three categories: educating people, establishing justice, and promoting welfare. Many Islamic scholars are concerned about the so-called *Maqasid al-Shari'ah* Index as a socio-economic mixture based index to measure the Islamic bank's performance comprehensively reflected in financial, social, material, and spiritual aspects. Imam Satibi is a well-known Islamic scholar who initially explains the *Maqasid al-Shari'ah* as a clear vision in practicing Islamic law. *Maqasid al-Shari'ah* reflects the holistic view of Islam which has to be looked at as a whole not in parts as Islam is a complete and integrated code of life and its goal encompasses the whole life, individual, and society, in this world and the Hereafter (Abozaid and Dusuki, 2007). According to Imam Satibi, there are five main objectives of practicing Islamic law: safeguarding the value of faith, rights and stake-holding, self, intellect, and social entity.

The argument behind this fundamental criticism is to clearly differentiate the paradigm of doing business in the financial industry following Islamic teaching in a holistic way. This leads us to ask: Should Islamic banks focus on how to create profit as much as possible resulting from *Shari'ah*-compliant products? Or should Islamic banking also consider how to narrow down the gap between the rich and the poor? According to the Islamic economics 'idealist' view, *Shari'ah* compliance as the ultimately distinguished parameter of Islamic financial institutions (IFIs) means that the IFIs (including Islamic banks) operate not only following the Islamic forms but also following the Islamic spirit or substance. Such paradigm gives direction and guidance on how to frame the ultimate goals in the

IFIs according to the spirit and value behind Islamic finance. The idealists respect Qur'an Surah 59 Verse 7:

> Whatever God restored to His Messenger from the inhabitants of the villages belongs to God, and to the Messenger, and to the relatives, and to the orphans, and to the poor, and to the wayfarer; so that it may not circulate solely between the wealthy among you. Whatever the Messenger gives you, accept it; and whatever he forbids you, abstain from it. And fear God. God is severe in punishment.

In the idealist view, the operation of Islamic banking should follow the *Maqasid al-Shari'ah* in which the ultimate goal is to promote human well-being reflected on economic and sustainable development, social justice, and social investing-oriented principles (Asutay, 2012; Chapra, 1992). Some scholars attempt to measure the unsatisfactory achievement (Martan *et. al.*, 1984; Asutay and Harningtyas, 2015). The idealists, however, ignore the important dimension such that banks as depository corporations are expected to pay the best effort to protect the interest (welfare) of their general depositors to maintain financial stability. For the purpose of avoiding the potential accumulation of non-performing credits which may trigger financial instability, in general, banks require the pledge of collateral for securing their financing. On the other hand, society should consider that poor people in general are categorized as unbankable or not-credible persons, thus the collateral condition becomes a serious constraint for poor people to access financing or credit from banks. Rahim (2007) implies that Islamic microfinance is still underdeveloped in Islamic finance.

This chapter aims to shed an analytical light on the current impact of Islamic microfinance – with the case of Islamic Saving–Loan and Financing Cooperatives in Indonesia – on poverty alleviation. Also this chapter aims to make a methodological contribution to the existing scientific method of impact assessment of microfinance by introducing the concept of 'artificial neural networks'. The outline of this chapter is as follows: Section 2 has a glimpse of the realities of Islamic microfinance in Indonesia. Section 3 reviews the limitations of the existing methods of impact assessment of microfinance. Section 4 describes the methodology in our analysis and proposes a methodological contribution to the existing scientific method. We discuss the concept of artificial neural networks. Section 5 argues and interprets the result of our analysis. Section 6 finally concludes.

2. The realities of Islamic microfinance in Indonesia

In Indonesia with the largest Muslim population in the world, the government requires Islamic banks to provide credit or financing facilities to micro-, small- and medium-sized enterprises (MSMEs) in a minimum amount of 20 percent of the total credit or financing (Bank Indonesia (BI) Regulation No. 17/12/PBI/2015 dated on June 25, 2015, as the amendment of BI Regulation No. 14/22/PBI/2012 dated on December 21, 2012). Banks which would fail to fulfill the required credit ratio are to be given administrative sanctions by the central bank. This regulation, however, may have given an ill-incentive for Islamic banks not to challenge the MSMEs credit risk beyond the minimum ratio (Figure 8.1).

As mentioned earlier, in general, banks as depository corporations have to pay the best effort to protect the welfare of their depositors. Under the current mode of profit-and-loss sharing (PLS), Islamic banks should be kept away from undertaking very high risk and uncertainty typically associated with the MSMEs financing. In exchange, society needs another type of IFIs so as to incubate MSMEs for the purpose of poverty alleviation. The main players in the Islamic microfinance sector in Indonesia include two types of financial institutions, namely 'Islamic rural banks' (*Bank Pembiayaan Rakyat Syariah*, BPRS) and 'Islamic microfinance cooperatives' also known as *Baitul Maal wat Tamwil* (BMT) (Bappenas, 2014).

BPRS as the micro-bank institution is regulated and supervised separately from Islamic commercial banks by Indonesian Financial Services Authority (FSA). The latter has two forms in its legal entity of Islamic microfinance cooperative, namely Islamic Financial Services Cooperatives (*Koperasi Jasa Keuangan Syariah/* KJKS) which is under the supervision of Ministry of Cooperatives and Small and Medium Enterprises, and Islamic Micro Financial Institution (*Lembaga Keuangan Mikro Syariah/*LKMS) which is under the supervision of FSA. Islamic Financial Services Cooperatives are replaced by Islamic Saving–Loan and Financing Cooperatives (*Koperasi Simpan Pinjam dan Pembiayaan Syariah/*KSPPS) based on Decree of Ministry of Cooperatives and Small and Medium Enterprises No. 16 Year 2015.

As of December 31, 2015 there were 163 BPRSs which operate in all areas of Indonesia. Meanwhile, there were only 18 units of Islamic Micro Financial Institution with total asset amounting to Rp 71 billion. In parallel, the number of Islamic Financial Services Cooperatives was 150,223 units including 4,000 units of Islamic-based cooperatives consisting of 1,197 units of Islamic Financial Services Cooperatives (*Koperasi Jasa Keuangan Syariah/*KJKS) and 2,163 units of Islamic Financial Services Unit/Windows (UJKS).

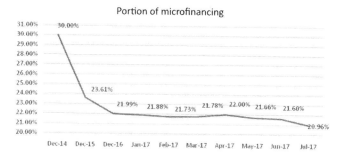

Figure 8.1 Portion of MSME financing in Indonesia's Islamic Banks

Source: FSA's Indonesian Banking Statistics

3. Limitations of existing impact assessment methodologies of microfinance

Hulme (2000) classifies three paradigms of impact assessment: the scientific method, the humanities tradition, and participatory learning and action (PLA). This classification was derived from the literature to improve the standard of measurement, sampling, and analytical technique. In fact, the existing literature has resulted in quite diverse conclusions on impact assessment of microfinance. For instance, Holcombe (1995), Hossain (1988), and Khandker (1998) conclude that microfinance gives benefits to both economic and social aspects. On the other hand, Adams and Von Pischke (1992), Buckley (1997), and Montgomery (1996) assert a different conclusion, that microfinance creates negative impacts on both the economic and social lives of people. There are researchers such as Hulme and Mosley (1996) and Mosely and Hulme (1998) who conclude that microfinance is beneficial economically but somehow does not benefit the poor through poverty alleviation.

Each paradigm of impact assessment has its own challenges. First, the scientific method is used to observe the parameters that microfinance could give impact to economic and social elements through experimentation. Hulme (2000) explains that this method lies under a specific condition which is perfectly under control. The statistical method that could be used is multiple regression, however, this method is rarely being used since the method requires a huge amount of data and strict assumptions. Otherwise, the research could experience problems of sample selection bias and misuse of parameters that fail to represent the population. The second problem lies in the humanities aspect. Hulme (2000) describes that the humanities tradition method initially belongs to the subjects of geography, rural sociology, and anthropology. This method is the opposite of the scientific method since it has nothing to do with statistics, probability, and samples. Due to the high intention of process involvement, the validity of the humanities tradition method relies on logical consistency, rigorous material, documents presented as evidence, degree of triangulation used to validate the evidence, and the quality of methodology and researchers. Therefore, the humanities tradition method seems to be qualitative, which needs a subjective approach to measure the quality of the research.

The participatory learning and action (PLA) approach of impact assessment strongly, on the other hand, relies on the side of the poor as the center of study. The assumption of this method is to cover the connection of parameters in the complex web. The scientific method is considered failed as it neglects the complexity, diversity, and contingency of winning livelihoods by reducing the complexity to unidirectional connections (Hulme, 2000). However, the problem addressed in this method is three-fold: (I) subjectivity on conceptualization in explaining the impact; (II) subjectivity on choosing and using data as parameters to observe the impact; (III) the condition of variation of a set of parameters used in different conditions which do not allow the drawing of a comparison.

Needless to say, there is no perfect way to conduct an impact assessment of microfinance. However, we should continue to challenge the improvement of impact assessment in fulfilling *Maqasid al-Shari'ah* in terms of poverty alleviation to realize 'social justice'. Here we attempt to contribute to the scientific method. First, we adopt a conventional model of impact chain proposed by Hulme (2000) which assumes that the Islamic microfinance institution acts as an intervention instrument to change the economic behavior of the poor and practice it somehow to achieve the desired outcome. We look at the internal variables of agents being intervened by microfinance institutions, following the work of Schreiner (2012). These variables include number of household members, education level, health condition, and economic condition in order to classify which parameters give the significant impact on poverty alleviation following business development and community empowerment program in the institution.

This method like other models has the weakness in regard to its assumption. Schreiner (2012) as the inventor of this method explains that a certain bias could be occurred since the future relationship between parameters and poverty is assumed to remain unchanged. However, as Desiere *et al.* (2015) explain, the bias could be reduced if the target parent population is not so specific and/or if the relationship between parameters and poverty is reasonably updated.

4. Methodology

To perform an impact assessment of microfinance on poverty alleviation, this research utilizes data consisting of 2,440 respondents among 136,675 members (as of September 2017) of an Islamic-based cooperatives namely KSPPS Benteng Mikro Indonesia as a case study. The data collection through its five branches is based on the stratified sampling method in calculating the necessary number of respondents in accordance with the population in several villages in each specific district which each branch is covering, so that the assessment may overcome the self-selection bias problem.

4.1 PPI scorecard

Measuring the impact on poverty alleviation is very complicated mainly because setting up the criteria for measuring it – how an 'absolute' criterion on the poverty line should be sought and how long we should monitor any positive or negative impact on poverty alleviation within a certain time frame – is extremely difficult. Needless to say, the data collection is time-consuming and very costly. In Indonesia, the government together with Mark Schreiner developed the Indonesian Progress out of Poverty Index (PPI) Scorecard as a tool for measuring the national poverty condition, mainly looking at four variables; the number of household members, the education level of the family head, the health condition, and the economic condition of each household (Schreiner, 2012). The scorecard is prepared using the national 2010 socio-economic survey conducted by the national statistical bureau of Indonesia. This scorecard is widely used as *rules of thumb* by Indonesian individuals or organizations to measure the poverty rates in targeted groups and parent population.

Schreiner (2012) explains the characteristics of the scorecard which uses ten parameters in four variables as follows: first, the parameters are selected, taking into account the cost for data collection, the clarity and coherence of setting the Q&As, and verifying them and the correlation with the changes in poverty status. Second, each parameter is quantified using a non-negative-integer score ranging from 0 (suggesting the significant correlation with living most likely below a poverty line) and 100 (least likely below a poverty line). Third, the parameters are selected and the score is given for each answer in each parameter according to the transformed function of statistical Logit coefficient which addresses the discriminatory power. The higher point is given to the answer which is its power in distinguishing the poor from the non-poor household is higher or otherwise (Desiere *et.al.*, 2015) [For instance, for the parameter of 'number of household members', six answers are prepared; (a) six or more, (b) five, (c) four, (d) three, (e) two, (f) one, then the point to each answers is assigned such as 0 to (a), 5 to (b), 11 to (c), 18 to (d), 24 to (e), 37 to (f), respectively. As for the parameter of 'level of education of family head', seven answers are prepared: (a) never go to school, (b) elementary school, (c) junior high school, (d) no family head/wife, (e) senior high school, (f) high school with special package, (g) diploma or bachelor and above, then the point to each answers is assigned as 0 to (a), 3 to (b), 4 to (c), 4 to (d), 4 to (e), 6 to (f), 18 to (g), respectively. As for the parameter of 'ownership status of a motorcycle/motor boat', all or nothing answers are prepared, 0 to 'no' and 9 to 'yes'. The details are available at 'Simple Poverty Scorecard® Indonesia']. The parameters are similar to those used in the model introduced by Noreen (2011) and Goetz and Gupta (1996).

Finally, the total score (PPI Score) is linked to the so-called percentage of purchase power parity (PPP) (see Table 8.1). The linkage of PPI score with the PPP exhibits the probability of a household that lives below the poverty line. The Indonesian PPI scorecard shows that, for example, a member in the category (Layer 3) of 10–14 PPI Score lives, with the probability of 98.3 percent, below the poverty line upon the US$ 2.50 income per day standard using the 2005 purchase power parity (US$ 2.50–2005 PPP) issued by the World Bank.

4.2 The process of poverty alleviation analysis

The analysis of the member's poverty status is very important especially for Islamic Saving–Loan and Financing Cooperatives including KSPPS Benteng Mikro Indonesia, since the cooperative has set its target for alleviating poverty so as to make the minimum income per day for each member reach Rp 30,000 or US$ 2.20. As discussed earlier, the survey of impact assessment on poverty alleviation is time-consuming and costly. Therefore, KSPPS Benteng Mikro Indonesia is very concerned about the rules of thumb for measuring the poverty rate of its members.

We calculate each PPI score of 2,440 respondents collected from the members of KSPPS Benteng Mikro Indonesia to check the member's poverty rate upon three criteria for the poverty line: (I) the international standard income of US$

Table 8.1 PPI scorecard for Indonesia

Layer	PPI score	PPP (in percentage)	
		$2.50	100% national
		Year 2005	(Indonesian standard)
1	0–4	99.6	66.3
2	5–9	99	60
3	10–14	98.3	48.4
4	15–19	96.5	34.1
5	20–24	95.2	25.2
6	25–29	91.5	17.3
7	30–34	87.7	10.3
8	35–39	79.7	5.8
9	40–44	68.4	3.2
10	45–49	54.7	1.4
11	50–54	40.1	0.6
12	55–59	26.9	0.2
13	60–64	17.6	0.1
14	65–69	9.1	0
15	70–74	6.9	0
16	75–79	3.7	0
17	80–84	0.2	0
18	85–89	0	0
19	90–94	0	0
20	95–100	0	0

Source: created from Indonesian PPI scorecard

2.50 per day, (II) the national poverty line standard as portrayed in 100 percent national purchase power parity, (III) the target income level of Rp 30,000 or US\$ 2.20 by using the extrapolated version of PPI scorecard upon the US\$ 2.50–2005 PPP (we adjust the US\$ 2.50–2005 PPP to the scale by [(US\$ 2.5 * Rp 13,630) - (US\$ 2.20 * Rp 13,630))/(US\$ 2.50 * Rp 13,630)][1] or 14 percent down.

Furthermore, we attempt to apply the method of 'artificial neural networks' (or the ANN method) to investigate how the individual factors are affecting poverty alleviation in the members of the cooperative. The cooperative is very concerned with which parameters (factors) would be more contributing to poverty alleviation for the members. Financial support to a household might be trickled down to society. Besides, the ANN method is expected to diagnose the hidden parameters which would be more contributing to alleviating the poverty of members in particular.

As mentioned earlier, we follow Schreiner (2012) in selecting input parameters as follows: number of household members (X1), all members aged 6 to 18 go to school (X2), level of education of family head (X3), material of the floor (X4), toilet arrangement (X5), main cooking fuel (X6), ownership status of gas cylinder

12 Kg (X7), ownership status of freezer (X8), ownership status of a motorcycle/ or motor boat (X9), and the main employment of family head (X10). On the other hand, we look at the PPI score (Y) as the proxy of life condition in each household. In passing, it is worth noting the statistical description of each parameter's score collected from 2,440 respondents (see Table 8.2).

4.3 Artificial neural networks

Here we wish to discuss the essence of artificial neural networks. This method is an early type of machine learning technique which simulates the way of the human brain in learning and understanding information. The human brain consists of billions of neurons that are interconnected. Specifically, the technique follows the function of the interconnection of neurons in receiving, processing, and transferring the valuable information to other neurons. Accordingly, the artificial neural networks technique is then designed in accordance with the information structure of neurons which consists of input function, weighted function, summation function, transformation function, and output function.

The designed structure supports the technique to analyze information resulting in pattern recognition which initially comes to input functions. The ability of this technique in understanding some patterns and translating them into information depends on the number of training given into the networks. This optimum number of training process is needed to develop data generalization and to enhance the potency of networks in improving the performance. Finally, the generalization ability can be used to perform powerful prediction and classification tasks.

The process of artificial neural networks in performing either prediction or classification tasks is as follows: First, there are some inputs coming to the neuron j marked with symbol x_{1j}, x_{2j}, x_{3j} to x_{ij}. Each input that comes into the neuron j has its different number of weight which differentiates its level of importance. Subsequently, the input is processed in the neuron using the activation function. The function calculates all inputs by summing up all the input value which the initial value has been multiplied with its respective weight. Furthermore, the calculation results will be compared to the threshold value which indicates minimum value that is allowed to be forwarded to other neurons as an output Yj. This threshold

Table 8.2 Statistical description of parameters

Statistical descriptive	X1	X2	X3	X4	X5	X6	X7	X8	X9	X10	Total score	PPI score
Minimum	1	0	0	0	0	0	0	0	0	0	6	0%
Maximum	6	2	18	5	4	5	6	8	9	6	64	60%
Median	4	2	3	5	4	5	0	8	9	1	40	3%
Std. deviation	1.2	1	2.6	1.3	1.5	0.9	1.77	3.35	2.85	1.13	8.0	8%
Average	4.03	1.2	4	4.61	3.1	4.84	0.58	6.19	7.98	1.66	38.1	7%

value is unique for each neuron when the net value originated from the sum-up calculation is bigger than the threshold value; therefore, the neuron will be activated to transfer the information as an output to other neurons. Currently, various types of activation function can be used in analysis, namely linear, sigmoid, and logistic.

The utilization of artificial neural networks in research is mostly in the form of multilayers which comprise sets of neurons (West *et.al.*, 1997). The group of neurons is then designed to become a specific structure to enhance the power of prediction making, and more often for doing classification tasks.

There are many techniques which can be used to do classification tasks including traditional statistical techniques such as linear discriminant analysis and logistic regression, and data-mining techniques such as artificial neural networks and support vector machine (Maroco *et al.*, 2011). Specifically, Nur Ozkan-Gunay and Ozkan (2007) argue that artificial neural networks outperform other statistical techniques such as Multi Discriminant Analysis (MDA) because the technique has adaptive capabilities in making adjustment of behavior changes of data distribution in the so-called nonlinear approach by transforming the data into a linearly separable feature space. Therefore, the technique results in better approximation by adaptively modifying the weighted function to promptly respond to the changes of data distribution behaviour. Meanwhile, the traditional statistic technique has limitations since the technique is conducted according to pre-assumptions that data are distributed in a linear behaviour, so-called multivariate normally distributed. Therefore, most of the traditional statistical techniques such as MDA will benefit the researchers if the parameters and basic underlying relationship are always in stable condition.

This is due to the fact that the utilization of artificial neural networks to do classification tasks has been extensively practiced in many fields (Yang, 2010). For Islamic banking research, Anwar and Ismal (2011) compare both techniques to predict the rate of return of Islamic banks' deposit products which conclude that artificial neural networks perform better in the context of capturing all patterns of data. Furthermore, Anwar and Mikami (2011) compare the pattern recognition ability to do predictions in Islamic banking between traditional statistical techniques and artificial neural networks and conclude that artificial neural networks result in better abilities in making predictions. The comparison is based on total classification accuracy and error rate.

To optimize the power of classification, artificial neural networks are constructed into multi stages comprising the input layer, the hidden layer functions as processing the weighted information coming from the input layer, and the output layer, whereas each layer consists of multi-units of neurons to enhance the power of classification.

Specifically, the input layer is a set of neurons which perform to collect information from outside. Subsequently, the collection of information is then feed forwarded into the hidden layer which detects the input signal and releases it to the output layer as an output. The output signal is actually the accumulation of the activation function of all neurons creating the hidden layer. Mathematically, the feed forward multi-layer structure of artificial neural networks is depicted in the following formula:

$$\hat{y}_t = f(x, \theta) + \varepsilon$$

where: $\hat{y}_t$ is an output value so-called target variable that is intended to be fore-casted or classified at observation time t. Meanwhile, x is the input variable vector which functions as an explanatory variable, θ is a weighted parameter of the input variable, and ε the component of random error. There are two types of activation functions which can be used to utilize feed forward artificial neural networks, namely the linear activation function and logistic activation function, both of which function as classifiers, which is located in the hidden layer. This research employs the linear activation function due to the output value being modeled being a numeric value which is formulated as:

$$f(x) = x$$

The classification resulted from this research is evaluated by following the work of Maroco et.al., (2011) when he classifies mild cognitive impairment among 400 people using two instruments namely sensitivity and specificity. Sensitivity means the ability to predict the condition when the condition is present meanwhile the specificity means the ability to predict the absence of the condition when the condition is not present.

In other words, this research empowers the ability of artificial neural networks to perform as classifier discriminant to measure the significance of the input parameters, which would be really contributing to alleviating poverty, in deter-mining the PPI score as the proxy of life conditions in each household. Finally, the output value as the classification result is to be evaluated using some statisti-cal techniques such as R^2, correlation coefficient, and actual vs. output graph to validate that the algorithm fits the data well enough.

This research utilizes the application Alyuda Neuro Intelligence which is widely used by many big companies for data mining and forecasting needs such as Microsoft, Hewlett-Packard, Boeing, Coca-Cola, General Electric etc. The application is used to develop the classifier algorithm which is initially trained in a certain number of iterations or epochs for a subset of the data, the so-called train set. The remaining subset of the data is categorized as the validation set and the test set. In the process of classifier algorithm development, the incre-ment number of iteration will upgrade the value of weight as an adjustment process to increase the correction rate of classification power at the same time to minimize the classification error. There are five subsequent steps conducted in this research to apply an artificial neural networks-based analysis using Aly-uda Neuro Intelligence software such as data preparation, data preprocessing, designing the architecture of the network, training the networks, and testing the networks.

5. Results and discussion

Islamic Saving–Loan and Financing Cooperative (KSPPS) Benteng Mikro Indonesia was established in June 2003 upon the modified Grameen microcredit model. Later, it officially started its operation upon the Islamic-compliant contract on March 20, 2013 and received its legal entity approval of Islamic Financial Services Cooperatives by the decree of the Minister of Cooperatives and MSMEs No. 486/BH/MENEG.I/V/2014.

We had an interview with the president director of KSPPS Benteng Mikro Indonesia (KSPPS-BMI) on October 27, 2017. According to the primary source, the number of cooperative members has reached 136,675 persons. KSPPS-BMI operates to serve those people living in Banten Province and West Java Province through five branches. The members of this cooperative are dominated by women (around 95 percent) and MSMEs entrepreneurs who are engaged mainly in running retailers, housing, and small restaurants. Basically, KSPPS-BMI offers its saving and investment accounts to members under the Islamic financial contracts of *mudharabah* (*mudharabah muqayayadah* or *mudharabah mutlaqha*). Additionally, KSPPS-BMI also channels funds from Islamic commercial banks and other Islamic microfinance institutions.

On the other hand, the asset side of the cooperative is accumulated mainly through the Islamic financial contracts of *murabaha* and *ijarah* in facilitating the demand of working capital from the members. The total financing was increased to Rp 486,221 million as of September 2017, increased by 26 percent from that in December 2016. Meanwhile, the ratio of non-performing financing (NPF) stays at about 0.4 percent.

5.1 Poverty rate analysis

The research collects the data from 2,440 respondents to calculate the PPI score of each household, classifying each of them into 20 categories (layers) according to PPI scorecard Indonesia. As discussed in Section 4, we check the member's poverty rate upon three criteria for the poverty line: (I) the international standard income of US$ 2.50 per day, (II) the national poverty line standard as portrayed in 100 percent national purchase power parity, (III) the target income level of Rp 30,000 or US$ 2.20 by using the extrapolated version of PPI scorecard upon the US$ 2.50–2005 PPP.

5.2 Poverty rate analysis of international standard

KSPPS-BMI's members are only classified into 12 layers of PPI Score (Table 8.3). In the highest layer (60 to 64), there are 15 respondents (representing 0.61 percent of the total) who are assumed to live, with the probability of 17.60 percent, under the poverty line upon the international standard. In contrast, in the lowest layer, there are 14 respondents or 0.57 percent who are assumed to live, with the probability of 99 percent, under the poverty line.

Table 8.3 KSPPS-BMI members' PPI score and PPP upon the international standard

	LAYER	PPI score	PPI table index	Number of respondents	Portion of total respondents	Average income/ day
	1	60–64	17.60%	15	0.61%	547.533
	2	55–59	26.90%	30	1.23%	208.186
	3	50–54	40.10%	57	2.34%	254.824
US$ 2.5 2005 PPP	4	44–49	54.70%	288	11.80%	189.204
	5	40–44	68.40%	872	35.74%	203.359
	6	35–39	79.70%	522	21.39%	182.355
	7	30–34	87.70%	310	12.70%	171.266
	8	25–29	91.50%	186	7.62%	146.550
	9	20–24	95.20%	94	3.85%	131.566
	10	15–19	96.55%	38	1.56%	99.647
	11	10–14	98.30%	17	0.70%	81.617
	12	5–9	99%	14	0.57%	103.000

This result suggests that the majority of the members (representing around 84 percent categorized into Layer 5 and above) are still likely to live under the poverty line upon the international standard. Also, we should note that the core members of the KSPPS concentrate on Layer 4 to 7. It is possible that the marginalized members categorized into Layer 8 and above, who are likely with the probability of more than 90 percent to live under the poverty line, have very limited access even to KSPPS.

5.3 Poverty rate analysis of national standard

The Indonesian government defines the poor as people who earn their income below Rp 374,500 or US$ 27.5 per month upon the latest exchange rate. According to Indonesian Statistic Bureau, nearly 30 million people are starving and living below the national poverty threshold. Table 8.4 shows KSPPS-BMI members' PPI Score and PPP upon the national standard. There are only 11 persons or 0.5 percent of the population (Layer 12) who have more than 50 percent probability to live under the poverty line upon the national standard.

It is worth noting here that the income per day of respondents in Layer 12 is higher than respondents in Layer 10 and 11. Table 8.5 shows the comparison of statistical description for each parameter. Looking at the difference in the score of X9 (ownership status of a motorcycle/or motor boat) between Layer 10 and 12, this anomaly might be explained by the hypothesis that the respondents in Layer 12 have to pay more expenses on public transportation despite earning higher income. However, explanation of the anomaly between Layer 12 and 11 entails further investigation.

5.4 Poverty rate analysis of KSPPS standard

Table 8.6 shows KSPPS-BMI members' PPI Score and PPP upon the KSPPS standard. An income of more than Rp 30,000 or US$ 2.20 per day should be

Table 8.4 KSPPS-BMI members' PPI score and PPP upon the national standard

	LAYER	PPI score	PPI table index	Number of respondents	Portion of total respondents	Average income/ day
100% national	1	60–64	0.1%	15	0.6%	547,533
	2	55–59	0.2%	30	1.2%	208,187
	3	50–54	0.6%	57	2.3%	254,825
	4	44–49	1.4%	288	11.8%	202,033
	5	40–44	3.2%	872	35.7%	203,360
	6	35–39	5.80%	522	21.4%	182,355
	7	30–34	10.3%	310	12.7%	161,525
	8	25–29	17.3%	186	7.6%	188,543
	9	20–24	25.2%	94	3.9%	131,567
	10	15–19	34.1%	38	1.6%	99,647
	11	10–14	48.4%	14	0.6%	81,618
	12	5–9	60%	11	0.5%	103,000

Table 8.5 Comparison of statistical description for each parameter

Statistical descriptive	X1	X2	X3	X4	X5	X6	X7	X8	X9	X10	
Minimum	1.00	0.00	0.00	0.00	0.00	0.00	0.00	0.00	0.00	0.00	LAYER 10
Maximum	6.00	2.00	4.00	5.00	4.00	5.00	6.00	8.00	9.00	3.00	
Median	4.00	0.00	3.00	5.00	0.00	5.00	0.00	0.00	0.00	1.00	
Std. deviation	1.46	0.92	1.44	2.52	1.73	2.44	0.97	1.81	4.02	0.91	
Average	*3.92*	*0.58*	*2.08*	*2.76*	*1.21*	*3.16*	*0.16*	*0.42*	*2.37*	*1.24*	
Minimum	1.00	0.00	0.00	0.00	0.00	0.00	0.00	0.00	0.00	0.00	LAYER 11
Maximum	6.00	0.00	3.00	5.00	0.00	5.00	0.00	0.00	0.00	1.00	
Median	2.50	0.00	0.00	2.50	0.00	0.00	0.00	0.00	0.00	0.50	
Std. deviation	1.58	0.00	0.95	2.64	0.00	2.42	0.00	0.00	0.00	0.53	
Average	*2.60*	*0.00*	*0.30*	*2.50*	*0.00*	*1.50*	*0.00*	*0.00*	*0.00*	*0.50*	
Minimum	1.00	0.00	0.00	0.00	0.00	0.00	0.00	0.00	0.00	0.00	LAYER 12
Maximum	6.00	0.00	3.00	5.00	0.00	5.00	0.00	0.00	0.00	1.00	
Median	2.50	0.00	0.00	2.50	0.00	0.00	0.00	0.00	0.00	0.50	
Std. deviation	1.58	0.00	0.95	2.64	0.00	2.42	0.00	0.00	0.00	0.53	
Average	*2.60*	*0.00*	*0.30*	*2.50*	*0.00*	*1.50*	*0.00*	*0.00*	*0.00*	*0.50*	

earned by its members. We find that KSPPS-BMI is still far away from achieving the target. As depicted in the table, there are only 520 respondents or 21.31 per-cent among the population who have below a 50 percent probability of living under the poverty line.

5.5 *Artificial neural networks*

As mentioned earlier, the utilization of artificial neural networks is addressed to classify the variables that give the most significant impact on determining the

Table 8.6 KSPPS-BMI members' PPI score and PPP upon the KSPPS standard

	LAYER	**PPI score**	**PPI table index**	**Number of respondents**	**Portion of total respondents**	**Average income/day**
	1	**70–74**	6.9%	12	0.49%	614,999
	2	**65–69**	9.10%	21	0.86%	231,742
	3	**60–64**	17.60%	22	0.90%	176,986
US$ 2.5 extrapolated	4	**55–59**	26.90%	89	3.65%	246,602
	5	**50–54**	40.10%	376	15.41%	197,815
	6	**44–49**	54.70%	742	30.41%	204,889
	7	**40–44**	68.4%	522	21.39%	182,355
	8	**35–39**	79.70%	257	10.53%	166,055
	9	**30–34**	87.70%	204	8.36%	188,305
	10	**25–29**	91.50%	97	3.98%	130,535
	11	**20–24**	95.20%	57	2.34%	114,722
	12	**15–19**	96.50%	19	0.78%	76,342
	13	**10–14**	98.3%	13	0.53%	80,348
	14	**5–9**	99%	8	0.33%	116,250

probability of KSPPS-BMI's members of living below the poverty line. In this regard, the data has been partitioned into three sets using random method as follows: the training set (a set of data that is used for training the networks) amounted to 68 percent of data, the validation set (a set of data that is used to validate the training process) amounted to 16 percent of data, and the test set (a set of data that is used to test the learning process of networks) amounted to 16 percent of data. In this preparation step, we set up 10 variables (X1, X2, X3, X4, X5, X6, X7, X8, X9, X10) as numeric and the others as categorical (Name, Villages, and Branches).

Further, we performed the preprocessing step to transform both the numerical and categorical variables into scaled-encoded numeric columns. This step also helps to encode the date and time variables to transfer source data into a convenient form for artificial neural networks analysis. As a result, we encoded 255 columns with scaling range of [-1,1]. Subsequently, we design the networks to perform further learning and adaptation processes. In this step, some parameters are set up as follow: (I) The input activation function is a linear function. (II) The output name is Score PPI. (III) The output error function is a sum-of-squares function. (IV) The output activation function is linear. The result of this step is a design of artificial neural networks architecture that consists of 342 neurons in the input layer, 2 neurons in the hidden layer, and 1 neuron in the output layer. The specific network to do PPI score classification is selected according to the proper fitness parameters of networks architecture as follows: (I) fitness value (0.860982), (II) train error value (0.044511), (III) validation error value (0.043639), (IV) correlation value (92.80 percent), and (V) R-squared value (86.09 percent).

The next step is training the networks. In this step, we trained the artificial neural networks to adapt and learn the behavior changes of data distribution. In this regard, we set up some training parameters as follows: (I) The training algorithm used is quick propagation in which parameters are set using 1.75 of quick propagation coefficient and 0.1 of learning rate. (II) The training process is stopped under certain conditions which are: Network MSE is 0.0000001 or 20.000 iterations, whichever comes first, and data set error is 0.0000001 or 20.000 iterations, whichever comes first.

Accordingly, the networks are trained; the process is depicted in Figure 8.2. The network error and R-squared figure describe the speed of networks in improving its forecasting ability. The ability actually shows us how good the networks are in adapting and learning the behavior changes of data distribution which brings the consequence that the networks will be able to make forecasts accurately. The networks successfully achieve the smallest network error at 12.000 iterations, meanwhile the best R-squared value is achieved before 2.000 iterations which depicts the goodness of fit in performing classification assignment. The training process is stopped when the value of R-squared almost reaches the threshold (1). It means that the variance of input variables will be correctly reproduced over learning processes.

The training process is crucial since it produces the input importance rate that indicates which variables give the strongest influence on the networks, as follows:

1 Ownership status of motorcycle or motor boat (X9) with the importance rate of 31.08 percent.
2 Ownership status of freezer (X8) with that of 25.80 percent.
3 Level of education of family head (X3) with that of 10.53 percent.
4 Number of household members (X1) with that of 8.89 percent.
5 Material of the floor (X4) with that of 8.20 percent.
6 Toilet arrangement (X5) with that of 7.02 percent.
7 Main cooking fuel (X6) with that of 2.54 percent.
8 The main employment of family head (X10) with that of 2.29 percent.
9 Ownership status of gas cylinder 12 Kg (X7) with that of 0.72 percent.
10 All members age 6–18 go to school (X2) with that of 0.19 percent.

As the final step, the networks testing process is to validate the classification process which results in the significant variables which determine the PPI Score. As shown in Figure 8.3, the result is convincing enough to say that artificial neural networks have performed very well in learning and adapting the changes of 2,440 data collected from the respondents according to correlation value (94.88 percent), R-squared value (88.99 percent), and mean absolute error (0.038009).

6. Conclusion

This chapter aimed to shed an analytical light on the current impact of Islamic microfinance – with the case of an Islamic Saving–Loan and Financing Cooperative

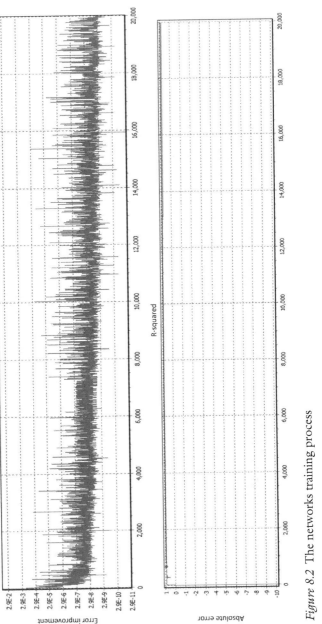

Figure 8.2 The networks training process

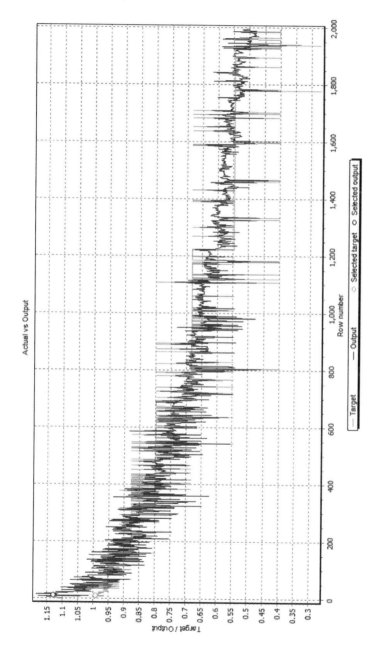

Figure 8.3 The validation evidence of artificial neural networks performance

in Indonesia – over poverty alleviation. We calculated the PPI Score representing their life condition from the respondents of the members of KSPPS Benteng Mikro Indonesia to estimate how many of their clients are likely to live under the poverty line upon the international standard, the national standard in Indonesia, and the KSPPS target, respectively. First of all, we should say that the national standard is a bit indulgent. In other words, it is applauded that KSPPS-BMI has set its target line which is closer to the international standard. Simultaneously, we find that even upon the KSPPS standard, around 78 percent of the respondents are likely to live under the poverty line (around 84 percent upon the international standard). We should be worried that the outreach of Islamic Saving–Loan and Financing Cooperatives to marginalized clients is perhaps very limited in Indonesia, though further examination on other KSPPS is required to make our hypothesis more conclusive.

This chapter also aimed to make a methodological contribution to the existing scientific method of impact assessment of microfinance by introducing the concept of 'artificial neural networks'. The training process in the ANN method is to produce the input importance rate that indicates which variables give the strongest influence on the networks. In this case of the respondents of KSPPS-BMI, we find that the variables of 'ownership status of motorcycle or motor boat' and 'ownership status of freezer' contribute on the networks much more greatly than the variables of 'number of household members' and 'level of education of family head' which are considered critical factors in the conventional methods like the PPI scorecard.

We may point out that the ANN method identifies a certain bias in the PPI scorecard utilization in KSPPS, though these preliminary findings entail further clarification. The 'all or nothing' scale for the variables of 'ownership status of motorcycle or motor boat' and 'ownership status of freezer' in the PPI scorecard should be reviewed. On the other hand, taking into consideration that the median values of these variables have reached the assigned maximum values (see Table 8.2), we could say that further improvement of these ownership statuses may contribute less to the PPI Score. In the parent population of this survey, we may hypothesize that the answers to the variables of 'number of household members' and 'level of education of family head', which are considered critical factors in the conventional method, might be narrowly distributed. If this hypothesis cannot be rejected, the lower importance rate indicated by the ANN method may suggest a higher potential for alleviating the poverty rate further. The interpretation of the result upon the ANN method entails further testing. To facilitate the discussion on how well or poorly Islamic finance could contribute to poverty alleviation, the method of impact assessment should be critically assessed for its improvement.

Note

1 We refer to the Rupiah/US$ exchange rate on November 2, 2017.

Part III
Dilemmas and challenges in governance structure

9 Anatomy of governance structure in the mode of Islamic finance

An emphasis on the governance over *Shari'ah* boards

Yasushi Suzuki, Sigit Pramono and Oni Sahroni

1. Introduction

There is little doubt that the role of the board members and advisors in the *Shari'ah* Supervisory Board (SSB) or the *Shari'ah* Committee, called in general '*Shari'ah* board' (SB), is inevitable in Islamic finance. Islamic Financial Institutions (IFIs) are usually governed by two boards; Board of Directors (BoD) and SB. The BoD has the same roles and characteristics of any traditional board, but the SB has a unique role of ensuring that all the IFIs are *Shari'ah* compliant (Garas and Pierce, 2010; Ginena and Hamid, 2015; Hassan, 2012). All the business and financial contracts in the framework of Islamic finance have to conform to the *Shari'ah* rules with the objective of helping to achieve *Maqasid* (objectives) *al-Shari'ah*. *Shari'ah* refers to a code of law or divine injunctions that regulate the conduct of human beings in their individual and collective lives (Ayub, 2007). The idea is having an SB to provide a third-party assurance – a proper 'check and balance' – that *Shari'ah* compliance is not being compromised. Besides, an SB is expected to provide the *Shari'ah* endorsement of the products dealt by IFIs (Bakar, 2016).

What are the expected duties and responsibilities undertaken by the SB members? For instance, the *Shari'ah Governance Framework for the Islamic Financial Institutions 2010* (BNM, 2010) introduced by Central Bank of Malaysia (Bank Negara Malaysia) provides a comprehensive guidance to the *Shari'ah* Committee members in discharging their duties and responsibilities for matters relating to *Shari'ah*. Their main duties and responsibilities are as follows: (a) to be responsible and accountable for all *Shari'ah* decisions, opinions and views provided by them. (b) To advise the board and provide input to the IFI on *Shari'ah* matters in order for the IFI to comply with *Shari'ah* principles at all times. (c) To endorse *Shari'ah* policies and procedures prepared by the IFI and to ensure that the contents do not contain any elements which are not in line with *Shari'ah*. (d) To endorse and validate relevant documentations including the terms and conditions contained in the forms, contracts, agreements or other legal documentations used in executing the transactions; and the product manual, marketing advertisements, sales illustrations and brochures used to describe the product comply with *Shari'ah* principles. (e) To assess whether the works carried out by *Shari'ah* review and *Shari'ah* audit are in order and compliance with *Shari'ah* matters which form part of their duties in providing their assessment of *Shari'ah* compliance and assurance information in the annual report. (f) To assist related parties of the IFI such as its legal counsel, auditor or consultant who seeks advice on *Shari'ah* matters from the *Shari'ah* Committee. (g) To advise on *Shari'ah* matters to be referred to the *Shari'ah* Advisory Council (SAC, Malaysian two-tier *Shari'ah* governance structure is discussed later) that could not be resolved. (h) To provide written *Shari'ah* opinions in circumstances where the IFI make reference to the SAC for further deliberation, or where the IFI submits applications to the Central Bank of Malaysia (Bank Negara Malaysia) for new product approval. Lewis and Algaoud (2001) opine that the SB has a vital role in the Islamic bank's corporate governance structure for two reasons. First, to ensure that the bank's operations are in accordance with *Shari'ah* principles and to maintain this compliance at all levels of the bank's organization. Second, the adherence to Islamic principles in conducting their business will become a response to the potential incentive problem and the agency theory issues in Islamic banks.

Nevertheless, it is worth noting that the position and role of SB has been changed in accordance with the development of Islamic banking and finance. As Nienhaus (2007) points out, at the primitive stage in development, SB was perceived, in general, as strictly conservative. However, as recent technological changes and intensifying uncertainty make the management of Islamic banking more complex, the practices by SB are increasingly being criticized as very permissive. Under this circumstance, it is becoming more important to review and well-design the SSB's duties and responsibilities for ensuring *Shari'ah* compliance in IFIs' business operations, while avoiding a 'merely procedural' adherence to Islamic principles.

To ensure that all these duties and responsibilities are carried out accordingly, many scholars have admitted that SB must be independent (Nienhaus, 2007; Syafei, 2010; Garas and Pierce, 2010; Othman *et al.*, 2013). According to Governance Standard for Islamic Financial Institutions No. 5, independence is defined as "an attitude of mind which does not allow the viewpoint and conclusions of its possessor to become reliant on or subordinate to the influences and pressures of conflicting interests. It is achieved through organizational status and objectivity" (AAOIFI, 2002, p. 44). Mautz and Sharaf (1961) refer to a categorization of independency as a "supervisory and audit function", pointing out that the SB's independence should include practitioners' independence in terms of performing their duties and responsibilities based on proper competence and capability. In addition, they point out that SB should have professional independence in order to make their decision-making unbiased and objective. Simultaneously we should be aware of the necessity of preparing a number of mechanisms in *Shari'ah* governance, including its members' appointment, composition, function and remuneration, to maintain SB's independence in the mentioned multiple contexts. On the other hand, there exist potential conflicts of interest as well as "a huge paradox" (Bakar, 2016) between *Shari'ah* scholars and the other stakeholders under the situation that the SB is appointed and remunerated by the financial institutions. This chapter aims to shed an analytical light on this paradox and to draw a prescription for it.

Section 2 aims to overview the multiple principal–agent structure in the mode of Islamic finance. Section 3 argues the current practices in nominating and decision-making process of the SB in Malaysia and Indonesia. Section 4 looks at an inside story of an SB member. Section 5 aims to draw a prescription upon the essence of the UK Corporate Governance Code. Section 6 presents the conclusion.

2. Anatomy of governance structure in the mode of Islamic finance

In the theory of microeconomics, the principal (P)–agent (A) problem of causing various types of 'market failure' such as moral hazard, adverse selection and credit crunch, may arise in the structure where (i) P cannot perfectly monitor A's activities, and/or (ii) P tends to think that the information held by P is too coarse for P's decision-making compared to that held by A (this is called as the asymmetry of information between the economic players).

To begin with, let us overview the multiple principal (P)–agent (A) structure in the mode of Islamic finance (see Figure 9.1); [1] Depositors (P)–Islamic banks (A): In the profit–loss sharing (PLS) mode of Islamic finance, the depositors are expected to share the risk and uncertainty which the Islamic banks are undertaking and sharing with their borrowers. Under the P–A structure where the depositors face the difficulty of screening and monitoring the skill of credit risk management in each Islamic bank, the depositors would have hesitated to place their funds as deposits to any bank. In practice, however, the depositors are not often asked to share the loss that the Islamic banks made. The banks would rather not lose their reputation which would be lost by sharing the loss with their depositors. The so-called displacement commercial risk by the depositors to withdraw their deposit from the banks that lost the reputation and confidence would discourage the banks to share any loss even if they made it. In this customary

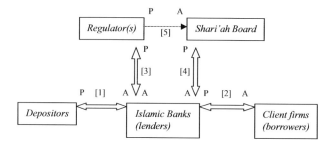

Figure 9.1 Multiple principal–agent structure in the mode of Islamic finance

practice, it appears that many depositors are not ready to share the loss. In this context, the typical problems from the P–A structure between depositors and banks would not often occur. Most depositors do not have strong incentives to monitor the banks on their own. Basically, it is considered in this mode that the depositors delegate the role of monitoring Islamic banks to the regulator and the *Shari'ah* board. On the other hand, the customary practice mentioned earlier in this chapter may have given a certain bias on the credit policy undertaken by the Islamic banks.

[2] Islamic Banks (P)–Client firms (A): In the PLS mode of Islamic finance, the Islamic banks as lenders are expected to share the profit and loss with the client firms as borrowers. Under the P–A structure without any condition of mitigating the information asymmetry or supporting the lender's limited capacity of monitoring, the banks would hesitate to invest in the borrowers, which may cause the 'credit crunch' situation. As was argued earlier, Islamic banks are, in practice, discouraged to share losses with their depositors. The 'displacement commercial risk' makes the banks' policy of portfolio selection 'risk-averse'. The so-called *murabaha* syndrome is due partly to this structure. Besides, the PLS structure may give the borrowers an ill-incentive of causing 'moral hazard'. For instance, in the current mode of Islamic banking, the banks are not allowed to charge any penalty as a threat on the borrowers for avoiding the occurrence of their delayed payment, because that situation calls for the loss sharing in accordance with a core principle of Islamic banking. This limited 'sanction' mechanism in contracting for protecting the lender's right may have given the banks and the borrowers an ill-incentive of causing 'credit crunch' and 'moral hazard'. Therefore, the regulator is expected to design an appropriate institutional framework for reasonably protecting the lender's right in contracting.

[3] Regulator (P)–Islamic Banks (A): Basically, the regulator tends to think that the regulator cannot perfectly monitor the regulated banks' activities. Therefore, it is intrinsically difficult for the regulator to find such an appropriate regulation that is not too severe as well as not too relaxed so as to avoid giving any ill-incentive to the regulated banks. If the regulation on banks is too severe, it would discourage the banks to mediate financial resources to the borrowers. If the regulation on banks is too gentle, for instance, the regulator's commitment to bail any bank out of any dismal portfolio, it would give a moral hazard effect on the banks to challenge high risk–high return-type investments even upon non-prominent monitoring skills, perhaps accumulating non-performing loans (NPL), consequently triggering the contagious runs by the bankruptcy of the troubled bank as a result of the accumulation of NPL. This is a systemic risk embedded in the banking industry.

[4] *Shari'ah* Board (P)–Islamic Banks (A): In the mode of Islamic finance, how the regulated banks comply the *Shari'ah* rules should be monitored. The regulator's limited capacity for supervising the regulated Islamic banks, particularly in the dimension of *Shari'ah* compliance, may urge the regulator to expect the role of SB. The idea of having an SB is to provide a third-party assurance – a proper 'check and balance' – that *Shari'ah* compliance is not being compromised.

Besides, an SB is expected to provide the *Shari'ah* endorsement of the products dealt by Islamic financial institutions (Bakar, 2016). However, in theory, the SB members tend to think that they cannot perfectly monitor the Islamic banks' activities. Besides, there exist potential conflicts of interest as well as 'a huge paradox' between *Shari'ah* scholars and the other stakeholders under the situation that the SB is appointed and remunerated by the financial institutions (Bakar, 2016). This leads us to ask, how can a proper check and balance be institutionally ensured?

[5] Regulator (P)–*Shari'ah* Board (A): According to Bakar (2016), there are two approaches in regulating SBs by regulators. In some jurisdictions like Malaysia, Sudan, Bahrain and Oman, the respective regulator will take the lead in providing the framework governing the SBs, either at the central bank or at the individual banks. These regulators would apply the same standard of robustness and due diligence on SB members as applied to other organs of the Islamic financial institution, such as the Board of Directors, appointment of the CEOs, the appointment of external auditors etc. Other regulators, on the other hand, would expect the individual Islamic financial institution to have their own internal standards and governance in dealing with their SB. (Bakar, 2016, p. 43). In the case of Malaysia, the National *Shari'ah* Advisory Council at the Central Bank (as well as the Securities Commission Malaysia) also needs to engage with the respective court of law quite actively, particularly when the courts refer Islamic finance to the Council to get its *Shari'ah* views. In essence, the *Shari'ah* Advisory Council will go through all the affidavits and submissions by both parties, namely the plaintiff and defendant, to identify the *Shari'ah* issue (if any) that needs a *Shari'ah* view (Bakar, 2016, p. 44).

As pointed out by a *Shari'ah* scholar, Dr Mohd Daud Bakar, at this point in time, in general, the *Shari'ah* advisors are not governed by any specific regulation. Therefore, "checks and balances, which is integral to any governance requirement may be lacking" (Bakar, 2016, p. 69). Though there is a standard by AAOIFI on the administrative procedures for the appointment of *Shari'ah* scholars and its related matters, "it is void of any governance language to provide a kind of checks and balances for the *Shari'ah* scholars" (*ibid.*, p. 69).

3. Current practices in nominating and decision-making process in the *Shari'ah* board

This section aims to describe the current practices in nominating and decision-making process in the *Shari'ah* board in Malaysia and Indonesia, respectively. The characteristics in each mode are summarized in Table 9.1.

3.1 Malaysia

As is mentioned earlier, Central Bank of Malaysia (CBM) has introduced a two-tier *Shari'ah* governance infrastructure comprising two vital components, (i) the *Shari'ah* Advisory Council (SAC) which is a centralized *Shari'ah* advisory

Table 9.1 Comparison of the governance mode over the *Shari'ah* board between Malaysia and Indonesia

	Malaysia	*Indonesia*
Governance structure	Two-tier *Shari'ah* governance: *Shari'ah* Advisory Council at Central Bank and *Shari'ah* Committee in each IFIs.	Two-tier *Shari'ah* governance: National *Shari'ah* Advisory Council (Dewan Syariah Nasional, 'DSN') at the Indonesian Ulama Council (*Majelis Ulama Indonesia/ MUI*) and *Shari'ah* Supervisory Board (Dewan Pengawas Syariah, 'DPS') in each IFIs.
Nominating process	Appointed by the BoD upon the recommendation of its Nomination Committee, subject to prior written approval of the Central Bank. The appointment shall be valid for a renewable term of two years.	Appointed by the DSN upon the recommendation and nomination from BoD of each IFIs. The appointment shall be valid for a renewable term of four years.
Number of SB members	Five in most of the IFIs.	At least three members in each IFI.
Decision-making process	Voting by majority. Opinions of the minority are to be written in *fatwa*.	Consensus among the SSB members and voting for the last alternate decision-making procedure.

body at CBM and (ii) the *Shari'ah* Committee which is an internal *Shari'ah* body formed in each respective IFI. This is important in ensuring that the overall Islamic financial system in Malaysia operates in accordance with the *Shari'ah* principles (Othman *et al.*, 2013). In 2010, CBM developed, introduced and issued the *Shari'ah* Governance Framework for the Islamic Financial Institutions with the primary objective of enhancing the role of the Board of Directors (BoD), the *Shari'ah* Committee and the management in relation to *Shari'ah* matters, including enhancing the relevant key organs having the responsibility to execute the *Shari'ah* compliance and research functions aimed at the attainment of a *Shari'ah*-based operating environment.

BNM (2010) has mentioned clearly that the *Shari'ah* Committee members shall be appointed by the BoD upon the recommendation of its Nomination Committee. The appointment and reappointment of a *Shari'ah* Committee member shall obtain prior written approval of Bank Negara Malaysia. The appointment shall be valid for a renewable term of two years. In approving the appointment and reappointment, Bank Negara Malaysia may impose necessary conditions it deems fit in addition to the requirements in these guidelines. The failure to comply with any of such conditions shall nullify the approval.

The members of the *Shari'ah* Committee shall be persons of acceptable reputation, character and integrity. Bank Negara Malaysia reserves the right to disqualify any member who fails to meet the requirements. In particular, any member may be disqualified due to any of the following breach of corporate governance: (i) he has acted in a manner which may cast doubt on his fitness to hold the position of a *Shari'ah* Committee member; (ii) he has failed to attend 75 percent of meetings scheduled for *Shari'ah* Committee in a year without reasonable excuse; (iii) he has been declared a bankrupt, or a petition under bankruptcy laws is filed against him; (iv) he was found guilty for any serious criminal offence, or any other offence punishable with imprisonment of one year or more; or (v) he is subject to any order of detention, supervision, restricted residence or banishment. Whereupon the discovery of any fact that any member of a *Shari'ah* Committee becomes subject to any ground of disqualification or otherwise becomes unfit to hold such appointment as provided in these guidelines and/or in the letter of approval from Bank Negara Malaysia, the Islamic financial institution shall terminate the appointment of the *Shari'ah* member.

The number of *Shari'ah* Committee members to be appointed must not be less than three. Othman *et al.* (2013), through their research by distributing and collecting the questionnaire to the respondents who are involved in IFI industries, report that most of the institutions have five members of *Shari'ah* Committee. Additionally, 75.3 percent of the respondents mention that they have five members, 16.0 percent of the respondents have more than five members while only 8.6 percent of respondents have fewer than five members. This is a very good indication as about 92.4 percent of the institutions have achieved the required numbers of the *Shari'ah* Committee members.

It is also the requirement of BNM (2010) that the majority of *Shari'ah* Committee members must possess strong knowledge in *Shari'ah* and be backed by the appropriate qualifications in that area. In this regard, every IFI is required to establish a *Shari'ah* Committee of which the majority shall comprise persons with appropriate qualifications and experience in *Shari'ah*. The competency and credibility of the *Shari'ah* Committee members provide the assurance that the IFI's operations are being monitored by a credible and competent committee. A member of a *Shari'ah* Committee shall be an individual. A company, institution or body shall not constitute a *Shari'ah* Committee for the purpose of these guidelines. The proposed member of the *Shari'ah* Committee shall at least either have qualification or possess necessary knowledge, expertise or experience in the following areas: (i) Islamic jurisprudence (*Usul al-Fiqh*); or (ii) Islamic transaction/commercial law (*Fiqh al-Mu'amalat*). It should however be noted that paper qualification on these subjects will not be mandatory as long as the candidate has the necessary expertise or experience in the areas specified in the qualifications list.

According to the survey by Othman *et al.* (2013), among the IFIs that have five *Shari'ah* Committee members (N=59), 44.1 percent (26 IFIs) assign five

Shari'ah Committee members who possess *Shari'ah* qualification, 40.7 percent (24 IFIs) do four, 15.2 percent (9 IFIs) do three. The requirement that each of the IFI must have a majority of *Shari'ah* Committee possess *Shari'ah* qualification was fulfilled. From another point of view, we may say that almost half of IFIs does not diversify the composition of SB to non-*Shari'ah* professionals.

3.1 Indonesia

In 1999, for the purpose of setting up the *Shari'ah* governance arrangement, the Indonesian Ulama Council (*Majelis Ulama Indonesia*, 'MUI') established the National *Shari'ah* Board (*Dewan Syariah Nasional*, 'DSN') in accordance with the Decree No. 754/MUI/II/1999. MUI is an organization of Islamic scholars (*Ulama*) in Indonesia which has its mission in empowerment, education and Islamic preaching programs for Muslim people. MUI was founded on 26 July 1975 in Jakarta upon the agreement in a convention that was attended by a large number of Islamic scholars and Muslim leaders who came from the majority of provinces over the nation. This event was known as 'the National Congress of Ulama I' and it released 'MUI establishment charter'. Specifically, MUI became an advisory body that takes a guiding role by giving religious decrees (*fatwa*) dealing with all the *Shari'ah* issues related from the individual life to the nation's matter. In this sense, MUI is perceived as a quasi-autonomous non-governmental organization in which it has been transformed to be a channel of aspiration for Muslim groups to influence government policies and benefitted from a special connection with the state (Lindsey, 2012; Choiruzzad and Nugroho, 2013).

The main responsibility of the National *Shari'ah* Board is to prepare *Shari'ah* regulatory support to the Islamic banking and finance industries (DSN-MUI and BI, 2006). Thus, the National *Shari'ah* Board has an important role in creating public trust and awareness of the *Shari'ah* compliance matters of the Islamic banking industry. It is worth noting that the National *Shari'ah* Board is an independent body from Bank Indonesia (Central Bank) or Financial Service Authority (FSA) interventions. This mechanism is different from the *Shari'ah* regulatory arrangement practiced in a number of other countries in support of Islamic banking. For instance, in Malaysia, the National *Shari'ah* Advisory Council (NSAC) as *Shari'ah* standards and regulatory body is placed under the control of Bank Negara Malaysia (BNM, the central bank) so that the NSAC seemingly is not an independent body from which the BNM's policy intervenes.

Similar to the *Shari'ah* governance structure in Malaysia, Indonesia has implemented a two-tier *Shari'ah* governance infrastructure through (i) the National *Shari'ah* Board as the *Shari'ah* opinion/*fatwa*-issuing body and comprehensively supervisory body for *Shari'ah* adherence in all IFIs, and (ii) *Shari'ah* Supervisory Board (SSB) as a *Shari'ah* compliance supervisory body which internally functions in each respective IFI.

In accordance with the Decree No. 3 Year 2000 of DSN (DSN-MUI and BI, 2006), each IFI in Indonesia should assign at least three members of their SSB. SSB members have to be approved by the DSN upon the recommendation and nomination from the BoD of each IFI. The remuneration of SSB is paid by each IFI. Some scholars and practitioners cast doubt on this mechanism which may cause conflicts of interest. Syafei (2010) reports that many Islamic bank managers consider that an alternative remuneration mechanism, for instance, fully remunerated by the regulator (e.g. Bank Indonesia, the central bank) would avoid the potential conflict of interest to improve the independence of the SSB.

The appointment for SSB members shall be valid for a renewable term of four years. Related to the concurrent position as member of SSB, this decree has arranged that every member of SSB in IFIs is only allowed to hold the maximum position in two Islamic banks and two non-bank Islamic financial institutions simultaneously. In the SSB's decision-making process, it is worth noting that seeking consensus among the SSB members is outweighed and voting is the last alternate in practice.

4. An inside story of a *Shari'ah* scholar

If the *Shari'ah* advisors are not governed by any specific regulation, as pointed by Bakar (2016), the performance would depend on the morale of the board members. Now, let us look at an inside story of a *Shari'ah* scholar. Dr Mohd Daud Bakar published a book in 2016, titled *Shariah Minds in Islamic Finance*. Having reflected on the author's 20 years of experience as a member as well as the chairman of many *Shari'ah* boards around the globe, this book offers an insightful work to shed light on the inner workings of '*Shari'ah* minds' in dealing with *Shari'ah* advisory, and how *Shari'ah* scholars respond to innovation as well as bottlenecks in a contemporary regulatory framework (Bakar, 2016).

In this book, the author begins with the explanation of what is the minimum quality and quantity of the knowledge that would make a person a *Shari'ah* scholar in Islamic finance (Bakar, 2016, Chapter 1). While admitting certain contributions in various ways by non-*Shari'ah* qualified or trained members of the SB, the author insists that only qualified and trained *Shari'ah* scholars or the majority of the *Shari'ah* minds are eligible to undertake the great responsibility of issuing any *fatwa*. The author raises three rules to be a *Shari'ah* scholar: First, to acknowledge that he/she is working in an environment that is not perfect and still requiring *Shari'ah* solutions. Second, to be cognisant that *Shari'ah* scholars do not work in isolation. Lastly, the most important aspect is to possess 'humility'. Good intellectual knowledge of both the *Shari'ah* and modern finance, as well as a good personality, are emphasized here. Then, he describes the roles of *Shari'ah* scholars in the industry of Islamic finance. The main function of the scholars is to provide assurance on *Shari'ah* compliance. The author describes the real working process of *Shari'ah* boards to draw the description of *Shari'ah* compliance as an apparatus of 'prevention' (Chapter 2). The author insists that the idea of having a *Shari'ah* board is to provide a third-party assurance – a proper 'check and balance' – that *Shari'ah* compliance is not being compromised. Besides, a *Shari'ah* board is expected to provide the *Shari'ah* endorsement of the products dealt by Islamic financial institutions (Chapter 4). He explains the

Shari'ah minds which need to deal with both *Shari'ah* rulings (which are Divine) and *fiqh* rulings (which are human in character). The author refers to the process of *ijtihad*, using one's best endeavours to arrive at the intended rulings of Allah the Almighty (Chapter 7). He also mentions the *Shari'ah* scholars' contributions to the Islamic finance industry. These contributions include: to install general 'confidence' by all the stakeholders in the industry, to establish a more robust *Shari'ah* compliance due diligence process, to brand Islamic finance by undertaking the role as 'global ambassadors' (Chapter 10).

Meanwhile, as mentioned earlier, the author describes potential conflicts of interest as well as 'a huge paradox' between *Shari'ah* scholars and the other stakeholders under the situation that the *Shari'ah* board is appointed and remunerated by the financial institutions (Chapter 8). He also refers to the concept of *Shari'ah* governance for *Shari'ah* scholars themselves (Chapter 3). He answers the question on how a *Shari'ah* scholar understands and scrutinizes financial products. *Shari'ah* advisory is, in his view, a daily learning process but all the experiences are stored in their brain for future use, consequently contributing to reach a *Shari'ah* solution for the development of the industry of Islamic finance (Chapter 5). The author raises a counter argument against the view of labelling the *Shari'ah* scholars as the '*Shari'ah*-compliant' proponents of mimicking conventional products. The author insists that the *Shari'ah* scholars would welcome and praise the move towards developing totally new structures and behaviours of Islamic financial products as '*Shari'ah* based' (Chapter 6).

Unlike conventional banks, Islamic banks have to absorb not only the credit risk but also the risk associated with the compliance of *Shari'ah*. In theory, the profit (the margin for security) earned by Islamic banks has to cover the necessary time and effort, what the economists call 'transaction cost', for seeking the compliance to maintain their reputation as prudent *Shari'ah* compliant lenders. In economics textbooks 'transaction cost' is defined as the economic equivalent of 'friction' in physical systems. His insight tells us how *Shari'ah* scholars, with the proper *Shari'ah* minds upon solid resolution and realism, play the important role as 'lubricant' for running the 'nervous system' in Islamic finance. However, it appears that the mechanism for monitoring the quality of lubricant is lacking in the industry. *Shari'ah* scholars, the regulatory authority and other professionals need to design an appropriate financial architecture which can create socially acceptable levels of margin opportunities for Islamic banks to avail the benefit from the variety of Islamic financing as declared by *Shari'ah*. '*Shari'ah* minds' must be a key for this design. However, the excess reliance on the morale in the board seems vulnerable.

5. A hint from the UK Corporate Governance Code

As argued earlier, there exist potential conflicts of interest as well as a huge paradox between *Shari'ah* scholars and other stakeholders under the situation that the *Shari'ah* board is appointed and remunerated by the financial institutions. How can the potential conflicts of interest be avoided?

One strategy is to pay the salary of the board members from the government's account to ensure the independence of the board. This strategy seems to be inspired by the practices that occur in various countries as an effort to maintain the independence of auditors of the public accountant firm who perform audits for the financial statements of banking and financial institutions. In this context, the remuneration paid to the *Shari'ah* Committee members will be charged to the government or regulator account (i.e. Central Bank, Financial Services Authority, Ministry of Finance) which may be sourced from the tax fund or membership contribution of each financial institution in the industry. Nevertheless, we should note that this strategy possibly will not resolve the basic dilemma of governance and decision-making process in the Islamic banking industry. As we discussed in Section 1, in the profit–loss sharing (PLS) mode of Islamic finance, the depositors are expected to share the risk and uncertainty which the Islamic banks are undertaking and sharing with their borrowers. Under the P–A structure, the depositors face the difficulty of screening and monitoring the skill of credit risk management in each Islamic bank. In particular, as Archer and Karim (2006) point out, a severe conflict of interest between the shareholders and the Investment Account Holders (IAH) may occur when Islamic banks mobilize the fund of IAH for the *mudaraba* and *musharaka* investment. Under the condition that IAH have no voting right at the Board of Directors (BoD) as well as the shareholders meeting, Islamic bank managers are able to shirk taking reasonable care of the IAH's interest by seeking profit opportunities only for the shareholders. This is a case of moral hazard. To avoid the case, some scholars suggest that a representative for IAH should be prepared in the BoD or the SSB (Nienhaus, 2007; Archer and Karim, 2007).

In the discussion with Prof. Mohammad Hashim Kamali, the founding CEO of International Institute of Advanced Islamic Studies (IAIS Malaysia) in November 2016, he was supportive for the remuneration strategy to be paid by the government. In the so-called Muslim countries such as Malaysia, the strategy would be politically supported and, to some extent justifiable, partly because the majority of the country would be benefited from the sound governance upon the independence of the SB over the Islamic banking industry. However, in our view, there exists a political hurdle to justify the strategy of using the national budget, because the government has to consider the utility of non-Muslim tax payers as well. Of course, as pointed out by Professor Kamali, the sound development of the Islamic banking industry would benefit not only the Muslim customers but also non-Muslim customers. In spite of it, the government has to ensure the 'level playing field' for the fair competition in the industry including the conventional banks within the country. Governmental support only to the Islamic banks would cause another dilemma.

Is there any other strategy to draw a prescription for the sound governance without using the national budget? For contributing to this argument, here we aim to get a hint from the essence of the UK Corporate Governance Code.

The UK Corporate Governance Code ('the Code') is a part of UK Company Law with a set of principles of good corporate governance aimed at companies listed on the London Stock Exchange. It is overseen by the Financial Reporting Council (FRC) and its importance derives from the Listing Rules by the Financial Conduct Authority. The Listing Rules themselves are given statutory authority under the Financial Services and Markets Act 2000 and require that publicly listed companies disclose how they have complied with the code, and explain where they have not applied the code – in what the code refers to as 'comply or explain'.[1] The Code adopts a principles-based approach in the sense that it provides general guidelines of best practice. This contrasts with a rules-based approach which rigidly defines exact provisions that must be adhered to.

The purpose of corporate governance is to facilitate effective, entrepreneurial and prudent management that can deliver the long-term success of the company. FRC (2016) refers to the first version of the Code (its paragraph 2.5) which was produced in 1992 by the Cadbury Committee as the classic definition of the context of the Code:

> Corporate governance is the system by which companies are directed and controlled. Boards of directors are responsible for the governance of their companies. The shareholders' role in governance is to appoint the directors and the auditors and to satisfy themselves that an appropriate governance structure is in place. The responsibilities of the board include setting the company's strategic aims, providing the leadership to put them into effect, supervising the management of the business and reporting to shareholders on their stewardship. The board's actions are subject to laws, regulations and the shareholders in general meeting.

Corporate governance is therefore about what the board of a company does and how it sets the values of the company. It is to be distinguished from the day-to-day operational management of the company by full-time executives. The Code is a guide to a number of key components of effective board practice. It is based on the underlying principles of all good governance: accountability, transparency, probity and focus on the sustainable success of an entity over the longer term. The Code has been enduring, but it is not immutable. Its fitness for purpose in a permanently changing economic and social business environment requires its evaluation at appropriate intervals. The new Code applies to accounting periods beginning on or after 17 June 2016 and applies to all companies with a premium listing of equity shares regardless of whether they are incorporated in the UK or elsewhere (FRC, 2016).

Following the 2014 Code amendments, which focussed on the provision by companies of information about the risks which affect longer-term viability, the FRC will continue to monitor compliance with these changes.

> One of the key roles for the board includes establishing the culture, values and ethics of the company. It is important that the board sets the correct 'tone from the top'. The directors should lead and ensure that good standards of behaviour permeate throughout all levels of the organisation. This

will help prevent misconduct, unethical practices and support the delivery of long-term success.

(Preface 4, FRC, 2016)

For the purpose of improving the governance, FRC emphasizes 'diversity' on the board.

One of the ways in which constructive debate can be encouraged is through having sufficient diversity on the board. This includes, but is not limited to, gender and race. Diverse board composition in these respects is not on its own a guarantee. Diversity is as much about differences of approach and experience, and it is very important in ensuring effective engagement with key stakeholders and in order to deliver the business strategy.

(Preface 3, FRC, 2016)

FRC raises 'Non-Executive Directors Main Principle'. The principle requires that as part of their role as members of a unitary board, non-executive directors should constructively challenge and help develop proposals on strategy.

Non-executive directors should scrutinise the performance of management in meeting agreed goals and objectives and monitor the reporting of performance. They should satisfy themselves on the integrity of financial information and that financial controls and systems of risk management are robust and defensible. They are responsible for determining appropriate levels of remuneration of executive directors and have a prime role in appointing and, where necessary, removing executive directors, and in succession planning.

(Section A.4, FRC, 2016)

FRC requires the board to appoint one of the independent non-executive directors[2] to be the senior independent director to provide a sounding board for the chairman and to serve as an intermediary for the other directors when necessary. The senior independent director should be available to shareholders if they have concerns which contact through the normal channels of chairman, chief executive or other executive directors has failed to resolve or for which such contact is inappropriate (Code Provisions A.4.1, FRC, 2016).

FRC supports for 'The Composition of the Board Main Principle' in which the board and its committees should have the appropriate balance of skills, experience, independence and knowledge of the company to enable them to discharge their respective duties and responsibilities effectively.

The board should include an appropriate combination of executive and non-executive directors (and, in particular, independent non-executive directors) such that no individual or small group of individuals can dominate the board's decision taking. The value of ensuring that committee membership is refreshed and that undue reliance is not placed on particular individuals should be taken into account in deciding chairmanship and membership of committees.

(Section B: Effectiveness B.1, FRC, 2016)

Drawing a hint from the UK Corporate Governance Code, we propose that the role of independent non-executive (non-*Shari'ah* or non-Muslim but professional) members in the SB be strengthened; at least, their job description should be clarified to ensure the independence of the SB. AAOIFI has offered some descriptions of a *Shari'ah* supervisory board:

> a *Shari'ah* supervisory board is an independent body of specialised jurist of *fiqh al-mu'amalah* (Islamic commercial jurisprudence). However, the *Shari'ah* supervisory board may include a member other than those specialised in *fiqh al-mu'amalah*, but who should be an expert in the field of Islamic finance and with knowledge of *fiqh al-mu'amalah*.
>
> (Bakar, 2016)

However, it seems that the expected role of non-*Shari'ah* members in the board is not yet clearly designated from the governance perspectives over the board.

According to Bakar, there are many different practices of admitting non-*Shari'ah* qualified personnel into *Shari'ah* supervisory boards.

> While some non-*Shari'ah* trained members would have voting rights in some practices and jurisdictions, they do not have this voting right in other practices and jurisdictions. In some other jurisdictions where they have voting rights, it is prescribed that majority of the *Shari'ah* supervisory board members must be *Shari'ah*-trained members.
>
> (Bakar, 2016, p. 8)

It seems that Bakar is conservative for the role of non-*Shari'ah* members:

> The *Shari'ah* minds must prevail in any potential conflict of perspectives. In short, only qualified and trained *Shari'ah* scholars or the majority of *Shari'ah* minds are eligible to undertake this great responsibility of issuing any *fatwa*. It would be damaging for a beginner in Islamic commercial law to embark on this assignment.
>
> (Bakar, 2016, p. 8)

His view from the *Shari'ah* scholar's viewpoint is understandable. However, it would be also damaging to put aside the diversity on the SB.

6. Concluding comments

The main objective of the paper is to shed an analytical light on the existence of potential conflicts of interest and 'a huge paradox' between SB and the other stakeholders under the 'client-patronage' independency since the SB is appointed and remunerated by the client financial institutions. In order to tackle various potential problems which may be caused under the multiple principal and agent structure, we should continuously seek a better mechanism for ensuring the proper 'check and balance' role and responsibility of the SB, which will contribute to the sound development of Islamic banking and finance industry. In this sense, a good *Shari'ah* governance must be attributable to the independence of SB. The independency of SB should be designed and monitored in various levels in the process of appointing its members and of determining its composition, scope and remuneration.

To design a perfect governance structure might be impossible. However, we should continuously seek it through a trial-and-error process. The strategy to compensate the remuneration for the SB members from the regulator's or government's account is one option for enhancing the independence of SB. However, as argued in the previous section, governmental support only to the Islamic banks would cause another dilemma. The strategy to assign independent and non-*Shari'ah* (but professional) members into the SB for its diversity would be another option. However, it is not so easy to designate the role and scope of non-*Shari'ah* qualified members in the SB in the light of strengthening the *Shari'ah* compliance. Again, to design a perfect governance structure might be impossible. However, we believe that seeking an appropriate governance structure will constitute the exercising of *ijtihad*.

Notes

1 FRC (2016) explains the comply or explain approach as follows: 1. The 'comply or explain' approach is the trademark of corporate governance in the UK. It has been in operation since the Code's beginnings and is the foundation of its flexibility. It is strongly supported by both companies and shareholders and has been widely admired and imitated internationally. 2. The Code is not a rigid set of rules. It consists of principles (main and supporting) and provisions. The Listing Rules require companies to apply the Main Principles and report to shareholders on how they have done so. The principles are the core of the Code and the way in which they are applied should be the central question for a board as it determines how it is to operate according to the Code. 3. It is recognized that an alternative to following a provision may be justified in particular circumstances if good governance can be achieved by other means. A condition of doing so is that the reasons for it should be explained clearly and carefully to shareholders, who may wish to discuss the position with the company and whose voting intentions may be influenced as a result. In providing an explanation, the company should aim to illustrate how its actual practices are consistent with the principle to which the particular provision relates, contribute to good governance and promote delivery of business objectives. It should set out the background, provide a clear rationale for the action it is taking and describe any mitigating actions taken to address any additional risk and maintain conformity with the relevant principle. Where deviation from a particular provision is intended to be limited in time, the explanation should indicate when the company expects to conform with the provision. 4. In their responses to explanations, shareholders should pay due regard to companies' individual circumstances and bear in mind in particular the size and complexity of the company and the nature of the risks and challenges it faces. While shareholders have every right to challenge companies' explanations if they are unconvincing, they should

not be evaluated in a mechanistic way and departures from the Code should not be automatically treated as breaches. Shareholders should be careful to respond to the statements from companies in a manner that supports the 'comply or explain' process and bearing in mind the purpose of good corporate governance. They should put their views to the company and both parties should be prepared to discuss the position. 5. Smaller listed companies, in particular those new to listing, may judge that some of the provisions are disproportionate or less relevant in their case. Some of the provisions do not apply to companies below the FTSE 350. Such companies may nonetheless consider that it would be appropriate to adopt the approach in the Code and they are encouraged to do so. Externally managed investment companies typically have a different board structure which may affect the relevance of particular provisions; the Association of Investment Companies' Corporate Governance Code and Guide can assist them in meeting their obligations under the Code. 6. Satisfactory engagement between company boards and investors is crucial to the health of the UK's corporate governance regime. Companies and shareholders both have responsibility for ensuring that 'comply or explain' remains an effective alternative to a rules-based system. There are practical and administrative obstacles to improved interactions between boards and shareholders. But certainly there is also scope for an increase in trust which could generate a virtuous upward spiral in attitudes to the Code and in its constructive use.

2 According to NASDAQ Rule 4200 a(15)) "independent director" is defined as a person other than an executive officer or employee of the company or any other individual having a relationship which, in the opinion of the issuer's board of directors, would interfere with the exercise of independent judgment in carrying out the responsibilities of a director. The following persons shall not be considered independent: (A) a director who is, or at any time during the past three years was, employed by the company or by any parent or subsidiary of the company; (B) a director who accepted or who has a family member ('family member' means a person's spouse, parents, children and siblings, whether by blood, marriage or adoption, or anyone residing in such person's home) who accepted any compensation from the company in excess of $60,000 during any period of 12 consecutive months within the three years preceding the determination of independence, other than the following: (i) compensation for board or board committee service; (ii) compensation paid to a family member who is an employee (other than an executive officer) of the company; or (iii) benefits under a tax-qualified retirement plan, or non-discretionary compensation. Provided, however, that in addition to the requirements contained in this paragraph (B), audit committee members are also subject to additional, more stringent requirements under NASDAQ Rule 4350(d). (C) a director who is a family member of an individual who is, or at any time during the past three years was, employed by the company as an executive officer; (D) a director who is, or has a family member who is, a partner in, or a controlling shareholder or an executive officer of, any organization to which the company made, or from which the company received, payments for property or services in the current or any of the past three fiscal years that exceed 5 percent of the recipient's consolidated gross revenues for that year, or $200,000, whichever is more, other than the following: (i) payments arising solely from investments in the company's securities; or (ii) payments under non-discretionary charitable contribution matching programs. (E) a director of the issuer who is, or has a family member who is, employed as an executive officer of another entity where at any time during the past three years any of the executive officers of the issuer serve on the compensation committee of such other entity; or (F) a director who is, or has a family member who is, a current partner of the company's outside auditor, or was a partner or employee of the company's outside auditor who worked on the company's audit at any time during any of the past three years.

10 A comparative study on *Shari'ah* compliance frameworks

Is the integrated or separated model well suited to Bangladesh?

S. M. Sohrab Uddin, Asif Nawaz Chowdhury and Yasushi Suzuki

1. Introduction

Besides Islamic countries, a handsome number of non-Islamic countries through-out the world use Islamic finance as a distinct approach of finance where Islamic *Shari'ah* (Islamic law) acts as the pivotal guiding element. However, there is evidence showing the breach of *Shari'ah* compliance due to lack of knowledge and awareness among employees, absence of an interest-free economy, government's inability to provide supportive rules and regulations, and adequate infrastructure for further development (Ullah, 2014). Some of these factors can be considered internal factors and some others external. Corresponding to the increasing demand for Islamic finance products and the rapid growth of Islamic banks and other financial institutions worldwide, *Shari'ah* compliance has received significant attention during the last few decades.

The *Shari'ah* compliance mechanism checks whether Islamic *Shari'ah* governs the process of origination of products and services, the execution of operations, and the reporting of financial and non-financial activities to the stakeholders of Islamic banks and financial institutions. Interestingly, *Shari'ah* compliance mechanisms differ from country to country based on the authority and delegation of responsibility of the central *Shari'ah* board. The existence of two fundamentally different compliance structures can be observed, namely the 'separated' model upon a very high degree of independence of the *Shari'ah* board, which is applied in Gulf Cooperation Council (GCC) countries including Kuwait, Saudi Arabia, Bahrain, Qatar, and the UAE, and in some other countries including Jordan, Yemen, and Gambia; and the 'integrated' model upon harmonizing with banking regulations, which is applied in Malaysia, Sudan, Pakistan, and Indonesia (Gintzburger, 2011; Hamza, 2013; Rahajeng, 2013). In the same way, Grassa (2013) categorizes the distinct available *Shari'ah*-compliance mechanisms as the Southeast Asian model and GCC model. On the other hand, it is quite unique to see that the existence of the *Shari'ah* board is not seemingly a prerequisite in Iran (Gintzburger, 2011, p. 314). Even deviations can be found in compliance practices among countries reported under the same compliance structure. According to Khan (2007, p. 288), the disparity in the opinions concerning *Shari'ah* creates unease among participants which, in turn, leads to profit-seeking behavior at the expense of misplacing the spirit of Islamic finance infrastructure.

Besides, some international bodies working on Islamic finance such as Accounting and Auditing Organization for Islamic Financial Institutions (AAOIFI), Islamic Development Bank (IDB), International Islamic Ratings Agency, International Islamic Centre for Reconciliation for Commercial Arbitration for Islamic Finance, Institute of Islamic Banking and Insurance (IIBI), International Institute of Islamic Finance (IIIF), and Islamic Financial Services Board (IFSB) provide guidelines and benchmarks on *Shari'ah* compliance, which largely influence the *Shari'ah* compliance mechanism. Malkawi (2013) categorizes various *Shari'ah* compliance structures as the internal *Shari'ah* board, the external *Shari'ah* board, and the regulatory and supervisory agency. The *Shari'ah* board of a particular Islamic bank or financial institution is regarded as the internal *Shari'ah* board. The external *Shari'ah* board is further divided into the national *Shari'ah* board, international *Shari'ah* board including AAOIFI and IDB, and consultant *Shari'ah* board including IIBI and IIIF. Finally, the IFSB is considered the regulatory and supervisory agency with a predominant aim to support the industry as a whole by promulgating adequate regulation and guidelines and by undertaking proper training and research.

The urgencies and rapid development of Islamic finance worldwide have enabled Bangladesh to operate Islamic finance activities throughout the country since 1983 with huge acceptability by its citizenry. Bangladesh Bank, the central bank of the country, has issued necessary guidelines to structure the *Shari'ah* compliance mechanism but it fails to provide the required solution whenever a conflict of interest occurs among participatory parties (Amanullah, 2015). Ullah (2014) finds a high degree of anomalies in *Shari'ah* compliance status of the Islamic banks in Bangladesh. With a variant approach, this chapter aims at identifying the *Shari'ah* compliance framework used by Islamic banks in Bangladesh and at examining the nonconformity in the compliance framework by linking the existing practice with the available compliance structures in the global arena and under the AAOIFI guideline.

The latter part of this chapter is divided into four segments. Section 2 highlights the literature review by demonstrating the *Shari'ah* compliance structures available in the international arena. Section 3 provides an overview of the Islamic banking sector of Bangladesh. Section 4 introduces the current *Shari'ah* compliance practices of Islamic banks and tries to identify an appropriate structure for Bangladesh. Section 5 concludes the paper with some policy recommendations for designing the future shape of the *Shari'ah* compliance framework.

2. Literature review

Shari'ah is an Arabic word which refers to Law of Allah used as religious precepts of Islam. Every aspect of a Muslim's life is required to be conducted as per *Shari'ah*.

There are four sources of Islamic *Shari'ah*: (i) interpretations of the *Qur'an* (The Holy Book of the Muslims consisting of the revelations made by God to the Prophet Muhammad (peace be upon him) during his Prophethood of about 23 years); (ii) interpretations of the *Sunnah/Hadith* (after the *Qur'an*, the *Sunnah* is the most important source of the Islamic faith and refers essentially to the Prophet's example as indicated by his practice of the faith); (iii) *Ijma*, consensus amongst scholars (consensus of the jurists on any issue of *fiqh* after the death of the Prophet (peace be upon him)/collective reasoning); and (iv) *Qiyas/Ijtihad* analogical deduction (individual reasoning).

(Ullah, 2014, p. 184)

All the activities must comply with at least any of these four sources in order to be considered Islamic. At the same time, activities have to be free from elements such as *riba* (interest), *maysir* (gambling), and *gharar* (uncertainty) (Adam and Bakar, 2014; Gintzburger, 2011).

Shari'ah compliance is a comprehensive issue which deals with a number of instruments including the *Shari'ah* supervisory board (SSB) and the *Shari'ah* governance framework. With the help of these instruments, *Shari'ah* is implemented by Islamic banks in designing their products and services, and in executing their operations. SSB is an independent body consisting of *Shari'ah* scholars who are specialized in *fiqh al-mu'amalat* (Islamic commercial law) and relevant proficiencies associated with the nucleus of Islamic finance mechanisms (Gintzburger, 2011; Hamza, 2013). The activities of SSB were first initiated in 1976 by the Faisal Islamic Bank in Egypt followed by Jordan and Sudan in 1978, Kuwait in 1979, Malaysia in 1983, and UAE in 1999 (Malkawi, 2013, p. 546). The members of SSB possess the right to interpret, review, and approve whenever there is a gap of opinions concerning any issue of *Shari'ah*. The process of interpretation is done through *ijthihad*, which refers to independent reasoning in finding a solution to a specific problem. Thus, SSB is predominantly responsible for reviewing, supervising, and directing the legal, contractual, and operating activities of Islamic banks. It provides guarantee and assures credibility to stockholders, stakeholders, and other related authorities that all activities of Islamic banks are performed as per *Shari'ah*, which is fundamental to the development of Islamic finance including Islamic banking since any non-compliance leads to the rise of *Shari'ah* risk and hampers the credibility of the sector as a whole (Hamza, 2013). Such non-compliance may violate market discipline too, as indicated by Khan (2007). SSB also plays a significant role in the process of constructing *Shari'ah*-compliant products besides pure *Shari'ah*-based products. In doing all of these, SSB considers the guidelines and benchmarks provided by international Islamic finance regulatory bodies including AAOIFI and IFSB. On the other hand, the *Shari'ah* governance is an organizational arrangement conducted by SSB for ensuring *Shari'ah* compliance and for conducting the *Shari'ah* audit in Islamic banks in order to identify any deviations of the *Shari'ah* rules. Of course, the *Shari'ah* governance framework is a part of corporate governance of Islamic banks, which is rather a complex blending of how firms are to be directed, governed, and controlled.

Two prominent models, the stockholder model and stakeholder model, are used to define the corporate governance structure in conventional finance.

The stockholder model suggests that a firm has one core objective, which is to maximize shareholder wealth. Thus, stockholders have the right to interfere in strategic decisions to maximize their wealth. On the other hand, the stakeholder model suggests maximizing both shareholders' and stakeholders' wealth. Here, 'stakeholder' is meant in a broader sense where stockholders along with other related entities are benefited. Hence, firms following the stakeholder model tend to have more responsibility to society. As an analogy, we can see the types of *Shari'ah* compliance structure; the 'separated' framework and the 'integrated' one in the light of the degree of independence of *Shari'ah* boards. The former puts the highest priority to the issue of *Shari'ah* compliance, while the latter intends to harmonize it with banking regulations at the centre.

Under the 'separated' model, SSB of each of the Islamic banks has the supreme power of authority. In this model, there is no powerful authority at the national level to structure and monitor institutional SSB. That is, SSBs in the institutional level are independent of the central bank and decisions taken by them concerning Islamic *Shari'ah* are deemed to be accepted without any external resistance in the case of the permissibility of contracts, *Shari'ah*-compliant financial products, and *Shari'ah* practices (Hamza, 2013). The GCC countries and Jordan, Yemen, and Gambia are the followers of the separated model as the *Shari'ah* compliance framework. However, anomalies exist among these followers of the separated model. For instance, even though there is no effective national authority in the level of the central bank in GCC countries, few of these countries such as Kuwait, Qatar, and UAE have higher *Shari'ah* authority. In Kuwait, the authority is known as the Ministry of Awqaf and Islamic Affairs; in Qatar, it is recognized as the Ministry of Awqaf; and in UAE, the authority is known as Higher *Shari'ah* Authority. Similarly, the decision of SSBs can only be influenced by Islamic *Fiqh* Academy (IFA) in the case of Saudi Arabia and by the National *Shari'ah* Board in the central bank in the case of Bahrain. Nevertheless, the higher authority can only advise if there are conflicts of opinion between or among the SSBs of Islamic banks or cases of *Shari'ah* interpretations or necessities for new *Shari'ah* issues (Grassa, 2013). As a result, with regard to *fatwa* (a scholarly opinion on a matter of Islamic law), inconsistencies may occur among the SSBs of Islamic banks or within the same SSB of an Islamic bank over the years. Table 10.1 provides a summary of the key issues associated with the separated model practiced by different GCC countries.

In contrast, the 'integrated' model assigns the essential authority to the central bank to pattern, control, advice, and follow up the Islamic banks on the conformity of *Shari'ah* in their products and services, procedure, and activities through a central SSB. Malaysia, Pakistan, Sudan, and Indonesia adopt, as Hamza (2013) calls it, the centralized *Shari'ah* framework (Hamza, 2013). In addition, evidence proves that Indonesia also follows the model (Rahajeng, 2013). In fact, under this model dual authority exists where the central authority at the national level guides, advises, and resolves *Shari'ah* issues related to Islamic banking. Individual SSB of respective Islamic banks are responsible for ensuring the compliance of the issues fixed by the central SSB at the institutional level. Thus, it is likely to observe

Table 10.1 Separated model in GCC countries

Issues	Bahrain	Kuwait	UAE	Qatar	Saudi Arabia
Authority for resolving *Shari'ah* conflict	National *Shari'ah* Board in the central bank	Ministry of Awqaf and Islamic Affairs	Higher *Shari'ah* Authority	Ministry of Awqaf	IFA
Responsibility of SSB in Islamic bank	Issuing *fatwa*. Ensuring *Shari'ah* review through a committee. Nomination of *Shari'ah* scholars. Allowing the presence of scholars in more than one Islamic bank.				
Shari'ah risk	Inconsistencies among *fatwas* of different SSBs or in the same SSB over the period due to the absence of an integrated SSB for all Islamic banks.				

Source: constructed by the authors based on Hamza (2013, p. 232–233)

a harmonized *Shari'ah* compliance practice under the integrated model, which is relatively free from inconsistencies concerning *fatwas* at the institutional level. In this regard, Hamza (2013) mentions that the integrated model ensures consistency of *fatwas* and explanations within the Islamic banking sector as a whole, though coordination among central SSB and SSBs of Islamic banks is still an issue. He asks for the formation of a council of all SSBs of Islamic banks in collaboration of the central bank for ensuring the harmonization of *Shari'ah* compliance. However, variations exist among countries practicing the integrated model, which are shown in Table 10.2. For instance, the members of central SSB are not allowed to be members of any SSB of an Islamic financial institution in Malaysia and Indonesia whereas it is allowed in Pakistan and Sudan. Yet again, unlike Sudan, the members of central SSB can be nominated as members of SSB of only one Islamic financial institution in Pakistan. In this regard, Malkawi (2013) argues that the situation of representing multiple SSBs leads to the erosion of perception by creating conflicts of interest and accordingly legal revisions are needed for prohibiting such sitting. In addition, the presence of *Shari'ah* scholars in more than one Islamic bank is allowed in Pakistan and Sundan but not in Malaysia and Indonesia.

3. Overview of the Islamic banking sector of Bangladesh

The Islamic banking sector of Bangladesh consists of full-fledged Islamic banks, Islamic banking branches of conventional banks, and Islamic banking counters or windows of conventional banks. Full-fledged Islamic banks refer to the institutions where all the products and activities are offered in such a way that complies with the Islamic *Shari'ah*. When one or more branches of a conventional bank offer Islamic banking they are regarded as Islamic banking branches of conventional banks, and when a conventional bank has an Islamic banking counter or window in its branches besides the conventional banking counter or window then it is called an Islamic banking window of a conventional bank. Table 10.3

Table 10.2 Integrated model in Malaysia, Pakistan, Sudan, and Indonesia

Issues	Malaysia	Pakistan	Sudan	Indonesia
Fatwa issued by central bank	Yes	Yes	Yes	Yes
Review and audit of *Shari'ah* compliance are done by Islamic banks	Yes	Yes	Yes	Yes
Appointment of *Shari'ah* scholars by Islamic banks	Yes, subject to the approval from the financial authorities.	Yes	Yes, subject to the approval from the central SSB.	Yes
Presence of scholars in more than one Islamic bank	No	Yes	Yes	No
Members of central SSB	Cannot be a member of any Islamic financial institution.	Can be a member of only one Islamic financial institution.	Can be a member of any Islamic financial institution.	Cannot be a member of any Islamic financial institution.
Authority for resolving *Shari'ah* conflict	Central SSB in the name of *Shari'ah* Advisory Council (SAC) at the central bank, Bank Negara Malaysia.	Central SSB in the name of *Shari'ah* board at the central bank, State Bank of Pakistan.	High *Shari'ah* Supervisory Board (HSSB) at the central bank.	*Majelis Ulama Indonesia* (MUI) (Indonesian Ulema Council or known as *Dewan Syariah Nasional – DSN*) is responsible for supporting the central bank, Bank Indonesia.
Shari'ah risk	Due to the absence of coordination among central SSB and SSBs of Islamic banks. May slow down the process of new product development.			

Source: constructed by the authors based on Gintzburger (2011), Hamza (2013, pp. 233–235), and Rahajeng (2013)

provides a summary of different types of banks involved in Islamic banking. It indicates that eight banks are engaged in Islamic banking services fully, which includes two banks that started their journey as conventional banks and later converted into full-fledged Islamic banks in 2004 and 2008, respectively. All of the full-fledged Islamic banks are under private ownership. In addition, 16 conventional banks are offering Islamic banking branches or windows out of which eight banks including seven private banks and one foreign bank are maintaining branches; and eight banks including three state-owned banks, three private banks, and two foreign banks are holding windows for such services. Most importantly,

Table 10.3 Initiation of and experience in Islamic banking by different types of banks

Bank	Type of ownership	Year of inauguration	Initiation of Islamic banking	Experience up to 2016
Full-fledged Islamic banks				
Islami Bank Bangladesh Ltd.	Private	1983	1983	34
ICB Islamic Bank Ltd.	Private	1987	1987	30
Social Islami Bank Ltd.	Private	1995	1995	22
Al-Arafah Islami Bank Ltd.	Private	1995	1995	22
Shahjalal Islami Bank Ltd.	Private	2001	2001	16
Union Bank Ltd.	Private	2013	2013	4
Converted Full-fledged Islamic Banks				
EXIM Bank Ltd.	Private	1999	2004	13
First Security Islami Bank Ltd.	Private	1999	2008	9
Conventional Banks with Islamic Banking Branches				
Prime Bank Ltd.	Private	1995	1995	22
The City Bank Ltd.	Private	1983	2003	14
Dhaka Bank Ltd.	Private	1995	2003	14
Premier Bank Ltd.	Private	1999	2003	14
Southeast Bank Ltd.	Private	1995	2003	14
Jamuna Bank Ltd.	Private	2001	2003	14
AB Bank Ltd.	Private	1982	2004	13
Bank Alfalah Ltd.	Foreign	1997	2003	14
Conventional Banks with Islamic Banking Windows				
Sonali Bank Ltd.	Govt.	1972	2010	7
Agrani Bank Ltd.	Govt.	1972	2010	7
Pubali Bank Ltd.	Govt.	1972	2010	7
Trust Bank Ltd.	Private	1999	2008	9
Bank Asia Ltd.	Private	1999	2008	9
Standard Bank Ltd.	Private	1999	2009	8
HSBC Bank Ltd.	Foreign	1996	2010	4*
Standard Chartered Bank Ltd.	Foreign	1972	2004	13

Source: constructed by the authors based on different annual reports of respective banks

Note: *HSBC Bank Ltd. closed all Islamic banking operations by the end of 2013

initiation of the Islamic banking sector in different time periods portrays the gap of experience of these banks varying from the highest experience of 34 years to the lowest of 4 years.

According to Bangladesh Bank (2016), the full-fledged Islamic banks contain 19.3 percent and 21.9 percent of the banking sector deposits and credits, respectively. On the other hand, banks with Islamic banking branches and windows hold 1.1 percent of deposits and 1.4 percent of credits of the sector. In aggregate, the marker share of the Islamic banking sector in terms of deposits and credits are 20.4 percent and 23.3 percent, respectively.

The full-fledged Islamic banks make a report concerning *Shari'ah* compliance in their published annual reports. All of these banks ensure the presence of at least three *Shari'ah* scholars in their SSB during the period 2012–2016. However, only Islamic Bank Bangladesh Ltd. has become the member of international bodies such as AAOIFI and IFSB. Variations are also observed among these full-fledged Islamic banks in terms of the number of meeting held of their SBBs and change in members of SSBs during the period 2012–2016, as shown in Table 10.4.

4. *Shari'ah* compliance in Bangladesh

Bangladesh is prevailed to have its own Islamic bank as the first Islamic bank in the name of Islami Bank Bangladesh Ltd., which started its operation in 1983.

Table 10.4 Number of meetings and change in members of SSB of full-fledged Islamic banks

Bank	2012	2013	2014	2015	2016
	Number of meetings of SBB				
Islami Bank Bangladesh Ltd.	NR	5	10	12	10
ICB Islamic Bank Ltd.	4	NR	NR	NR	NR
Social Islami Bank Ltd.	NR	NR	5	6	6
Al-Arafah Islami Bank Ltd.	NR	NR	NR	NR	NR
Shahjalal Islami Bank Ltd.	9	4	5	5	6
EXIM Bank Ltd.	NR	NR	NR	NR	6
First Security Islami Bank Ltd.	7	NR	NR	NR	NR
Union Bank Ltd.	NR	NR	8	10	NR
	Change in members of SSB				
Islami Bank Bangladesh Ltd.	No	No	Yes	Yes	Yes
ICB Islamic Bank Ltd.	Yes	Yes	Yes	Yes	Yes
Social Islami Bank Ltd.	Yes	Yes	No	No	Yes
Al-Arafah Islami Bank Ltd.	NR	NR	NR	NR	NR
Shahjalal Islami Bank Ltd.	Yes	Yes	Yes	Yes	Yes
EXIM Bank Ltd.	NR	Yes	Yes	Yes	No
First Security Islami Bank Ltd.	No	No	No	No	No
Union Bank Ltd.	NR	NR	No	No	No

Source: constructed by the authors based on different annual reports of respective banks

Note: 'NR' stands for not reported

For ensuring *Shari'ah* compliance in Islamic banking products and service, Bangladesh has arrangements at both the national and institutional levels. At the national level, there is a central *Shari'ah* board known as Central *Shari'ah* Board for Islamic Banks of Bangladesh (CSBIBB). At the same time, Bangladesh Bank has issued Guidelines for Conducting Islamic Banking. At the institutional level, every Islamic bank has its own SSB. Though there is a CSBIBB, it is not backed by sufficient authority needed to harmonize, control, and rule over Islamic banks. According to Section III of the Guidelines for Conducting Islamic Banking issued in November 2009 by Bangladesh Bank:

> It will be the responsibility of the board of directors of the respective banks to ensure that the activities of the banks and their products are *Shari'ah* compliant. The Board of the Islamic banks/subsidiary company/conventional commercial banks having Islamic branches, therefore, is constituted with directors having requisite knowledge and expertise in Islamic Jurisprudence. The Board may form an independent *Shari'ah* Supervisory Committee with experienced and knowledgeable persons in Islamic Jurisprudence. However, the Board shall be responsible for any lapses/irregularities on the part of the *Shari'ah* Supervisory Committee.
>
> (p. 10)

CSBIBB started its journey in 2001 mainly to assist and provide necessary advice to member banks following the similar procedure and unanimous action of *Shari'ah* principles and to supervise the implementation of *Shari'ah* principles in the activities and operations of member banks. Table 10.5 highlights the registered members of CSBIBB during the period 2012–2016. It shows that seven full-fledged Islamic banks have been the members of CSBIBB during the period 2012–2016. In 2012, the registered number of conventional banks with Islamic branches or windows was 10, which rose to 13 in 2016. However, one full-fledged Islamic bank and two conventional banks offering Islamic banking still remain unregistered in CSBIBB. In aggregate, it includes 7 full-fledged Islamic banks, 8 conventional banks having Islamic banking branches, 5 conventional banks having Islamic banking windows, and 1 Islamic financial institution, leading to a total of 21 registered institutional members. CSBIBB also has 65 individual members. The board organizes trainings, workshops, capacity building, and knowledge-sharing programs for Islamic banking practitioners of the country on a regular basis.

Table 10.5 Number of banks registered in CSBIBB

Types of bank	2012	2013	2014	2015	2016
Full-fledged Islamic banks	7	7	7	7	7
Conventional banks with Islamic banking branches/windows	10	10	13	13	13

Source: constructed by the authors based on different annual reports of Bangladesh Bank

Table 10.6 provides involvement of the 52 individual members (for whom data are available) of CSBIBB in banks offering Islamic banking services. According to the table, 22 members engage in full-fledged Islamic banks; 14 in banks with Islamic banking branches; 11 in banks with Islamic banking windows; 1 in banks with Islamic branches and banks with Islamic windows; and 1 in Islamic banks, banks with Islamic branches, and banks with Islamic windows. Only three of them are independent as they are not involved in any Islamic bank or financial institution. On the other hand, 12 members are involved in SSB of banks offering Islamic banking, 36 engage in management of banks offering Islamic banking, 1 participates in both SSB and management, and 3 of them are not involved in either of the two roles (see Table 10.7). Among 12 members engaged in the SSB of Islamic banks, 10 are involved in an individual bank, one concurrently serves the SSB of six banks, and 1 is associated with five banks simultaneously. However, Malkawi (2013) urges limiting the number of seats that *Shari'ah* scholars can hold simultaneously even though he acknowledges the shortage of experienced scholars as a shortcoming to be resolved quickly.

There are a few differences between the integrated model and the model practiced in Bangladesh. For instance, CSBIBB as the central SSB does not have the sole authority to issue *fatwa*. At the same time, it is not mandatory to follow CSBIBB's rulings for Islamic banks, which is a fundamental issue under the

Table 10.6 Involvement of the members of CSBIBB in banks engaging in Islamic banking

Member of CSBIBB	Only in full-fledged Islamic banks	Only in banks with Islamic branches	Only in banks with Islamic windows	Banks with Islamic branches and banks with Islamic windows	In Islamic banks, banks with Islamic branches, and banks with Islamic windows	Not in banks offering Islamic banking
52 out of 65	22	14	11	1	1	3

Source: constructed by the authors based on different annual reports of respective banks

Table 10.7 Nature of involvement of the members of CSBIBB in banks offering Islamic banking

Member of CSBIBB	Member of SSB of banks offering Islamic banking	Engage in management of banks offering Islamic banking	Engage in SSB and management of banks offering Islamic banking	Not engage in SSB or management of banks offering Islamic banking
52 out of 65	12	36	1	3

Source: constructed by the authors based on different annual reports of respective banks

integrated model. On the other hand, like the separated model, SSBs enjoy the power of authority in Islamic banks of Bangladesh and are independent from the central bank concerning decision-making based on *Shari'ah*. Some other basic features of the separated model including *fatwa* issued by Islamic banks, review of *Shari'ah* compliance done by Islamic banks, and presence of scholars in other Islamic banks are also observed in the model used by Islamic banks. However, unlike the separated model, there is no specific authority to resolve *Shari'ah* conflict in Bangladesh. Table 10.8 makes a summary of the issues associated with the *Shari'ah* compliance framework practiced by Islamic banks. Interestingly, it is a bit confusing as it follows the shared features of both separated and integrated models. At the same time, nonexistence of specific authority for solving the conflicts of interest among SSBs and the involvement of the members of CSBIBB in any number of banks ranging from a minimum of one bank to a maximum of six banks can be regarded as country-specific issues. Seemingly, a hybrid model with the features of both separated and integrated models along with some country-specific issues exists in the *Shari'ah* compliance framework practiced by Islamic banks of Bangladesh.

In order to assess if banks in Bangladesh follow the guidelines set by AAOIFI, an analysis is made on all full-fledged Islamic banks during the period 2012–2016 based on the contents mentioned in Table A2 in the Appendices. It is observed

Table 10.8 Issues associated with the *Shari'ah* compliance framework of Islamic banks in Bangladesh

Separated	• Responsibility of providing necessary *Shari'ah* advice to member banks delegated to CSBIBB. • *Fatwa* issued by the SSB of Islamic banks. • Islamic banks are responsible for ensuring that all activities comply with the Islamic *Shari'ah*.
Integrated	• Members of central SSB, that is, CSBIBB, are allowed to participate in the *Shari'ah* compliance of Islamic banks and financial institutions. • Members of CSBIBB can be involved with more than one bank. • Islamic banks are authorized to appointment *Shari'ah* scholars in their SSBs as per the criteria including educational qualification; experience and exposure; track record; solvency and financial integrity; and integrity, honesty, and reputation set by Bangladesh Bank. The details of these criteria are reported in Table A1 in the Appendices.
Bangladesh specific issues	• Authority for resolving *Shari'ah* conflict is not clearly specified within the system. • Members of CSBIBB can be involved with any number of banks, ranging from a minimum of one bank to a maximum of six banks. • Members of CSBIBB are allowed to take part in the management of Islamic banks and financial institutions.

Source: constructed by the authors

that all of the banks follow the guidelines such as composition of SSB including maximum five years of members as experts, existence of full members, and minimum of three members; selection of SSB members at an annual general meeting; reporting regarding remuneration provided to SSB members; periodic meetings with the management; and inclusion of title, opinion paragraph containing an expression of opinion about the compliance of the Islamic financial institution with Islamic *Shari'ah* rules, and signatures of the members of SSB in the SSB report. On the other hand, appointment and dismissal mechanisms of SSB members are not clearly mentioned by these banks in their annual reports. However, inconsistencies are found concerning the issues including invited members in the SSB; no dual position with SSB and management of other Islamic banks and financial institutions; and addressee, opening or introductory paragraph, scope paragraph describing the nature of the work performed, and date of the SSB report.

5. Conclusion

This chapter has intended to provide insights regarding *Shari'ah* compliance of Islamic banks in the international arena along with Bangladesh. It is found that the compliance mechanism practiced by the Islamic banks in Bangladesh is different from the two broad categories followed by the GCC countries and the Southeast Asian countries. Interestingly, the model of Bangladesh consists of a few country-specific features such as the absence of the authority for resolving *Shari'ah* conflict, involvement of the members of CSBIBB with any number of banks, and allowance of the members of CSBIBB to take part in the management of Islamic banks and financial institutions. Moreover, CSBIBB does not have the right to issue *fatwa* and Islamic banks are not bound to follow rulings issued by the CSBIBB. The findings reveal that Bangladesh needs to establish a powerful central SSB with the authority to pattern the *Shari'ah* compliance structure, deal with the disagreement of opinions, lead the increasing trend of Islamic banking throughout the country, and provide sufficient direction and necessary rulings for Islamic banks and financial institutions. At the national level, the CSBIBB structure should be reviewed and necessary steps should be taken so that it can act as an authoritative central board with sufficient power to issue *fatwa* and control the SSB at the institutional level. There should also be operational mechanism regarding the committee member selection and for dealing with conflicts of interest among SSBs in CSBIBB. At the institutional level, Islamic banks should follow the international standard both in *Shari'ah* compliance and in *Shari'ah* reporting.

Appendices

Table A1 Criteria for selecting members for SSB of Islamic banks

Qualification	Issues
Educational qualification	• Graduate and postgraduate degrees in Islamic studies, Arabic, Islamic law, Islamic economics, or Islamic banking with insightful knowledge in the Arabic language.
Experience and exposure	• Must have at least three years of experience in teaching or research work in Islamic jurisprudence/Islamic law/Islamic banking-related subject. • Three years of experience as a member of any *fatwa* board in giving *Shari'ah* rulings on Islamic trade and commerce/banking and financial matters or publication of three exclusive articles on Islamic trade and commerce, Islamic banking, Islamic economics, and Islamic commercial jurisprudence in any recognized journal or publication of three books on the same subjects.
Track record	• Must have an impeccable record of accomplishment in social, economic, and financial dealings. • Has not been terminated or dismissed in the capacity of an employee or director/chairman from any institution, firm, or company.
Solvency and financial integrity	• Has not been involved in any illegal/improper activity particularly relating to banking business. • Has not been in default of payment of dues owed to any bank or financial institution and/or default in payment of any taxes in an individual capacity or as a proprietary concern.
Integrity, honesty, and reputation	• Has not been convicted in any civil/criminal offence or involved in financial impropriety and moral turpitude. • Has not been subject to any adverse findings or any settlement in civil/criminal proceedings particularly, in regard to investments, financial/business, misconduct, fraud etc. • Has not contravened any of the requirements and standards of the regulatory system or the equivalent standards of requirements of any regulatory authority. • Has not been debarred from giving religious rulings by any religious institution/body.

Source: constructed by the authors based on Section III of the Guidelines for Conducting Islamic Banking issued by Bangladesh Bank

Table A2 AAOIFI compliance items

AAOIFI: IFSB independence elements of SSB members

Appointment mechanism
Maximum five years among the experts
Composition and competencies:
 Full member
 Invited member
 Minimum three members
Selection at an annual general meeting
Dismissal mechanism recommended by the board of directors
No dual position with other Islamic financial institution and with board, e.g. as
 director
Remuneration
Periodical meetings with the management

AAOIFI: basic elements of the SSB's report

Title of the SSB
Addressee
Opening or introductory paragraph
Scope paragraph describing the nature of the work performed
Opinion paragraph containing an expression of opinion concerning the compliance
 of the Islamic financial institution with the *Shari'ah* rules and principles
Date of report
Signatures of the members of the SSB

Source: constructed by the authors based on Rahajeng (2013) and Vinnicombe (2010)

11 Alternative views upon the 'division of work' and 'specialization' towards a new mode of profit–loss sharing

Yasushi Suzuki and Mohammad Dulal Miah

1. Introduction

It is observed that exorbitant dominance of *murabaha* financing has remained unchanged over the years. This is alarming as per the explanation of major Islamic finance literature. Many studies state that at the beginning of Islamic finance, jurists were a bit lenient in endorsing *murabaha* concentration on the pretence that such a practice might help infant Islamic finance grow rapidly. Once this model of finance reaches a competitive stage it may strive to shift gradually from the mark-up based/*Shari'ah*-compliant financing to participatory/trust-based financing upon the pure mode of 'profit–loss sharing' (PLS) (Ahmad, 1993). Contrary to this expectation, Islamic financial institutions have been maintaining their financing dominance on *murabaha*. Many Islamic scholars insist that being *Shari'ah* compliant does not automatically embody the spirit of Islamic finance. Thus, they are very critical about the current practice of Islamic banks (Kuran, 1995; El-Gamal, 2006; Çizakça, 2011).

The literature, however, provides some explanations as to why Islamic banks do not readily participate in PLS. Iqbal and Molyneux (2005) identify moral hazard and adverse selection problems as the key to *murabaha* concentration of Islamic banks. They further emphasize that the monitoring cost required for resolving these problems functions as an obstacle towards PLS-based financing. Aggarwal and Yousef (2000) contend that banks' attempts to avoid agency problems rationalize their preference for debt-like finance. Similarly, Chong and Liu (2009) argue that reducing the mark-up dominance of Islamic banks calls for the mitigation of agency problems. Some studies however emphasize entrepreneurs' moral hazard problem associated with *ex post* information asymmetry (Mills and Presley, 1999; Dar and Presley, 2000; Hamza, 2016). Farooq (2007), on the other hand, argues that the reason for not materializing the expected growth of PLS lies with the nature of partnership. He provides evidence showing that partnership is the least common form of business organization because of some legal predicaments involved with it. Khan (2010) lists several obstacles that discourage banks from engaging in PLS. He insists that entrepreneurs' moral hazard, particularly their tendency to hide critical information as well as non-cooperative attitude, fades Islamic banks' interest in participatory finance.

We argue that these issues are important but secondary only as far as Islamic banking is concerned. The primary issue cements the question of whether Islamic banks should ideally be allowed to deal with risk and uncertainty embedded in participatory/trust-based financing and/or with the financing towards marginal clients under the current mode of loose PLS. Banks, regardless of whether they are Islamic or conventional, are special and sensitive because they are entrusted with the use-power of people's savings for commercial purpose. If incentives for commercial banking are tightly aligned with banks' higher risk-appetite, depositors' interest would be at stake. Thus, depository corporations have to put their best effort in protecting the welfare of the depositors by avoiding high risk and uncertainty in lending activities. As long as financial instruments of asset-backed financing are *Shari'ah* compliant, it is surprising why Islamic banks are criticized so much for their focus on this technique. Second, conventional banks are tightly regulated for many credible reasons including the avoidance of systemic financial catastrophe. If so, how far is it logical to suggest Islamic banks to assume higher risk involved with participatory financing or financing for marginal clients?

Our analysis in this chapter rests on the following understanding. An expansion of the mode of PLS is essential to materialize the social justice sought in the *Shari'ah* norm. However, banks regardless of their philosophical orientation are not in a position to solely perform this task. Islamic banks are still expected to mobilize the 'safety' fund from the *risk-averse* depositors who are not yet willing to engage in the mode of PLS. At the same time, Islamic banks should protect the welfare of these depositors which requires that Islamic banks should minimally be involved with participatory financing and/or financing for marginal clients. Other financial institutions including Islamic venture capital and microfinance institutions can be developed and supported to greatly contribute to the PLS mode of finance because these institutions possess comparative advantage in dealing with PLS compared to depository corporations. Banks' appetite for higher risk stemming from participatory financial contracts and/or financing for marginal clients may lead financial institutions to financial fragility. Therefore, Islamic banks like their conventional counterparts should be conservative for the risk and uncertainty embedded in the participatory mode of finance.

The chapter has been structured as follows: Section 2 describes the feasibility of Islamic banks to finance PLS-based projects under the existing financial and regulatory framework. Section 3 offers an alternative model based on the specialization and division of work of Islamic financial institutions to enhance PLS. Section 4 focuses on other contemporary issues discussed in the existing literature as obstacles towards PLS finance and the possible ways to address them. This is followed by a brief conclusion.

2. Participatory finance and bank's risk exposure

Many Islamic finance scholars ask: Why do Islamic banks not actively participate in equity-like financing instead of their current debt-like financing? This is a right question but wrongly directed because suggesting that banks take more risk associated with participatory finance is contrary to the long-standing practice of the banking industry, though there is a debate on how equity-like financing would prevent banks from undertaking excess credit risks.

It is rational for the greater stability of a financial system that Islamic banks simply should not be encouraged to accept high risk because bankruptcy of a single bank can lead a country-wide bank run which in turn, through its ripple effect, may trigger financial and economic crisis (Krugman, 2012). In the case of bankruptcy of a depositary corporation it is usually the depositors who lose their deposited money beyond the amount insured under the deposit insurance. On the other hand, they are ultimately the tax payers who would pay the socio-economic cost for insurance. Even worse, once it happens, depositors lose their confidence on the financial system, which would often lead to the disinterme-diation of financial resources resulting in economic slowdown. Evidence shows that the failure of financial institutions results in macroeconomic instability and bail out costs (Caprio and Klingebiel, 2002; Englund, 1999; Angkinand, 2009). Honohan and Klingebiel (2003) show that the cost of cleaning up financial mess accounts for on average 12.8 percent of national GDP in their sample of 40 epi-sodes. The calculated cost is higher (14.3 percent) for developing countries and some crises have claimed much larger outlays of about 40–55 percent of GDP. Because of huge social cost involved with the bankruptcy of depository corpora-tions, they are rescued during the time of their financial distress by injecting tax payers' money. This external social cost justifies tight regulation on the banking industry for preventing banks from undertaking excess credit risks.

One may insist that banks' limited liability and the existence of 'quasi' flat rate deposit insurance could encourage banks to assume more risk which is termed in the literature as 'moral hazard'. However, there arises confusion in this story between the rescue of a bank (or depositors) and the rescue of the owners or managers who are responsible for the creation of the situation which creates the need for a rescue.

> To the manager, it is not much of a consolation that his/her firm is saved by the government, if the rescue operation involves the termination of his/her contract. So, if a manager knows that his/her job would be in jeopardy if the firm performs badly, there is little moral hazard.
>
> (Chang, 2000, p. 782)

In the *incentive* approach, solvency regulations are modeled as solutions to prin-cipal–agent problems between a public insurance system and private banks. Since regulators' insurance is costly, solvency regulations are required to create incen-tives that limit the potential cost in terms of public funds being used to bail out depositors, by way of keeping banks away from excess credit risks.

If the conventional banking system is regulated tightly to avoid potential finan-cial catastrophe and to maintain depositors' confidence in the financial system, it is equally rational to ask Islamic banks to keep away from dealing with high risk and fundamental uncertainty involved with participatory financing (or the financing to marginal clients) under the current mode of PLS. If Islamic banks fail to share the loss incurred from the accumulation of non-performing credit, it is ultimately the tax payers who are supposed to pay the socio-economic cost under the deposit insurance for protecting the general depositors (in particular, saving account holders). Under the PLS-based contract, banks' function is confined merely to financial intermediaries. Ideally they bear no risk of clients because they can transfer the risks associated with the borrowers to the depositors (for instance, investment account holders). This structure would, however, cause serious principal–agent problems between depositors (investors) and Islamic banks, which actually drain the 'risk fund' as resources that are needed for participatory financing. Under the existing banking model, capital owners (investment account holders) appoint Islamic banks as their agent for making various decisions such as determining the PLS ratio, re-investment prospects and terms of funds, liquidation of projects etc. Banks have their own shareholders who represent in the board of a bank. In such a circumstance, it is uncertain how far banks strive to protect the right of the investment account holders instead of maximizing the welfare of shareholders of the bank.

More importantly, the depositors of Islamic banks like their conventional counterparts are mostly small savers who are assumed to be risk-averse (Muljawan *et al.*, 2004; Nienhaus, 2007). A wholesale transfer of risk may keep this group of depositors away from the formal financial system. The fact is that we should not view Islamic and conventional banks as competitors to each other. But rather, the operation of Islamic banks can be seen as complementary, to a great extent, to the conventional banking model at least, in regard to financial inclusion and financial stability.

We do not deny the claim that PLS-based Islamic finance is associated with greater potentials. Our point of departure from the 'idealist' Islamic economists is that promoting participatory financing (or the financing to marginal clients) under the current mode of PLS upon the risk-averse nature of small investors would be problematic to the banks. As Chapra (2002, p. 222) states, "there may be nothing basically wrong in a reasonable amount of short-term debt that is used for financing the purchase and sale of real goods and services." From this perspective, let the Islamic banks finance on the basis of mark-up at a reasonable amount. Participatory financing (or financing for marginal clients) needs can be satisfied by other Islamic financial institutions like Islamic venture capital firms and microfinance institutions.

3. Alternative views upon division of work and specialization in Islamic finance

Most studies of Islamic 'idealist' literature attribute the rise of *murabaha* concentration to agency problems. As a result, policy prescriptions for shifting from a debt-like financing to PLS-based financing centers on resolving agency problems (Maurer, 2002; Khalil et. al, 2002; Farooq, 2007). In so doing, the literature, however, treats agency problems embedded in *musharaka* and *mudaraba* in the same manner although the nature of agency problems is different for these two contracts. For instance, *musharaka* is a partnership contract where agency problems are evident. In contrast, *mudaraba* is a trust-based contract which does not entail agency risk ostensibly, because the *rab-ul-mal* (financier) trusts the *mudarib* (entrepreneur).

Here, we support the view that Islamic banks should be kept away from trust-based financing because they are responsible for paying the best effort to protect the welfare of their depositors. In a *mudaraba* contract, financiers 'trust' the entrepreneurs in regard to their sincerity and dedication to the project's success as well as honesty in dealing with financial information that affects the contract. Khalil *et al.* (2002) find that project attributes, the quality of the entrepreneur, and religious considerations are the three most important agency-contractual problems in *mudaraba* financing. These attributes while critical for *mudaraba* contract are unobservable. Islamic banks as depository corporations cannot simply rely on these intangible attributes of entrepreneurs given the fact that individuals vary greatly in terms of their belief in the omnipotence. Also, individuals' dedication to religious and spiritual belief fluctuates over time. Hence Islamic banks find it difficult to extend depositors' funds to finance projects based on *mudaraba*.

Islamic banks may show similar conservative behavior in financing small and medium enterprises. It is reported in many studies that firms at their infant stage find it difficult to access the capital market for their necessary financing (Cosh and Hughes, 2003; Fraser, 2005; Cowling *et al.*, 2012). This can be attributed to the firms' lack of sufficient information and a proper track record of business which are considered the prerequisites for accessing finance (Berger and Udell, 1998; Revest and Sapio, 2012). These start-ups tend to rely heavily on bank-based financing besides their limited self-financing. Given various modes of finance offered by Islamic banks, these start-ups may prefer participatory financing which does not essentially meet the conditions of collateral. Moreover, newly established firms look for partners so that the associated risks and uncertainties of projects can be shared. Islamic banks on the other hand have their own business strategies in terms of risk-appetite and profitability. They may perceive young and small firms to be highly risky. At the same time, they may be dubious about the personal attributes of the entrepreneur. Thus, Islamic banks tend to be very conservative in engaging with young and small enterprises.

While we support Islamic banks' conservative behavior for financing *mudaraba* as well as start-up projects, we however argue that financing needs of these projects can be met by other financial institutions which possess a comparative advantage over Islamic banks in financing these enterprises. Islamic venture capital (VC) is one among them. Many Islamic VC firms are established by Islamic banks as their venture capital wing dedicated to venture capital financing. However, this should be modeled after special purpose entity (SPE/SPV) so that the depositors of mainstream Islamic banking operations remain unaffected by the economic outcome of the SPE/SPV. It is logical to assume that some risk-neutral investors devoted to the Islamic faith live in society and prefer higher returns at the exchange of higher risk. These investors are unlikely to be tapped by the traditional Islamic banking system that offers benchmark returns to the investment account holders. Thus, independent VC firms are expected to become the effective vehicle to bring these risk-neutral investors into Islamic financial systems. We consider this strategy a less cumbersome alternative to a strategy of naively expecting Islamic banks to expand participatory financing, although the emergence of a large and diversified base of risk-neutral investors which are willing to sufficiently absorb various types of risk and uncertainty embedded in innovative start-ups is a prerequisite for the strategy (see Chapter 5 of this book for the reality in the Islamic VC industry).

Islamic banks are also facing the difficulty of sharing risk and uncertainty embedded in microfinance towards marginal clients. Recently, microfinance institutions (MFIs) such as Grameen Bank have got widespread coverage in empowering the poor. They appear to possess some comparative advantage in mitigating risks and uncertainties associated with their marginal clients. One of the important institutional settings for successful MFIs is to be able to raise concessional funds from the donors and NGOs enough to absorb the associated risk and uncertainty (see Chapter 7 of this book for the details). Although microfinance entails a huge potential and can simply be accommodated to the *Shari'ah* principles, the sector did not grow expectedly. Suzuki and Miah (2015) identify some critical constraints that restrict the growth of Islamic microfinance. They argue that the key constraint to the development of this segment of small-scale finance is the inadequate supply of funds. Although many Islamic microfinance institutes work under the auspices of Islamic banks, the supply of funds is very scanty *vis-à-vis* the demand (Suzuki and Miah, 2015).

Traditionally, financing needs of start-up firms were satisfied by the venture capitalists, while financing needs of marginal clients were nurtured by the initiatives of MFIs. In the same way, it would make sense to seek the 'division of work' and 'specialization' in Islamic finance. Islamic VC firms are expected to mobilize more 'risk funds' from a relatively large and diversified base of investors who are willing to absorb risk and uncertainty embedded in innovative start-ups. On the other hand, Islamic MFIs are expected to mobilize more 'concessional funds' from *waqf/zakat* or Islamic multinational financial organizations or donors who are ready to contribute to poverty alleviation by empowering the poor.

Given the nature of commercial banks as depository corporations, it makes sense for Islamic banks to concentrate on the mark-up based financing on their attempt to protect the welfare of depositors. This 'division of work' and 'specialization' strategy by Islamic banks would contribute to mediate more 'safety' idle money from the general risk-averse depositors who are limitedly willing to absorb risk and uncertainty, as well as meet the still-strong demand of asset-based investment, partly contributing to further economic development through the credit multiplier.

An expansion of participatory financing undertaken by Islamic VC or an increased participation of MFIs for catering to the financing needs of small and marginalized borrowers requires some issues, discussed in the following section, to be properly addressed.

4. Issues to be resolved for expanding participatory financing

4.1 *Mitigating agency problems*

The genesis of agency problems is the asymmetry of information and moral hazard problems. Thus, the key to mitigating agency problems lies in how to reduce these twin problems. In the developed countries, credit rating agencies reduce information asymmetry to a greater extent. Developing countries where most Islamic financial institutions are based lack this particular institution because the system would be excessively costly. This calls for an alternative mechanism to be devised. A national system of information repository can be maintained particularly for small and medium enterprises (SMEs), what can be called the 'SME Foundation'. This foundation would aim to keep record of relevant information about SMEs, especially their financing structure and the history of debt repayment habit. Moreover, the success of projects initiated by a particular entrepreneur can be accounted for.

Although this information is difficult to retrieve, cooperation among and between different branches of the state may facilitate necessary information collection. For instance, a start-up is required to receive a license from the concerned office of the country or region; it needs clearance from the central banks for applying for a loan; it is also supposed to acquire tax certificates for the business purpose. Digitalization of these systems can automatically track an entrepreneur and can generate some necessary information for any financiers to consider. An SME Foundation can be digitally linked to the information database of a particular entrepreneur. Based on different criteria, the SME Foundation can rank an individual's financial traits in a transparent manner which can be used by financial institutions such as VC or MFIs (also Islamic banks in financing *musharaka*) in deciding if it is logical to partner with an entrepreneur or finance the marginalized borrowers. Financial institutions would seriously consider the provided information because they can share the fortune of a successful project whereas entrepreneurs would be willing to provide data because doing so would enhance their chance of being financed.

Of course, the system mentioned earlier in the chapter is unlikely to check entrepreneurs' moral hazard once the project is financed. It is to be noted that asymmetry of information does not harm the contract if parties do not behave opportunistically. Williamson (1985) epitomizes the contracting problem admitting two important aspects of human behavior: bounded rationality and opportunism. If we assume that the human brain possesses unlimited calculative power, problems stemming from opportunism can be tackled by writing a comprehensive contract *ex ante*. Also, *ex post* opportunism can be averted by taking every future contingency into account. Similarly, if human behavior is non-opportunistic, contracting problems arising *ex post* due to bounded rationality can be overcome because parties have agreed to cooperate and disclose all the relevant information that affects the contract. Since human-bounded rationality should be admitted, effective PLS contracting requires that contracting parties do not behave opportunistically.

Moral hazard of entrepreneurs that hurts the interest of financiers, in most instances, may take the form of underreporting of profit or over invoicing of costs. These instances can be safeguarded by initiating an interim audit of the project. Financiers should have the discretion to initiate surprising audit as and when they deem fit. Provisions for imposing severe penalties can be prescribed in case the audit finds any anomalies in the profit or expense items which negatively affect the interest of financiers. A sincere and honest entrepreneur should have no objection to this provision. This arrangement would protect the interest of both parties in the contract. Also, two other necessary steps can be useful in mitigating the actor's moral hazard. First, strategies are to be made to reduce the unaccounted cash flow of any project; and second, attempts are to be made so that the level of discretionary cost is minimized. These strategies are believed to squeeze entrepreneurs' scope of over or underreporting of cash flows.

4.2 Trust and relation-based contracting

Islamic finance during the time of the Prophet and the subsequent Caliphates was based on *mudaraba*. Agency problems were not highly pronounced because most transactions were accomplished based on trust and morality. Abdul-Rahman et al. (2014) contend that trust was developed from the financier's knowledge of the entrepreneur's conviction to noble values and his esteemed personality. This informal institution reduces the designing and implementing cost of formal rules and regulations. Abdul-Rahman et al. (2014) further note that formal institutions unlikely to replace the deep-seated trust developed through interactions between financiers and entrepreneurs. The Muslim community, besides creating wealth in business, should be striving to achieve rewards for the life hereafter by being moral and honest. If so, entrepreneurs would be more compelling by putting their sincere efforts into making the project successful and revealing the true performance of firms.

Although trust is an intangible attribute and difficult to ascertain, lending and borrowing activities relying on trust and relation in the modern world are not rare either. For instance, Japan and Germany during their economic and financial heyday practiced a distinct financial system known as a 'relation-based' system. Unlike the Anglo-American market-based financial system in which the capital market meets the major financing needs of corporations, firms in the bank-based system rely extensively on the banking system to meet their financing needs. In Japan, a specific bank worked as a lead bank called the *main bank* (*hausbank* in Germany) that supplied the major share of a client's total external financing need. A tightly knit relationship between the main bank and a borrower facilitated the free flow of information as well as reduced moral hazard of the borrower. The system was incentive compatible in the sense that clients during their financial distress received financial and advisory assistance from the lending banks. In exchange, the lending banks used to enjoy 'rent' or more than competitive market rates during the high profit period of clients' firms. The foundation of the system relied on trust and cooperation between the interacting parties. They were committed to honor and respect the trust regardless of business outcome. Any breach in trust resulted in serious social and economic repercussion.

This trust-based relationship system is highly compatible with the participatory Islamic banking model. Toriqullah Khan (1995) argues that the contractual relationships and trust between parties are the two fundamental building blocks of an Islamic economic system. It is mentioned in the Holy Qur'an (Chapter 23, Verses 1 and 8) that "successful are the believers those who are faithfully true to their *amanat* (all the duties which Allah has ordained: honesty, moral responsibility, and trust) and to their covenants." Although cultural artifacts significantly influence the level of trust held by the members of a society, the Islamic mode of finance has the greater possibility to adapt to this system because the contracting parties themselves share similar characteristics, notably a common faith that affects their economic and financial behavior. Clients believing in the Islamic faith should disclose relevant information that affects the contract. If Islamic banks can build the trust exemplified by the Prophet and his companions, agency problems can be reduced to a greater extent.

Although less revealed and formally analyzed, trust- and relation-based financing are practiced in some instances. Abalkhail and Presley (2002) show that Saudi informal financiers rely heavily on the trust of their clients. Their study shows that among the top five entrepreneurial criteria, 'trust' ranks second after the entrepreneur's success in ventures in the past. Karim (2002) presents a case of Bank Muamalat showing that the bank has been successful in initiating *mudaraba* and *musharaka* financing through a cooperative financing system in which the bank has emphasized reducing the non-observable cash flow as well as discretionary expenses. Similarly, Sadr and Iqbal (2002) have investigated the nature of trust-based investment undertaken by Agriculture Bank of Iran (ABI). The authors argue that through continuous and frequent supervision, the ABI has established a very solid and trusting relationship with the partners. By investing in supervision, the bank seems to be able to learn about profitable investment opportunities in various agricultural regions and about the entrepreneurial and moral characteristics of its partners. They show that in 1996, an 80 percent recovery rate of the total outstanding debt was left over to the borrowers. Recovery rate on Islamic contracts is impressive and ranges between 95 and 99 percent. An insightful analysis of these cases is necessary to disintegrate the elements of trust contained in them for an expansion of Islamic participatory finance.

No doubt, trust and relations are intangible features of human beings which are susceptible to be exploited by any opportunist entrepreneur. Like the proverb 'good fences make good neighbors', strict formal regulations force people to be loyal and trustworthy. Thus, the level of trust in society is the function of its formal and informal rules. Formal rules should be updated and implemented effectively. On the other hand, there should be a system of informal punishment for breaking trust. The genesis of formal rules should start with the protection of one's rights.

4.3 Efficient structure of property rights

Well-defined property rights are a prerequisite for PLS contracts. Lenders or financiers' rights are at stake due to the lack of legal protection under the current mode of PLS. As hinted earlier, man-made rules are required because honesty and faith in the life hereafter are unobservable traits of human beings. The foundation of any man-made institution should be the institution of efficient property rights. Although Islamic tradition believes that the sole ownership of property remains to Allah and property owners in this world are simply the custodians, there is no prohibition of owning private property for the purpose of generating profit, creating employment, increasing investment and prosperity (Azid *et al.*, 2007). Strong property rights tend to provide financiers with a sense of security about the return of their investment and if possible with some addition. If financiers find *ex post* that entrepreneurs are shirking or hiding information that may hurt the interest of the financiers in the project, financiers can resort to the court to protect their interest. Strong enforcement of contracts may accompany the reduction of the moral hazard problem.

PLS contracts are deemed to be less attractive because property rights in most Muslim countries are not properly defined or protected (Farooq, 2007). It is not enough that the rules and regulations of a country are prevalent. It is important to ensure that these rules are pragmatic and implemented at the lowest cost. In the context of Islamic finance, there are many issues which may seem to be new or not historically practiced by the legal system in many societies. Thus, Islamic jurists should be equipped well with *fiqh* knowledge and modern financing techniques to clearly understand the respective rights in a contract. It is not uncommon that in many developing countries winding up or bankruptcy procedures of firms take years to be finished. Such a cumbersome legal system even if strong may not render expected services due to legal inertia or exorbitant costs. Thus, a strong and simplified nature of property rights should supplement the *Shari'ah* principles in this particular regard for expanding PLS-based finance.

4.4 Islamic jurisprudence on risk-hedging tools

Chapter 3 has outlined in detail the existing debate in regard to acceptable limits of *gharar*. Islam encourages participatory financing which is associated with fundamental uncertainty of entrepreneurs. On the other hand, *Shari'ah* rules prohibit economic agents from dealing with excessive *gharar*. Although Islamic jurists have distinguished between major or excessive *gharar* (El-Gamal, 2006), the problem is that the extent of uncertainty which makes any transaction *haram* has not been clearly defined (Ayub, 2007). Although this excuse should not be put forward to justify the current accumulation of mark-up financing of Islamic banks, non-clarity in regard to acceptable *gharar* may provide Islamic banks a moral ground to shun away from PLS-based financing.

Moreover, PLS-based financing is embedded in risk which financial institutions may wish to hedge through using some available financial mechanisms.

The conventional derivative products are unsuitable because they are most often involved with *maysir* (gambling). Although *Aurbun* is an allowed hedging technique, some *Madhabs* disagree on some clauses of *Aurbun*. It is essential that the Islamic *Fiqh* Council initiates an in-depth research on the analysis of Qur'anic terms and Prophetic Sunnah to arrive at a consensus in regard to issues which are currently not clearly understood by the general practitioners of Islamic finance. *Gharar* is one example of these blurred issues. At the same time, the *Fiqh* Council should come into a consensus through seeking experts' opinions on the suitable nature of derivatives permissible for Islamic financial institutions. If currently practiced derivatives are unsuitable for them the new risk-hedging tools should be invented.

Moreover, sustainable development of participatory finance requires long-term vision of developing Islamic scholars with the knowledge of finance. Morais (2007) reports that about 20 *Shari'ah* scholars are available worldwide who have the necessary stature to certify something as *Shari'ah* compliant. He further reports that these scholars sit on 40–50 *Shari'ah* boards each. Perhaps because of time constraints of these *Shari'ah* scholars, Khan (2010, p. 817) argues that they

> are satisfied if the IBF (Islamic Banking and Financial) institutions convince their customers that they are partaking in something exclusively Islamic, something that reinforces the borrower's 'Islamic identity' rather than in ensuring that the financial products on offer are truly different.

This requires international governing bodies to formulate policies on how to equip qualified Islamic scholars with financial knowledge.

4.5 Profit management

The current mark-up financing mode of Islamic banking is criticized on the ground that it is a costlier alternative to the conventional banking model (Kuran, 1996) in the sense that the model serves the same purpose as does the conventional banking model but the former incurs additional transaction costs because multiple parties' involvement is required to accomplish a single transaction. Despite this criticism, the mark-up financing is *Shari'ah* compliant whereas the conventional bank lending is not. In this sense, the mark-up model is better than a state of no-*Shari'ah* compliance financing for clients devoted to the Islamic faith.

Islamic banks have to compete with conventional banks in both the deposit and lending markets. While it is true that depositors and investors having faith in Islamic teaching should strive to comply with Islamic principles instead of looking for conventional alternatives, it is not clear whether this judgement can remain valid if the mainstream conventional alternatives offer higher returns on deposit and thinner interest on lending compared to Islamic banks. This compels Islamic banks to focus on mark-up financing which is considered less risky than the PLS financing in the sense that the return on debt-contracts is fixed whereas return on participatory financing is variable and uncertain.

As hinted earlier, given the risk-neutral characteristics of the depositors of Islamic banks, it is infeasible on the part of banks to function simply as intermediary between the depositors and the entrepreneurs so that banks can simply transfer the risk involved with the projects to the depositors. Although some studies find that Muslim depositors do not really care about a promised return for deposit (Abdullah *et al.*, 2016), the fact is not universal. Erol and El-Bdour (1989) find that religious motives did not stand out as being the major significant motive for depositors in considering motives responsible for selecting Islamic banks as depository institutions. This indicates that Islamic banks should offer depositors competitive rates in commensuration with conventional banks. Most Islamic banks thus stabilize the rate through managing profit. They create profit equalization reserves (PER) and investment risk reserves (IRR). During economic upturn which is expected to bring above average profit, Islamic banks retain a portion of this earning and distribute to the depositors in a year of comparatively bad returns on investment. Banks benchmark to the market interest rate in deciding an appropriate percentage on investment to be paid to depositors. Thus, it is not surprising that the return on deposits of Islamic banks coincides with the market rate.

Although this policy may hypothetically help banks avoid displaced commercial risk, such a profit management mechanisms is redundant at best because more than 90 percent of Islamic banks' financing is based on fixed or mark-up return. While the demand side of funds remains dominated by fixed returns, it is rather irrational to see neutralizing the fluctuation of return in the supply side. We argue that profit management mechanisms would be worth more if a reasonable amount of investment in Islamic banks takes place in the form of PLS such as *musharaka*. This implies that the current practice of profit management is irrelevant which would make great sense if Islamic banks participate reasonably in the participatory financing mode. Thus, *Shari'ah* boards should carefully permit PER and IRR of Islamic banks unless their PLS-based financing reaches a certain threshold.

5. Conclusion

Scholars of Islamic finance are in consensus that the true spirit of Islamic finance lies in the widespread use of PLS. The existing practice thus falls short of this expectation. In the equity-based Islamic financing model, banks as financial intermediaries can do very little to change the dominance of mark-up-based practices because the risk banks undertake by extending finance to investors can be shifted, in an ideal case, to the depositors if they are risk neutral. Islamic banks should face no difficulty in transferring the risk at this circumstance. On the contrary, if depositors are risk-averse, direct transfer of risk is infeasible. Here comes the role of banks. They absorb part of the investors' risk before shifting it to the depositors. Banking as an industry is very special and sensitive which means that banks possess only limited capacity for absorbing risk. Thus, it is logical for them to avoid risky investments to such an extent that does not defy the existing legal system. Since debt-like or *murabaha* financing is endorsed by the *Shari'ah* board as *Shari'ah* compliant, concentration of Islamic banks to this mode is rather a rational choice.

We have further argued that Islamic banking is a demand-driven industry which claims enormous popularity in Muslim-majority countries. Thus, any regulatory changes aiming to curb banks' reliance on *murabaha* financing may adversely affect the industry in different ways. For instance, any restriction on *murabaha* financing is likely to compel banks to gorge higher risk involved with participatory financing which may result in overall financial catastrophe. On the other hand, banks' strategy to transfer the risk to depositors may end up with losing the deposit base. Either way, the scarce fund will be dried up from the formal financial system. Based on this argument, we propose the division of work and specialization of Islamic banks in which the mainstream operations will remain mark-up dominant to protect the welfare of depositors whereas independent venture capital firms and microfinance institutes would dedicate themselves to catering to the equity financing needs of entrepreneurs and the financing of marginal clients, respectively.

Of course, Islamic banks can increase their participation in equity-based finance to a reasonable extent through *musharaka* contracts. However, some institutional settings are required to encourage banks as well as VCs and Islamic MFIs towards this end. Salient among them are instituting a strong property right so that all the parties' interests in the contract are adequately protected. We believe that a strong legal system should supplement the moral sentiment of financiers which may facilitate trust- and relation-based participatory finance. Furthermore, it is essential for Islamic scholars to endorse some risk-hedging financial tools. Since equity-based financing of Islamic banks is accompanied with higher risk, banks' risk-hedging strategy is vital to encourage Islamic banks for *musharaka* financing.

Conclusion

Yasushi Suzuki and Mohammad Dulal Miah

The phenomenal growth of Islamic finance in the last couple of decades has attracted considerable attention from scholars and policymakers alike. Various issues including the distinctive nature of Islamic finance, its impact on the development and stability of the financial system, the long-term sustainability of the model and its competitive advantage over the conventional counterpart occupy the center of academic discussion. One of the distinct characteristics of Islamic finance is risk sharing. The financier and the entrepreneur mutually absorb the risk involved with a project through equity and/or equity-like participation. This in turn results in the spread of venture firms leading to larger business activities and economic progress. While these expected benefits cannot be neglected, a large segment of the Muslim population has not yet fully embraced Islamic finance as a way of their economic lives due to various reasons. According to some scholars, the current practice of Islamic finance conforms less to the substance of Islamic teaching because Islamic finance is dominated by the banking industry that prefers debt-like financing over PLS contracts, although diversity in Islamic financial products, to some extent, very recently can be noted.

The book has attempted to explain the logic of *murabaha* or mark-up bias of Islamic banks. In so doing the book takes the view of modern banking theories which explain the sensitive nature of banks and the repercussion that may result from financial intermediaries' excessive risk appetite. An analysis of banking and financial fragility supports the proposition that most financial crises precede an event of excess risk-taking. In this sense, risk-neutral behavior of financial intermediaries augurs well for the economy. Just criticizing *murabaha* concentration or conservative behavior of Islamic banks is unfair at best.

On the other hand, conservative behavior of Islamic banks creates an obvious challenge as to how the Islamic financial system should be designed to expand equity-like PLS-based finance where Islamic banks, being the dominant players in the Islamic financial system, shy away from investing in the participatory mode. Unfolding this challenge occupies the central theme of the book. In the existing debate it has been argued that as long as *murabaha* is allowed without limit, Islamic banks are unlikely, and rationally so, to be engaged with equity-like PLS-based financing. The reason is that *murabaha* is an incentive-compatible mode of finance for Islamic banks in terms of risk–return tradeoff. At this circumstance, any attempt to increase the PLS-based Islamic finance may require regulatory authority either to emphasize other types of Islamic financial institutions or to impose an outright restriction on the use of *murabaha*.

The latter view is not economically convincing because there is no guarantee that a restriction on the use of *murabaha* is accompanied by an increase in PLS. Although *murabaha* contracts specify pre-agreed fixed returns it is the sale-based transaction which is allowed in Islamic *Shari'ah*. The asset-backed *murabaha* financing facilitates and supports the economic activities of, in particular, the merchants in the Muslim economy. In this perspective, restricting *murabaha* entails financial disintermediation which may prove to be welfare-reducing for the economy.

Thus, the general arguments of this book echo the proposition that an alternative mode of PLS system is welfare enhancing. In this regard, we have put our views towards a new mode of Islamic finance in the previous chapter. It is not an easy task to design an alternative mode of achieving a delicate balance in mobilizing funds from risk-averse depositors while creating and accumulating the wealth in society enough for incubating risk-neutral investors or donors who would be willing to absorb various types of risk and uncertainty exposed to innovative start-ups or to empower marginalized people. Now it is time to conclude our argument, which can be summarized as follows.

First, safety of the banking industry is utmost important for the greater stability of a financial system. Islamic banks as depository corporations have to pay the best effort to protect the welfare of their general depositors. As a consequence, suggesting Islamic banks to assume higher risk involved with trust-based *mudaraba* finance is less compelling. Due to their economic and social role of intermediating depositors' funds, the ethical mode of trust-based finance is unsuitable for Islamic banks. On the other hand, the participatory form of financing or *musharaka* would be feasible in accordance with the effective power retained by Islamic banks to monitor and discipline the clients or partners. However, under the current regulation for encouraging the mode of PLS, Islamic banks are not given adequate incentives to develop the 'hands-on' skill and knowledge necessary for the effective monitoring of entrepreneurs. This implies that under the current mode of PLS, Islamic banks are to be discouraged to engage in participatory *musharaka* financing, too.

Second, Islamic venture capital (VC) firms are expected to engage in participatory finance. However, the Islamic VC industry is still underdeveloped. Several cases of Islamic venture capital operating in different Muslim countries have been analyzed to show their contribution to the economy measured by various yardsticks. Also, the future prospects of these funds as well as the impediments that may come across their growth have been examined. The success of this industry depends on how to diversify and absorb the risk and uncertainty embedded in the innovative start-ups. It is mentioned that Islamic virtues of altruism and reciprocity urge wealthy individuals to help the fellow entrepreneurs who lack necessary financial strength to start a project. However, due to the difficulty of observing one's dedication to the religious belief, financiers who subscribe to a strong sense of reciprocity may be reluctant to finance the entrepreneurs. While individuals' moral commitment should be emphasized and respected, the book endorses the view that there is a need for designing institutions to protect the financier's rights in the contracts. In particular, the national system of property rights should be effectively implemented and simplified so that transaction costs remain low.

Third, Islamic banks show very little interest in financing small and marginalized borrowers. Since deposits are the major source of funds for banks, they must place all sorts of feasible attempts in securing assurance from the entrepreneurs that the promised amount will be recovered. Small borrowers, in most instances, fail to provide such reliable and feasible assurances because they lack tangible collateral or proven business track records. Taking these facts into account, the book portrays the role of Islamic microfinance institutes (MFI) to assess if they can cater to the needs of small and marginal borrowers. The success factors of conventional MFI have been singled out and examples have been presented showing how Islamic MFI can be remodelled for accomplishing this goal. One critical constraint highlighted in the book is that, unlike their conventional counterparts, Islamic MFI suffers from being short of funds. This has been attributed to the failure of these MFIs in their attempts to convince the potential donors about the distinct features as Islamic MFIs. There is a dilemma in which many Islamic MFIs are operated under the patronage of Islamic banks that are not always willing to undertake the credit risk of marginalized borrowers.

Apart from an idealistic view, the Islamic financial system should, in our view, take a trial-and-error process to evolve upon the 'specialization' and 'division of work' in credit risk screening activities and monitoring functions. In this context, Islamic banks should play a specialized function as depository corporations and fund providers mainly for small- and middle-sized merchants and manufacturers, Islamic VC firms should act as incubators, and Islamic MFIs should act as financial intermediaries for empowering marginalized clients. A policy prescription requiring tax advantages for incubating Islamic VC and microfinance industries should be paid more attention.

The book has also stressed the need for some key institutional design for mitigating multiple principal–agent problems embedded in Islamic finance. For instance, the book is unequivocal in suggesting the independence of *Shari'ah* boards. The current practice of the appointment and remuneration system may compromise boards' independence, at least 'in appearance' if not 'in practice'. The book has explicitly mentioned the feasibility of arranging payment to board members facilitated by the state mediators like the central bank or other such centrally governed enterprises, though governmental support only to the Islamic banks would cause another dilemma because the government has to ensure the 'level playing field' for fair competition in the industry including the conventional banks within the country. The governance system also entails a trial-and-error process to evolve.

The book emphasizes that there is no ready-made solution to the expansion of Islamic participatory finance and Islamic microfinance. It requires a concerted effort from the concerned stakeholders including market participants, regulatory authority, and *Shari'ah* boards. Participants' understanding on the divine reward and punishment as well as the moral and spiritual advantage derived from adopting the sacred concept of PLS and seeking for social justice is essential. At the same time, it is duly acknowledged that such institutional design for the expansion of PLS requires costs. The innate benefit derived from facilitating participatory finance, empowering the poor, and strengthening the governance structure is expected to outweigh the costs even in the economic sense.

References

AAOIFI (2002) 'Governance standard for Islamic financial institutions', No.5, Manama.

AAOIFI (2003) *Sharia Standard No. 17, Investment Sukuk*. Accounting and Auditing Organization for Islamic Financial Institutions (AAOIFI), Manama, Bahrain

Abalkhail, M., and Presley, J. (2002) 'How Informal Risk Capital Investors Manage Asymmetric Information in Profit/Loss-Sharing Contracts, in Iqbal, M., and Llewellyn, D. (eds.) *Islamic Banking and Finance: New Perspectives on Profit Sharing and Risk*. Cheltenham: Edward Elgar, pp. 111–134.

Abduh, M. (2016) *Foundation of Islamic Finance*. Kuala Lumpur: IIUM Press.

Abdullah, S., Hassan, S., and Masron, T. (2016) 'Switching Intention of Muslim Depositors in Islamic Deposit Account', *International Journal of Economics, Management and Accounting*, 24(1), pp. 83–106.

Abdul-Rahman, A., Latif, R. A., Muda, R., and Abdullah, M. A. (2014) 'Failure and Potential of Profit-Loss Sharing Contracts: A Perspective of New Institutional Economics (NIE) Theory', *Pacific-Basin Finance Journal*, 28, pp. 136–151.

Abozaid, A., and Dusuki, A. W. (2007) 'The Challenges of Realizing Maqasid Al-Shariah in Islamic Banking and Finance', paper presented at the *International Conference on Islamic Banking and Finance Research and Development*, Kuala Lumpur, 23–25 April, 2007.

Abu Zaharah, M. (1997) *Usul al-Fiqh*. Cairo, Dar al-Fikr al-Arabi.

Adam, N. L., and Bakar, N. A. (2014) 'Shariah Screening Process in Malaysia', *Procedia – Social and Behavioral Sciences*, 121, pp. 113–123.

Adams, D., and von Pischke, J. D. (1992) Microenterprise Credit Programs: Deja vu. *World Development*, 20, pp. 1463–1470.

Aggarwal, R., and Yousef, T. (2000) 'Islamic Banks and Investment Financing', *Journal of Money, Credit and Banking*, 32(1), pp. 93–120.

Ahmad, A. (1993) 'Contemporary Practices of Islamic Financing Techniques' Islamic Development Bank', *Islamic Research and Training Institute Research Paper #20*, retrieved from http://ieaoi.ir/files/site1/pages/ketab/english_book/contemporary_practices_of_islamic_financing_techniques.pdf (on October 15, 2017).

Ahmad, K. (1980) *Studies in Islamic Economics*. Leicester: Palgrave Macmillan.

Ahmed, E., Islam, A., Alabdullah, T., and Ariffin, K. (2015) 'Islamic *Sukuk*: Pricing Mechanism and Rating', *The Social Sciences*, 10(2), pp. 178–183.

Ahmed, H. (2002) 'Financing Microenterprises: An Analytical Study of Islamic Microfinance Institutions', Islamic Economic Studies, 9(2), pp. 27-64.

Ahmed, S. (2009) 'Microfinance Institutions in Bangladesh: Achievements and Challenges', *Managerial Finance*, 35(12), pp. 999–1010.

Ali, A. E. E. S. (2015) 'Islamic Microfinance: Moving Beyond Financial Inclusion', *European Scientific Journal*, 11(10), pp. 297–310.

Ali, S. S. (2011) 'Islamic Banking in MENA Region, Financial Flagship', *Islamic Research and Training Institute*, World Bank, retrieved from http://siteresources.worldbank.org/INTMNAREGTOPPOVRED/Resources/MENAFlagshipIslamicFinance2_24_11.pdf (on October 19, 2017).

Al-Mubarak, T. (2011) 'Rural Development Scheme (RDS) of the Islamic Bank Bangladesh Limited (IBBL) and the Conventional Microfinance Institutes in Bangladesh: A Comparative Analysis', paper presented at 2nd International Conference on Inclusive Islamic Financial Sector Development, held on 9-11 October at Khartoum, Sudan

Al-Qaradawi, Y. (2013) *The Lawful and the Prohibited in Islam*, (translated by Kamal El-Helbawy, Moinuddin Siddiqui, Syed, Shukry). Kuala Lumpur: Islam, Islamic Book Trust.

Al-Saati, A. R. (2003) 'The Permissible Gharar (Risk) in Classical Islamic Jurisprudence', *Journal of King Abdulaziz University: Islamic Economics*, 16(2), pp. 3–19.

Alzahrani, M., and Megginson, W. L. (2017) 'Finance as Worship: A Survey of Islamic Finance Research', *CEIF Discussion Paper (4/2017)*, retrieved from https://ssrn.com/abstract=2967619 (on September 12, 2017).

Amanullah, M. (2015) 'Criteria of Sharī'ah Supervisory Committee: A Comparative Study between Guidelines of Bangladesh Bank and Bank Negara Malaysia', *Intellectual Discourse*, 23, pp. 453–473.

Amit, R., Brandera, J., and Zotta, C. (1998) 'Why Do Venture Capital Firms Exist? Theory and Canadian Evidence', *Journal of Business Venturing*, 13(6), pp. 441–466.

Angkinand, A. (2009) 'Banking Regulation and the Output Cost of Banking Crises,' *Journal of International Financial Markets, Institutions and Money*, 19(2): pp. 240–257.

Anwar, S., and Ismal, R. (2011) 'Robustness Analysis of Artificial Neural Networks and Support Vector Machine in Making Prediction', Paper presented in *The 9th IEEE International Symposium on Parallel and Distributed Processing With Applications*, Busan, Korea, 26–28 May, 2011.

Anwar, S., and Mikami, Y. (2011) 'Comparing Accuracy Performance of ANN, MLR, and GARCH Model in Predicting Time Deposit Return of Islamic Bank', *International Journal of Trade, Economics and Finance*, 2(1), pp. 44–51.

Archer, S., and Karim, R. A. A. (2006) 'Corporate Governance, Market Discipline, and Regulation of Islamic Banks', *The Company Lawyer*, 27(5), pp. 134–145.

Archer, S., and Karim, R. A. A. (2007) 'Specific Corporate Governance Issues in Islamic Banks', in Archer, S., and Karim, R. (eds.) *Islamic Finance: The Regulatory Challenge*. Singapore: John Wiley & Sons (Asia), pp. 310–341.

Ariff, M., and Rosly, S. (2011) 'Islamic Banking in Malaysia: Unchartered Waters', *Asian Economic Policy Review*, 6(2), pp. 301–319.

Arikan, A. T. (2008) 'Institutional Transformation during the Emergence of New York's Silicon Valley', in Phan, P., Venkataraman, S., and Velamuri, S. (eds.) *Entrepreneurship in Emerging Regions Around the World Theory, Evidence and Implications*. Cheltenham: Edward Elgar Publishing Limited, pp. 92–121.

Arrow, K. (1974) *The Limits of Organization*. New York: W.W. Norton.

Ashraf, M. A., and Ibrahim, Y. B. (2013) 'An Investigation into the Barrier to the Rural Poor Participation in MFIs: The Case of Bangladesh', *International Journal*, 1(2), pp. 1–17.

Asian Development Bank (2017) *Basis Statistics 2017*, Economic Research and Regional Cooperation Department, Asian Development Bank. Retrieve from www.adb.org/sites/default/files/publication/298061/basic-statistics-2017.pdf (on September 24, 2017).

Asutay, M. (2012) 'Conceptualizing and Locating the Social Failure of Islamic Finance: Aspirations of Islamic Moral Economy vs. the Realities of Islamic Finance', *Asian and African Area Studies*, 11(2), pp. 93–113.

Asutay, M., and Harningtyas, A. F. (2015) 'Developing Maqasid Al-Shari'ah Index to Evaluate Social Performance Of Islamic Banks: A Conceptual And Empirical Attempt', *International Journal of Islamic Economics and Finance Studies*, 1(1), 5–64.

Audretsch, D. B., Bonte, W., and Mahagaonkar, P. (2012) 'Financial Signaling by Innovative Nascent Ventures: The Relevance of Patents and Prototypes', *Research Policy*, 41(8), pp. 1407–1421.

Ayub, M. (2007) *Understanding Islamic Finance*. West Sussex: John Wiley & Sons.

Ayub, M. (n.d.) 'Derivatives and Islamic Finance', Working Paper, State Bank of Pakistan Karachi, retrieved from www.sbp.org.pk/departments/ibd/derivatives_islamic.pdf (on 30 August, 2012).

Azid, T., Asutay, M., and Burki, U. (2007) 'Theory of the Firm, Management and Stakeholders: An Islamic Perspective', *Islamic Economic Studies*, 15(1), pp. 1–30.

Bahrain Islamic Venture Capital Report (2016) *Venture Capital: Building the Next Phase of Economic Development in Bahrain*. Bahrain: Thomson Reuters.

Bakar, M. D. (2016) *Shariah Minds in Islamic Finance: An Inside Story of A Shariah Scholar*. Kuala Lumpur: Amanie Media.

Bakar, M. D. (2017) *An Insightful Journey into Emirates Airline Sukuk: Pushing the Boundaries of Islamic Finance*. Kuala Lumpur: Amanie Media.

Bangladesh Bank (2016), Bangladesh Bank Annual Report 2015-2016 (Financial Market, chapter 8), retrived from https://www.bb.org.bd/pub/annual/anreport/ar1516/chap8.pdf (on September 12, 2017)

Bangladesh Bank (various years), *Annual Report*, Bangladesh Bank archive, retrived from https://www.bb.org.bd/pub/publictn.php (on Jnaury 12, 2018).

Bank Indonesia. (2009) *Indonesian Islamic Banking Outlook 2010*. Jakarta: Bank Indonesia.

Bank Indonesia. (2016) *Pemetaan dan Strategi Peningkatan Daya Saing UMKM dalam Menghadapi Masyarakat Ekonomi ASEAN (MEA) 2015 dan Pasca MEA 2025*. Jakarta: Bank Indonesia, retrieved from www.bi.go.id/id/umkm/penelitian/nasional/kajian/Documents/Pemetaan%20dan%20Strategi%20Peningkatan%20Daya%20Saing%20UMKM%20dalam%20Menghadapi%20Masyarakat%20Ekonomi%20ASEAN%20(2015)%20dan%20Pasca%20MEA%202025.pdf (on October 24, 2017).

Bank Negara Malaysia. (2010) *Shari'ah Governance Framework for the Islamic Financial Institutions 2010*. Bank Negara Malaysia.

Bank Negara Malaysia. (2016) *Global Sukuk market: A Record Year of Sukuk Issuance*. Kuala Lumpur: Bank Negara Malaysia.

Bank Negara Malaysia, and Suruhanjaya Sekuriti. (2009) *Malaysian Debt Securities and Sukuk Market*. Kuala Lumpur: Bank Negara Malaysia.

Bappenas. (2014) *Masterplan Arsitektur Keuangan Syariah di Indonesia*. Jakarta: Badan Perencanaan Pembangunan Nasional (Bappenas).

Beck, T., Demirgüç-Kunt, A., and Merrouche, O. (2013) 'Islamic vs. Conventional Banking: Business Model, Efficiency and Stability', *Journal of Banking & Finance*, 37(2), pp. 433–447.

Bergemann, D., and Hege, U. (1997) 'Venture Capital Financing, Moral Hazard and Learning', *CentER Discussion Papers*, Vol.108, Tilburg University.

Berger, A., and Udell, G. (1998) 'The Economics of Small Business Finance: The Roles of Private Equity and Debt Markets in the Financial Growth Cycle', *Journal of Banking & Finance*, 22(6), pp. 613–673.

Bertoni, F., Colombo, M. G., and Grilli, L. (2011) 'Venture Capital Financing and the Growth of Hightech Start-ups: Disentangling Treatment from Selection Effects', *Research Policy*, 40(7), pp. 1028–1043.

Bertoni, F., Ferrer, M. A., and Martí, J. (2013) 'The Different Role Played by Venture Capital and Private Equity Investors on the Investment Activity of Their Portfolio Firms', *Small Business Economics*, 40(3), pp. 607–633.

Besley, T., and Coate, S. (1995) 'Group Lending, Repayment Incentives and Social Collateral', *Journal of Development Economics*, 46(1), pp. 1–18.

Bhambra, H. (2007) 'Supervisory Implications of Islamic Finance in the Current Regulatory Environment', in Archer, S., and Karim, R. (eds.) *Islamic Finance: The New Regulatory Challenge*. Singapore: John Wiley & Sons, pp. 198–212.

Block, H. J., Fisch, C. O., and Praag, M. V. (2017) 'The Schumpeterian Entrepreneur: A Review of the Empirical Evidence on the Antecedents, Behavior and Consequences of Innovative Entrepreneurship', *Industry and Innovation*, 24(1), pp. 61–95.

Boateng, I. A., and Agyei, A. (2013) 'Microfinance in Ghana: Development, Success Factors and Challenges', *International Journal of Academic Research in Accounting, Finance and Management Sciences*, 3(4), pp. 153–160.

Bond Pricing Agency Malaysia. (2015) *Malaysia Bond and Sukuk Almanac*. Kuala Lumpur: Bond Pricing Agency Malaysia.

Bowles, S. (2012) *The New Economics of Inequality and Redistribution*. New York: Cambridge University Press.

Broughman, B. (2010), 'Investor Opportunism, and Governance in Venture Capital', in Cumming, D. J. (ed.) *Venture Capital: Investment Strategies, Structures, and Policies*. Hoboken, NJ: John Wiley & Sons, Inc. pp. 347–346.

Buckley, G. (1997) 'Microfinance in Africa: Is It Either the Problem or the Solution?', *World Development*, 25 (7), pp. 1081–1094.

Calomiris, C. W., and Haber, S. H. (2014) *Fragile by Design: The Political Origins of Banking Crises and Scarce Credit*. Princeton: Princeton University Press.

Caprio, G., and Klingebiel, D. (2002) 'Episodes of Systemic and Borderline Banking Crises', in Klingebiel, D., and Laeven, L. (eds.) *Managing the Real and Fiscal Effects of Banking Crises*. Washington, DC: The World Bank, pp. 31–49.

Castanhar, J. C., Dias, J. F., and Esperança J. P. (2008) 'The Entrepreneurial Drivers of Regional Economic Transformation in Brazil, in Phan, P., Venkataraman, S., and Velamuri, S. (eds.) *Entrepreneurship in Emerging Regions around the World Theory Evidence and Implications*. Cheltenham: Edward Elgar Publishing Limited, pp. 47–91.

Chang, H. (2000) 'The Hazard of Moral Hazard: Untangling the Asian Crisis', *World Development*, 28(4), pp. 775–788.

Chapra, M. U. (1992) *Islam and the Economic Challenge*. Leicester: Islamic Foundation

Chapra, U. (2002) 'Alternative Visions of International Monetary Reform', in Iqbal, M., and Llewellyn, D. (eds.), *Islamic Banking and Finance: New Perspectives on Profit Sharing and Risk*, Cheltenham: Edward Elgar, pp. 219–238.

Chemmanur, T. J., Krishnan, K., and Nandy, D. K. (2011) 'How does Venture Capital Financing Improve Efficiency in Private Firms? A Look beneath the Surface', *Review of Financial Studies*, 24(12), pp. 4037–4090.

Choiruzzad, S. A. B. and Nugroho, B. E. (2013) 'Indonesia's Islamic Economy Project and the Islamic Scholars', *Procedia Environmental Science*, 17, pp. 957–966.

Chong, B., and Liu, M. (2009) 'Islamic Banking: Interest-Free or Interest-Based?', *Pacific-Basin Finance Journal*, 17(1), pp. 125–144.

Choudhury, M. A. (2001) 'Islamic Venture Capital: A Critical Examination', *Journal of Economic Studies*, 28(1), pp. 14–33.

Choudhury, M. A. (2007) 'Development of Islamic Economic and Social Thought', in Hassan, K., and Lewis, M. (eds.) *Handbook of Islamic Banking*. Cheltenham: Edward Elgar, pp. 21–37.

Chung, S., Choi, Y. K., Lee, J., Park, S., and Shin, H. (2008) 'Policy Intervention in the Development of the Korean Venture Capital Industry', in Phan, P., Venkataraman, S., and Velamuri, S. (eds.) *Entrepreneurship in Emerging Regions Around the World Theory, Evidence and Implications*. Cheltenham: Edward Elgar Publishing Limited, pp. 206–236.

Çizakça, M. (2011) *Islamic Capitalism and Finance: Origins, Evolution and the Future*. Cheltenham: Edward Elgar.

Cohen, D., and Knetsch, J. L. (1992) 'Judicial Choice and Disparities between Measures of Economic Values', in Kahneman, D., and Tversky, A. (eds.) *Choices, Values, and Frames*. Cambridge: Cambridge University Press, pp. 424–450.

Colombo, M. G., and Grilli, L. (2010) 'On Growth Drivers of High-tech Start-ups: The Role of Founders' Human Capital and Venture Capital', *Journal of Business Venturing*, 25(6) pp. 610–626.

Consultative Group to Assist the Poor. (2008) *CGAP Annual Report 2008*. Retrieve from: www.cgap.org/publications/cgap-annual-report-2008 (on September 20, 2017).

Conti, A., Thursby, M., and Rothaermel, F. T. (2013) 'Show Me the Right Stuff: Signals for High-tech Startups', *Journal of Economics & Management Strategy*, 22(2), pp. 341–364.

Cosh, A., and Hughes, A. (Eds.) (2003) *Enterprise Challenged: Policy and Performance in the British SME Sector 1999–2002*. Cambridge: ESRC Centre for Business Research.

Cowling, M., Liu, W., and Ledger, A. (2012) 'Small Business Financing in the UK Before and During the Current Financial Crisis', *International Small Business Journal*, 30(7), pp. 778–800.

Crotty, J. (2005) 'The Neoliberal Paradox: the Impact of Destructive Product Market Competition and "Modern" Financial Markets on Nonfinancial Corporation Performance in the Neoliberal Era,' in Epstein, G. (ed.) *Financialization and the World Economy*. Aldershot: Edward Elgar, pp. 77–110.

Cumming, D. J. (2005) 'Agency Costs, Institutions, Learning, and Taxation in Venture Capital Contracting', *Journal of Business Venturing*, 20(5), pp. 573–622.

Dar, H. A., and Presley, J. R. (2000) 'Lack of Profit Loss Sharing in Islamic Banking: Management and Control Imbalances', *International Journal of Islamic Financial Services*, 2(2), pp. 3–18.

Davis, E. P. (1995) *Debt Financial Fragility and Systemic Risk*. Oxford: Clarendon Press.

Deloach, S. B., and Lamanna, E. (2011) 'Measuring the Impact of Microfinance on Child Health Outcomes in Indonesia', *World Development*, 39(10), pp. 1808–1819.

Desiere, S., Vellema, W., and D'Haese, M. (2015) 'A Validity Assessment of the Progress Out of Poverty Index', *Evaluation and Program Planning*, 49, pp. 10–18.

Dewan Syariah Nasional-Majelis Ulama Indonesia, and Bank Indonesia (2006) *Himpunan Fatwa DSN-MUI*, Jakarta: DSN MUI-BI.

Dewi, M. K., and Kasri, R. A. (2011) 'SMEs Financing Innovation Application of Hawalah in Islamic Cooperative', *International Journal of Excellence in Islamic Banking and Finance*, 1(2), pp. 1–15.

Dogarawa, A. B. (2011) 'Financial Inclusion in Nigeria and the Prospects and Challenges of Islamic Microfinance Banks', retrieved from https://papers.ssrn.com/sol3/papers.cfm?abstract_id=1956653 (on July 12, 2017).

Dore, R. (2000) Stock Market Capitalism: Welfare Capitalism, Japan and Germany versus the Anglo-Saxons, Oxford: Oxford University Press.

Dore, R. (2008) 'Financialization of the Global Economy', *Industrial and Corporate Change*, 17(6), pp. 1097–1112.

Dore, R. (2011) *Kinyu Ga Nottoru Sekai Keizai*. Tokyo: Chuko-shinsho.

Drucker, P. F. (1985) *Innovation and Entrepreneurship: Practices and Principles*. New York: Harper & Row Publishers Inc.

Durrani, M. (2006) 'Business Ethics and Venture Capital in Islam', in Durrani, M., and Boocock, G. (eds.) *Venture Capital, Islamic Finance and SMEs: Valuation, Structuring and Monitoring Practices in India*. Basingstoke: Palgrave Macmillan, pp. 148–169.

Dusuki, A. W. (2007) 'The Ideal of Islamic Banking: A Survey of Stakeholders' Perceptions', *Review of Islamic Economics*, 11(3), pp. 1–32.

Dymski, G. (1993) 'Keynesian Uncertainty and Asymmetric Information: Complementary or Contradictory', *Journal of Post Keynesian Economics*, 16(1), pp. 49–54.

El Tiby, A. M. (2011) *Islamic Banking: How to Manage Risk and Improve Profitability*. New York: Wiley.

El-Gamal, A. M. (2006) *Islamic Finance: Law, Economics, and Practice*. Cambridge: Cambridge University Press.

Elsiefy, E. (2013) 'Towards a Model for Islamic Venture Capital', *Business Journal for Entrepreneurs*, 1(1), pp. 39–56.

Elsiefy, E. (2014) 'Fundamental Requirements for Building an Islamic Venture Capital Model', *Accounting and Finance Research*, 3(1), pp. 55–66.

Elster, J. (2006) 'Altruistic Behaviour and Altruistic Motivations', in Serge-Christophe K., and Ythier, J. M. (eds.) *Handbook of the Economics of Giving, Altruism and Reciprocity*, Vol. 1. Amsterdam: Elsevier, pp. 183–206.

Englund, P. (1999) 'The Swedish Banking Crisis: Roots and Consequences', *Oxford Review of Economic Policy*, 15(3), pp. 80–97.

Epstein, G., and Power, D. (2003) 'Rentier Incomes and Financial Crises: An Empirical Examination of Trends and Cycles in Some OECD Countries', *Canadian Journal of Development Studies*, 29(2), pp. 230–248.

Erhardt, E. C. (2017) 'Microfinance Beyond Self-Employment: Evidence For Firms in Bulgaria', *Labour Economics*, 47, pp. 75–95.

Erol, C., and El-Bdour, R. (1989) 'Attitudes, Behaviour, and Patronage Factors of Bank Customers towards Islamic Banks', *International Journal of Bank Marketing*, 7(6), pp. 31–37.

Eslter, J. (1986) *An Introduction to Karl Marx.* Cambridge: Cambridge University Press.

Farook, S., and Farooq, M. O. (2011) 'Shariah Governance for Islamic Finance: Challenges and Pragmatic Solutions', Working Paper, Bahrain Institute of Banking and Finance.

Farooq, M. O. (2009) 'The Riba-Interest Equation and Islam: Reexamination of the Traditional Arguments', *Global Journal of Finance and Economics*, 6(2), pp. 99–111.

Farooq, M. O. (2012) 'Exploitation, Profit and the Riba-Interest Reductionism', *International Journal of Islamic and Middle Eastern Finance and Management*, 5(4), pp. 292–320.

Farooq, O. (2007) 'Partnership, Equity Financing, and Islamic Finance: Whither Profit Loss Sharing?', *Review of Islamic Economics*, 11, pp. 67–88.

Financial Reporting Council. (2016) *The UK Corporate Governance Code.* London: The Financial Reporting Council Company Limited.

Financial Services Agency. (2012) *Taxation of J-Sukuk Q&A*, retrieved from www.al-mirsal.com/files/2012/06/Taxation-of-J-Sukuk-QA1.pdf (on September 12, 2017).

Financial Services Authority. (2016a) Finance Institutions Statistics 2015. Jakarta: FSA, Indonesia, retrieved from www.ojk.go.id/id/kanal/iknb/data-dan-statistik/lembaga-pembiayaan/Documents/Buku%20Statistik%20Lembaga%20Pembiayaan%202015.pdf (on August 09, 2017).

Financial Services Authority. (2016b) Indonesian Banking Statistics 2015. Jakarta: FSA, Indonesia, retrieved from http://www.ojk.go.id/en/kanal/perbankan/data-dan-statistik/statistik-perbankan-indonesia/Documents/Pages/Indonesia-Banking-Statistic-December-2015/Indonesia%20Banking%20Statistic%20December%202015.pdf (on August 09, 2017).

Financial Services Authority. (2017a) Finance Institutions Statistics 2016. Jakarta: FSA, Indonesia, retrieved from www.ojk.go.id/id/kanal/iknb/data-dan-statistik/lembaga-pembiayaan/Documents/Pages/Buku-Statistik-Lembaga-Pembiayaan-2016/Buku%20Statistik%20Lembaga%20Pembiayaan%202016.pdf (on September 10, 2017).

Financial Services Authority. (2017b) Indonesian Banking Statistics 2016. Jakarta: FSA, Indonesia, retrieved from http://www.ojk.go.id/en/kanal/perbankan/data-dan-statistik/statistik-perbankan-indonesia/Documents/Pages/Indonesia-Banking-Statistics---December-2016/SPI%20December%202016.pdf (on September 10, 2017).

Fine, B., and Saad-Filho, A. (2004) *Marx's Capital.* London: Pluto Press.

Fisher, M. S. (2011) *Are Muslims Distinctive: A Look at the Evidence.* Oxford: Oxford University Press.

Fong, C. M. (2007) 'Evidence From an Experiment on Charity to Welfare Recipients: Reciprocity, Altruism, and the Empathic Responsiveness Hypothesis', *The Economic Journal*, 117, pp. 1008–1024.

Foster, J. B. (2007) 'The Financialization of Capitalism', *Monthly Review*, 58(11), pp. 1–12.

Frank, H. K. (1921) *Risk, Uncertainty and Profit.* Boston: Hart, Schaffner & Marx, Houghton Mifflin Co.

Fraser, S. (2005) *Finance for Small and Medium Sized Enterprises: A Report on the 2004 UK Survey of SME Finances.* Warwick Business School, Coventry.

Fukuyama, F. (1995) *Trust: The Social Virtues and the Creation of Prosperity.* New York: Free Press.

Garas, S. N. and Pierce, C. (2010) 'The Independence of the *Shari'ah* Supervisory Board in the Islamic Financial Institutions of the GCC countries', *Corporate Board: Role, Duties & Composition*, 6(2), pp. 20–34.

Ginena, K., and Hamid, A. (2015) *Foundations of Shari'ah Governance of Islamic Banks.* West Sussex: John Wiley & Sons Ltd.

Gintzburger, A. S. (2011) 'An Analysis of Global Trends and Regional Pockets in the Application of Islamic Financial Contracts in Malaysia and the Gulf Cooperation Council', in Hassan, K., and Mahlknecht, M. (eds.) *Islamic Capital Markets: Products and Strategies.* West Sussex: John Wiley & Sons, pp. 307–339.

Glaubitt, K., Hagen, H. M., Feist, J., and Beck, M. (2008) 'Reducing Barriers to Microfinance Investments: The Role of Structured Finance', in Matthäus-Maier, I., and Pischke, J. (eds.) *New Partnerships for Innovation in Microfinance.* Berlin: Springer, pp. 349–378.

Godlewski, C. J., Turk-Ariss, R., and Weill, L. (2013) '*Sukuk* vs. Conventional Bonds: A Stock Market Perspective', *Journal of Comparative Economics*, 41, pp. 745–761.

Goetz, A. M., and Gupta, R. S. (1996) 'Who Takes The Credit? Gender, Power, and Control Over Loan Use in Rural Credit Programs in Bangladesh', *World Development*, 24(1), pp. 45–63.

Gompers, P. A., and Lerner, J. (1999a) *The Venture Capital Cycle.* Cambridge: MIT Press.

Gompers, P. A., and Lerner, J. (1999b) 'An Analysis of Compensation in the U.S. Venture Capital Partnership', *Journal of Financial Economics*, 51(1), pp. 3–44.

Gompers, P. A., and Lerner, J. (2001) 'The Venture Capital Revolution', *Journal of Economic Perspectives*, 15(2), pp. 145–168.

Grassa, R. (2013) 'Shariah Supervisory System in Islamic Financial Institutions New Issues and Challenges: A Comparative Analysis between Southeast Asia Models and GCC Models', *Humanomics*, 29(4), pp. 333–348.

Grassa, R., and Miniauoi, H. (2017) 'Corporate Choice between Conventional Bond and Sukuk Issuance: Evidence From GCC Countries', *Research in International Business and Finance*, retrieved from http://dx.doi.org/10.1016/j.ribaf.2017.07.179 (on August 23, 2017).

Green, W. S. (2005), 'Introduction: Altruism and the Study of the Religion', in Nuesner, J., and Chilton, B. (eds.) *Altruism in World Religions.* Washington, DC: Georgetown University Press.

Hammond, P. (1975), 'Charity: Altruism or Cooperative Egoism?', in Edmund, S. P. (ed.), *Altruism, Morality, and Economic Theory.* New York: Russell Sage, pp. 115–131.

Hamoudi, H. (2007) 'Muhammad's Social Justice or Muslim Cant: Langdellianism and the Failures of Islamic Finance', *Cornell International Law Journal*, 40(1), pp. 90–133.

Hamza, H. (2013) 'Sharia Governance in Islamic Banks: Effectiveness and Supervision Model', *International Journal of Islamic and Middle Eastern Finance and Management*, 6(3), pp. 226–237.

Hamza, H. (2016) 'Does Investment Deposit Return in Islamic Banks Reflect PLS Principle?', *Borsa Istanbul Review*, 16(1), pp. 32–42.

Haque, M. S., and Yamao, M. (2011) 'Prospects and Challenges of Islamic Micro-finance Programmes: A Case Study in Bangladesh', *International Journal of Economic Policy in Emerging Economies*, 4(1), pp. 95–111.

Haron, S., and Azmi, N. (2009) *Islamic Finance Banking System*. Singapore: McGraw-Hill.

Hasan, B. R., Mikail, S. A., and Arifin, M. (2011) 'Islamic Law, Historical Development of Islamic Venture Capital: An Appraisal', *Journal of Applied Sciences Research*, 7(13), pp. 2377–2384.

Hasan, Z. (2014) *Islamic Banking and Finance: An Integrated Approach*. Oxford: Oxford University Press.

Hassan, K. (2010) 'An Integrated Poverty Alleviation Model Combining Zakat, Awaqaf, and Micro-finance', paper presented at the *Seventh International Conference – The Tawhidi Epistemology: Zakat and Waqf Economy*, Bangi, Malaysia, 6–7 January, 2010.

Hassan, Z. (2012) *Shari'ah Governance in Islamic Banks*. Edinburgh: Edinburgh University Press.

Healy, P. M., and Palepu, K. G. (2001) 'Information Asymmetry, Corporate Disclosure, and the Capital Markets: A Review of the Empirical Disclosure Literature', *Journal of Accounting and Economics*, 31(1), pp. 405–440.

Hellmann, T., and Puri, M. (2000) 'The Interaction between Product Market and Financing Strategy: The Role of Venture Capital', *Review of Financial Studies*, 13(4), pp. 959–984.

Hellmann, T., and Puri, M. (2002) 'Venture Capital and the Professionalization of Start-Up Firms: Empirical Evidence', *The Journal of Finance*, 57(1), pp. 169–197.

Hirukawa, M., and Ueda, M. (2011) 'Venture Capital and Innovation: Which is First?', *Pacific Economic Review*, 16(4), pp. 421–465.

Holcombe, S. (1995) *Managing to Empower: The Grameen Bank's Experience of Poverty Alleviation*. London: Zed Press.

Homerin, L. E. (2005) 'Altruism in Islam', in Nuesner, J., and Chilton, B. (eds.) *Altruism in World Religions*. Washington, DC: Georgetown University Press, pp. 67–87.

Honohan, P., and Klingebiel, D. (2003) 'The Fiscal Cost Implications of an Accommodating Approach to Banking Crises,' *Journal of Banking & Finance*, 27(8), pp. 1539–1560.

Hossain, M. (1988) *Credit for Alleviation of Rural Poverty: The Grameen Bank in Bangladesh*. Washington, DC: IFPRI

Hossain, M. B. T., Siwar, C., and Al-Mubarak, T. (2008) 'Determination of The Efficiency Ways Microfinance For Islamic Bank To Eliminate Poverty: An Empirical Investigation', *Working Papers in Islamic Economics and Finance*, No. WIEF0826, University Kebangsaan Malaysia (UKM), Selangor, Malaysia.

HSBC Bank Malaysia Berhad. (2015) 'Japan Is Right To Seek *Sukuk* Success', *News Release on 27 April 2015*, retrieved from www.hsbc.com.my (on July 12, 2017).

Hsu, H. D. (2004) 'What Do Entrepreneurs Pay for Venture Capital Affiliation?', *Journal of Finance*, 59(4), pp. 1805–1844.

Hsu, H. D. (2007) 'Experienced Entrepreneurial Founders, Organizational Capital, and Venture Capital Funding', *Research Policy*, 36 (5), pp. 722–741.

Hsu, H. D., and Ziedonis, R. H. (2013) 'Resources as Dual Sources of Advantage: Implications for Valuing Entrepreneurial-Firm Patents', *Strategic Management Journal*, 34(7), pp. 761–781.

Hulme, D. (2000) 'Impact Assessment Methodologies for Microfinance: Theory, Experience And Better Practice', *World Development*, 28(1), pp. 79–98.

Hulme, D., and Mosley, P. (1996) *Finance Against Poverty*. Vols. 1 and 2. London: Routledge.

Hunt, G. K. (1990), *Philosophy and Politics*. Cambridge: Cambridge University Press.

IFSB. (2014) *Islamic Financial Services Industry Stability Report 2014*.

IFSB. (2017) *Another Year of Slowdown in Global Islamic Finance*, retrieved from www.islamicfinance.com/2017/06/ifsb-another-year-slowdown-global-islamic-finance/ (on September 01, 2017).

Imai, K. S., Arun, T., and Annim, S. K. (2010) 'Microfinance and Household Poverty Reduction: New Evidence From India', *World Development*, 38 (12), pp. 1760–1774.

Imai, K. S., Gaiha, R., Thapa, G., and Annim, S. K. (2012) 'Microfinance and Poverty – A Macro Perspective', *World Development*, 40(8), pp. 1675–689.

Iqbal, M., and Molyneux, P. (2005). *Thirty Years of Islamic Banking: History, Performance and Prospects*. Basingstoke: Springer.

Itoh, M., and Lapavitsas, C. (1999) *Political Economy of Money and Finance*. Basingstoke: Palgrave Macmillan.

Jabeen, Z., and Javed, M. T. (2007) 'Sukuk Structures: An Analysis of Risk-Reward Sharing and Wealth Circulation', *The Pakistan Development Review*, 46(4), pp. 405–419.

Kamali, M. H. (2000) *Islamic Commercial Law: An Analysis of Futures and Options*. Cambridge: Islamic Texts Society.

Kamarudin, F., Kamaludin, N., Manan, S., and Ghani, G. (2014) 'Defaulters Profile in Malaysia Sukuk Market', *Procedia-Social and Behavioral Science*, 145, pp. 277–278.

Kaplan, S. N., Sensoy, B. A., and Stromberg, P. (2009) 'Should Investors Bet on the Jockey or the Horse? Evidence From the Evolution of Firms from Early Business Plans to Public Companies', *Journal of Finance*, 64(1), pp. 75–115.

Karim, A. (2002) 'Incentive-Compatible Constraints for Islamic Banking: Some Lessons from Bank Muamalat, in Iqbal, M., and Llewellyn, D. (eds.) *Islamic Banking and Finance: New Perspectives on Profit Sharing and Risk*. Cheltenham: Edward Elgar, pp. 95–108.

Karim, N., Tarazi, M., and Reille, X. (2008) 'Islamic Microfinance: An Emerging Market Niche', *Focus Note* 49, CGAP.

Kettell, B. (2011) *Introduction to Islamic Banking and Finance* (Vol. 1). West Sussex, UK: John Wiley & Sons.

Keynes, J. M. (1936) *The General Theory of Employment, Interest and Money* (Vol. VII). London and Basingstoke: Palgrave Macmillan.

Keynes, J. M. (1937) 'The General Theory of Employment', *Quarterly Journal of Economics*, 51, pp. 209–23.

Khalil, A. F. A., Rickwood, C., and Murinde, V. (2002) 'Evidence on Agency-Contractual Problems in Mudārābah Financing Operations by Islamic Banks, in Iqbal, M., and Llewellyn, D. (eds.) *Islamic Banking and Finance: New Perspectives on Profit Sharing and Risk*. Cheltenham: Edward Elgar, pp. 57–94.

Khalil, E. L. (2004) 'What is Altruism?' *Journal of Economic Psychology*, 25(1), pp. 97–123.

Khan, F. (2010) 'How "Islamic"is Islamic banking?', *Journal of Economic Behavior & Organization*, 76(3), pp. 805–820.

Khan, M. F. (2007) 'Setting Standards for *Shariah* Application in the Islamic Financial Industry', *Thunderbird International Business Review*, 49(3), pp. 285–307.

Khan, M. S., and Mirakhor, A. (1987) 'The Framework and Practice of Islamic Banking', in Khan, M., and Mirakhor, A. (eds.) *Theoretical Studies in Islamic Banking and Finance*, Texas: The Institute for Research and Islamic Studies, pp. 32–40.

Khan, T. (1995) 'Demand For and Supply of Mark-Up and PLS Funds in Islamic Banking: Some Alternative Explanations', *Islamic Economic Studies*, 3(1), pp. 39–78.

Khandker, S. R. (1998) *Fighting Poverty with Microcredit: Experience in Bangladesh*. Washington, DC: Oxford University Press for the World Bank.

Kindleberger, C. (2000) *Manias, Panics and Crashes* (4th ed.). London and Basingstoke: Palgrave Macmillan.

Klein, P. O., and Weil, L. (2016) 'Why Do Companies Issue Sukuk?', *Review of Financial Economics*, retrieved from http://dx.doi.org/10.1016/j.rfe.2016.05.003 (on July 1, 2017).

Klonowski, D. (2010) *The Venture Capital Investment and Process*. New York: Palgrave Macmillan.

Knight, F. (1921) 'From Risk, Uncertainty and Profit', in Putterman, L. (Ee.) (1996) *The Economic Nature of the Firm, A Reader 2nd Edition*. Cambridge: Cambridge University Press, pp. 60–65.

Kortum, S., and Lerner, J. (2000) 'Assessing the Contribution of Venture Capital to Innovation', *RAND Journal of Economics*, 31(4), pp. 674–692.

Krugman, P. (2012) 'Why We Regulate', Op-Ed, *New York Times*, May 13.

Kuckertz, A., Berger, E. S. C., and Allmendinger, M. P. (2015) 'What Drives Entrepreneurship? A Configurational Analysis of the Determinants of Entrepreneurship in Innovation-Driven Economies', *Die Betriebswirtschaf Business Administration Review*, 75(4), pp. 273–288.

Kuran, T. (1995) 'Islamic Economics and the Islamic Subeconomy', *Journal of Economic Perspectives*, 9(4), pp. 155–173.

Kuran, T. (1996) 'The Discontents of Islamic Economic Morality', *American Economic Review*, 86(2), pp. 438–442.

Lackmann, B. G. (2015) 'Types of Sukuk (Islamic Bonds) and History of Japanese Company Issuance', *Nomura Journal of Capital Markets*, 6(3), pp. 1–20.

Lapavitsas, C. (2003), 'Money as Money and Money as Capital in a Capitalist Economy', in Saad-Filho, A. (ed.) *Anti-Capitalism: A Marxist Introduction*, London: Pluto Press, pp. 59–72.

Lawson, T. (2006) 'The Nature of Heterodox Economics', *Cambridge Journal of Economics*, 30(4), pp. 483–505.

Lee, F. (2009) *A History of Heterodox Economics: Challenging the Mainstream in the Twentieth Century*. Oxon: Routledge.

Lee, F., and Jo, T. (2011) 'Social Surplus Approach and Heterodox Economics', *Journal of Economic Issues*, 45(4), pp. 857–876.

Lewis, M. K. (2007) 'Comparing Islamic and Christian Attitudes to Usury', in Hasan, K., and Lewis, M. (eds.) *Handbook of Islamic Banking*. Cheltenham: Edward Elgar, pp. 64–84.

Lewis, M. K., and Algaoud, L. M. (2001) *Islamic Banking*. Cheltenham: Edward Elgar.

Lindsey, T. (2012) 'Between Piety and Prudence: State Syariah and the Regulation of Islamic Banking in Indonesia', *Sydney Law Review*, 34, pp. 107–127.

Lohmann, L. (2011) 'Capital and Climate Change' *Development and Change*, 42(2), pp. 649–668.

Looft, M. (2014) *Inspired Finance: The Role of Faith in Microfinance and International Economic Development*. Basingstoke: Palgrave Macmillan.

Macmillan, C. I., Kulow, D. M., and Khoylian, R. (1989) 'Venture Capitalists' Involvement in Their Investments: Extent and Performance', *Journal of Business Venturing*, 4(1), pp. 27–47.

Malkawi, B. H. (2013) 'Shari'ah Board in the Governance Structure of Islamic Financial Institution', *The American Journal of Comparative Law*, 61(3), pp. 539–577.

Maroco, J., Silva, D., Rodrigues, A., Guerreiro, M., Santana, I., & de Mendonça, A. (2011) Data mining methods in the prediction of Dementia: A real-data comparison of the accuracy, sensitivity and specificity of linear discriminant analysis, logistic regression, neural networks, support vector machines, classification trees and random forests. BMC Research Notes, 4(1), 299, retrieved from https://www.ncbi.nlm.nih.gov/pmc/articles/PMC3180705/ (on January 11, 2018).

Martan, A. F., Jabarti, A., and Sofrata, H. (1984) 'Islamic vis-a-vis Traditional Banking-A Fuzzy Set Approach', *Journal of Research in Islamic Economics*, 2(1), pp. 31–41.

Marx, K. (1959) Capital: *A Critique of Political Economy, Volume III (The Process of Capitalist Production)* (Edited by Fredric Engles). Institute of Marxism-Leninism: USSR.

Maurer, B. (2002) 'Anthropological and Accounting Knowledge in Islamic Banking and Finance: Rethinking Critical Accounts', *Journal of the Royal Anthropological Institute*, 8(4), pp. 645–667.

Mautz, R. K., and Sharaf, H. A. (1961) *The Philosophy of Auditing*. American Accounting Association Monograph No. 6, FL, USA.

Mawdudi, S. A. A. (2011) *First Principles of Islamic Economics* (translated by Ahmad Imam Shafaq Hashemi). Leicestershire: The Islamic Foundation.

Mazumder, M. S., and Lu, W. (2015) 'What Impact does Microfinance Have on Rural Livelihood? A Comparison of Governmental and Non-governmental Microfinance Programs in Bangladesh', *World Development*, 68, pp. 336–354.

McKernan, S. M. (2002) 'The Impact of Microcredit Programs on Self-employment Profits: Do Non Credit Program Aspects Matter?', *The Review of Economics and Statistics*, 84(1), pp. 93–115.

Metwally, M. M. (1997). Differences Between the Financial Characteristics of Interest-Free Banks and Conventional Banks', *European Business Review*, 97(2), pp. 92–98.

Miah, M. D., and Sharmeen, K. (2015) 'Relationship Between Capital, Risk and Efficiency: A Comparative Study Between Islamic and Conventional Banks of Bangladesh', *International Journal of Islamic and Middle Eastern Finance and Management*, 8(2), pp. 203–221.

Miah, M. D., and Uddin, H. (2017) 'Efficiency and Stability: A Comparative Study Between Islamic and Conventional Banks in GCC Countries', *Future Business Journal*, 3(2), pp. 172–185.

Microcredit Regulatory Authority. (2015) *Annual Report*, Microcredit Regulatory Authority, Dhaka, Bangladesh. Retrieve from: www.mra.gov.bd/images/mra_files/Publications/annual2016upd.pdf (on March 12, 2016).

Mills, P., and Presley, J. (1999) *Islamic Finance: Theory and Practice*. Basingstoke: Palgrave Macmillan.

Ministry of Cooperative and Small and Medium Enterprises. (2010) *Statistic of Micro and Small and Medium Enterprises Year 2008–2009*, Republic of Indonesia, retrieved from www.depkop.go.id/pdf-viewer/?p=uploads/tx_rtgfiles/narasi_statistik_umkm_2008-2009_-_komplittbl_grafik_tanpa_pemerintah.pdf (on June 7, 2017).

Minsky, H. (1977) 'A Theory of Systemic Fragility', in Altman, E., and Sametz, A. W.(eds.) *Financial Crises; Institutions and Markets in a Fragile Environment*. New York: Wiley, pp. 138–52.

Minsky, H. P. (1975) *John Maynard Keynes*. Columbia: Columbia University Press.

Mirghani, M., Mohammed, M., Bhuiyan, A. B., and Siwar, C. (2011) 'Islamic Micro-credit and Poverty Alleviation in the Muslim World: Prospects and Challenges', *Australian Journal of Basic and Applied Sciences*, 5(9), pp. 620–626.

Montgomery, H., and Weiss, J. (2011) 'Can Commercially-oriented Microfinance Help Meet the Millennium Development Goals? Evidence from Pakistan', *World Development*, 39(1), pp. 87–109.

Montgomery, R., Davies, R., Saxena, N. C., and Ashley, S. (1996) *Guidance Materials for Improved Project Monitoring and Impact Review Systems in India*. Centre for Development Studies, University College, Swansea, UK.

Morduch, J. (2000) 'The Microfinance Schism', *World Development*, 28(4), pp. 61–629.

Morais, T. (2007) 'Don't Call It Interest', *Forbes*, July 7.

Morrison, S. (2013) 'Islamic Bonds Unbound: Japan's Samurai Sukuk', *The Newsletter*, No. 65, International Institute for Asian Studies.

Mosely, P., and Hulme, D. (1998) 'Microenterprise Finance: Is There A Conflict between Growth And Poverty Alleviation', *World Development*, 26(5), pp. 783–790.

Muhammad, S. D. (2010) 'Microfinance Challenges and Opportunities in Pakistan', *European Journal of Social Sciences*, 14(1), pp. 88–97.

Mukunda, G. (2014) 'The Price of Wall-Street's Power', *Harvard Business Review*, 92(6), pp. 70–78.

Muljawan, D., Dar, H., and Hall, M. (2004) 'A Capital Adequacy Framework For Islamic Banks: The Need to Reconcile Depositors' Risk Aversion With Managers' Risk Taking', *Applied Financial Economics*, 14(6), pp. 429–441.

Nader, Y. F. (2008) 'Microcredit and the Socio-Economic Wellbeing of Women and Their Families in Cairo', *Journal of Socio-Economics*, 37(2), pp. 644–656.

Nagano, M. (2016) 'Who Issues Sukuk and When? An Analysis of the Determinants of Islamic Bond Issuance', *Review of Financial Economics*, 31, pp. 45–55.

Nagel, T. (1970) *The Possibility of Altruism*. Princeton: Princeton University Press.

Naqvi, S. N. H. (2003), *Perspectives on Morality and Human Well-Being*. Leicestershire: The Islamic Foundation.

Nelson, S. C., and Katzenstein, P. J. (2014) 'Uncertainty, Risk, and the Financial Crisis of 2008', *International Organization*, 68(2), pp. 361–392.

Nienhaus, V. (2007) 'Governance of Islamic Banks,' in Hassan, K., and Lewis, M. (eds.) *Handbook of Islamic Banking*. Cheltenham: Edward Elgar, pp. 128–143.

Noreen, U. (2011) *Impact of Microfinance on Poverty*. Frankfurt: Lap Lambert Academic Publications.

North, D. (1981) *Structure and Change of Economic History*. New York: W. W. Norton.

North, D. (1990) *Institutions, Institutional Change and Economic Performance*. Cambridge: Cambridge University Press.

North, D. (2005) *Understanding the Process of Economic Change*. New York: Princeton University Press.

NRSP Microfinance Bank Limited. (2016) *Annual Report 2016*, NRSP Microfinance Bank Limited, Pakistan.

Nur Ozkan-Gunay, E., and Ozkan, M. (2007) 'Prediction of Bank Failures in Emerging Financial Markets: An ANN Approach', *Journal of Risk Finance*, 8(5), pp. 465–480.

Obaidullah, M. (2007) 'Role of Microfinance in Poverty Alleviation: Lessons from Experiences in Selected IDB Member Countries', Islamic Development Bank, Jeddah: IRTI/IDB, retrieved from https://papers.ssrn.com/sol3/papers.cfm?abstract_id=1506077 (on June 25, 2017).

Olson, D., and Zoubi, T. A. (2008) 'Using Accounting Ratios to Distinguish between Islamic and Conventional Banks in the GCC Region', *The International Journal of Accounting*, 43(1), pp. 45–65.

Othman, A. A., Hassan, R., Omar, M. N., Napiah, M. D. M., Ariffin, M., Yusoff, A., Khatimin, N., and Zaharim, A. (2013) '*Shari'ah* Governance for Islamic Financial Institutions in Malaysia on the Independency of *Shari'ah* Committee and Efficiency of Its *Shari'ah* Decisions', *Recent Advantages in Management, Marketing and Finances*, Proceedings of the 7th WSEAS International Conference on Management, Marketing and Finances (MMF '13), Cambridge, MA, USA, 30 January–1 February 2013.

Pacces, A. M. (2010) 'Uncertainty and the Financial Crisis', *Journal of Financial Transformation*, 29, pp. 79–93.

PMN (Pakistan Microfinance Network) (2016) Pakistan Microfinance Review 2015: Annual Assessment of the Microfinance Industry.

PMN (Pakistan Microfinance Network) (2017) Pakistan Microfinance Review 2016: Annual Assessment of the Microfinance Industry.

Parker, M. (2010) 'Payment Delays and Defaults', *Arab News*, retrieved from www.arabnews.com/node/349438 (on August 20, 2017).

Pitt, M., and Khandker, S. (1996) 'Household and Intra-household Impact of the Grameen Bank and Similar Targeted Programs in Bangladesh', Discussion Paper No. 320, Washington, DC: World Bank.

Porter, M. E. (1990) *The Competitive Advantage of Nations*. New York: Free Press.

PT Permodalan Nasional Madani (Persero) (2015, 2016) *Annual Report*.

PT PNM Ventura Syariah (2015, 2016) *Audited Report*.

PT PNM Venture Capital (2015, 2016) *Audited Report*.

Rahajeng, D. K. (2013) 'Sharia Governance: Sharia Supervisory Board Model of Islamic Banking and Finance in Indonesia', retrieved from http://ssrn.com/abstract=2366722 (on September 15, 2017).

Rahim A. R. (2007) 'Islamic Microfinance: A Missing Component in Islamic Banking', *Kyoto Bulletin of Islamic Area Studies*, 1–2, pp. 38–53

Rahman, A. R., and Dean, F. (2013) 'Challenges and Solutions in Islamic Microfinance', *Humanomics*, 29(4), pp. 293–306.

Raihan, S., Osmani, S. R., and Khalily, M. B. (2015) 'Contribution of Microfinance to the Gross Domestic Product (GDP) of Bangladesh', Working Paper No. 44, Institute of Microfinance, retrieved from http://inm.org.bd/wp-content/uploads/2016/01/Workingpaper44.pdf (on October 25, 2017).

Ramli, R. (2015) 'Beyond Sovereign Issuers: Strategies to Facilitate the Sukuk Market to a Broader Pool of Issuers: The Malaysian Experience' paper presented at *The World Islamic Banking Conference*, 04 June, 2015 Singapore.

Revest, V., and Sapio, A. (2012) 'Financing Technology-based Small Firms in Europe: What Do We Know?', *Small Business Economics*, 39(1), pp. 179–205.

Riwajanti, N. I. (2015) 'Islamic Microfinance: Challenges and Development', *Journal of Research and Applications: Accounting and Management*, 1(1), pp. 42–53.

Roche, F., O'Shea, R., Allen, T. J., and Breznitz, D. (2008) 'The Dynamics of an Emerging Entrepreneurial Región in Ireland', in Phan, P., Venkataraman, S., and Velamuri, S. (eds.) *Entrepreneurship in Emerging Regions around the World Theory, Evidence and Implications*. Cheltenham: Edward Elgar Publishing Limited, pp. 9–46.

Rosly, S., and Bakar, M. (2003) 'Performance of Islamic and Mainstream Banks in Malaysia', *International Journal of Social Economics*, 30(12), pp. 1249–1265.

Sadr, K., and Iqbal, Z. (2002) 'Choice between Debt and Equity Contracts and Asymmetrical Information: Some Empirical Evidence, in Iqbal, M., and Llewellyn, D. (eds.) *Islamic Banking and Finance: New Perspectives on Profit Sharing and Risk*, Cheltenham: Edward Elgar, pp. 139–151.

Sahlman, W. A. (1990) 'The Structure and Governance of Venture-Capital Organizations', *Journal of Financial Economics*, 27(2), pp. 473–521.

Sarkar, A. A. (2009) 'Islamic Finance Progress in Bangladesh', *New Horizon*, 170, p. 26.

Sarkar, A. A. (2015) 'Islamic Monetary Policy Instruments', *Thoughts on Economics*, 25(1&2), pp. 7–48.

Schreiner, M. (2012) *A Simple Poverty Scorecard for Indonesia*. Mimeo, retrieved from www.progressoutofpoverty.org (on August 25, 2017).

Schuler, S. R., Hashemi, S. M., and Riley, A. P. (1997) 'The Influence of Women's Changing Roles and Status in Bangladesh's Fertility Transition: Evidence From a Study of Credit Programs and Contraceptive Use', *World Development*, 25(4), pp. 563–576.

Schumpeter, J. A. (1934) *The Theory of Economic Development An Inquiry into Profits, Capital, Credit, Interest, and the Business Cycle*. Cambridge, MA: Harvard University Press.

Schumpeter, J. A. (1994) [1942] *Capitalism, Socialism and Democracy*. London: Routledge.

Securities Commission Malaysia (SCM) (2015) *Guidelines on the Registration of Venture Capital and Private Equity Corporations and Management Corporations*. Kuala Lumpur: Securities Commission Malaysia, retrieved from www.sc.com.my/wp-content/uploads/eng/html/resources/guidelines/VC/guidelines_vcpe_150309.pdf (on July 23, 2017).

Seelos, C. and Mair, J. (2005) 'Social Entrepreneurship: Creating New Business Models to Serve the Poor', *Business Horizons*, 48, pp. 241–246.

Segal, U., and Sobel, J. (2007) 'Tit For Tat: Foundations of Preferences For Reciprocity in Strategic Settings', *Journal of Economic Theory*, 136(1), pp. 197–216.

Servin, R., Lensink, R., and Berg, M. V. (2012) 'Ownership and Technical Efficiency of Microfinance Institutions: Empirical Evidence from Latin America', *Journal of Banking and Finance*, 36, pp. 2316–2144.

SESRIC (Statistical, Economic and Social Research and Training Centre for Islamic Countries). (2009) 'Islamic Finance and Banking System: A Potential Alternative in the Aftermath of the Current Global Financial Crisis (Part II)', *SESRIC Monthly Report*, October-November 2009, pp. 1–11.

Shane, S. (2000) 'Prior Knowledge and the Discovery of Entrepreneurial Opportunities', *Organization Science*, 11(4), pp. 448–469.

Shane, S. (2003) *General Theory of Entrepreneurship: The Individual-Opportunity Nexus*. Cheltenham: Edward Elgar.

Shepherd, D. A., and Zacharakis, A. L. (2001) 'The Nature of Information and Over-confidence on Venture Capitalists Decision Making', *Journal of Business Venturing*, 16(4), pp. 311–332.

Siddiqi, M. N. (2004) *Riba, Bank Interest and the Rationale of Its Prohibition*. Jeddah, Saudia Arabia: Islamic Research and Training Institute.

Siddiqui, S. H. (2001) 'Islamic Banking: True Modes of Financing', *New Horizon*, 109, May–June, pp. 21–22.

Simon, H. (1993) 'Altruism and Economics', *American Economic Review*, 83, pp. 156–161.

Simon, H. (1996) *The Sciences of the Artificial* (3rd ed.). New York: The MIT Press.

Simon, H. A. (1961) *Administrative Behavior* (2nd ed.). London, NY: Palgrave Macmillan.

Smith, L. R., and Smith, K. J. (2000) *Entrepreneurial Finance*. New York: John Wiley & Sons

Soroglou, V. (2013) 'Religion, Spirituality, and Altruism', in Kenneth I. Pargament, Julie J. Exline, and James W. Jones (eds.) *APA Handbook of Psychology, Religion and Spirituality* (Vol. 1). pp. 439–457, Washington, DC: American Psychological Association.

Stiglitz, J. (2012) *The Price of Inequality*. New York: W.W. Norton.

Supapol, A. B., Fischer, E., and Pan, Y. (2008) 'The Founding Conditions of Entrepreneurial Firms as a Function of Emerging Institutional Arrangements in China', in Phan, P., Venkataraman, S., and Velamuri, S. (eds.) *Entrepreneurship in Emerging Regions around the World Theory, Evidence and Implications*. Cheltenham: Edward Elgar, pp. 239–268.

Surahanjaya Sekurity. (2017a) *Islamic Capital Market Statistics*, retrieved from www.sc.com.my/data-statistics/islamic-capital-market-statistics/ (on August 12, 2017).

Surahanjaya Sekurity. (2017b) *Legislation and Guidelines*, retrieved from www.sc.com.my/legislation-guidelines (on August 20, 2017).

Suzuki, Y. (2013) 'A Post-Keynesian Perspective on Islamic Prohibition of Gharar', *International Journal of Islamic and Middle Eastern Finance and Management*, 6(3), pp. 200–210.

Suzuki, Y., Barai, M. K., Adhikary, B. K., and Wanniarachchige, M. K. (2011) 'The Grameen Bank "Empowering the Poor" Model of Microcredit: An Institutional Comparison With the Traditional Mode of the Japanese Banking System', *Journal of Comparative Asian Development*, 10(1), pp. 129–156.

Suzuki, Y. Miah, D., Wanniarachchige, M., and Uddin, S. (eds.) (2017) *Banking and Economic Rent in Asia: Rent Effects, Financial Fragility, and Economic Development*. London, NY: Routledge.

Suzuki, Y., and Miah, M. D. (2015) 'A New Institutional Approach in Explaining the Underdevelopment of Islamic Microfinance', *Islam and Civilisational Renewal*, 6(4), pp. 468–488.

Suzuki, Y., and Miah, M. D. (2016) 'Altruism, Reciprocity and Islamic Equity Finance', *International Journal of Islamic and Middle Eastern Finance and Management*, 9(2), pp. 205–221.

Suzuki, Y., and Uddin, S. (2014) 'Islamic Bank Rent: A Case Study of Islamic Banking in Bangladesh', *International Journal of Islamic and Middle Eastern Finance and Management*, 7(2), pp. 170–181.

Suzuki, Y., Uddin, S. M. S., and Pramono, S. (2018) 'Do Islamic Banks Need to Earn Extra Profits? A Comparative Analysis on Banking Sector Rent in Bangladesh and Indonesia', *Journal of Islamic Accounting and Business Research*, forthcoming.

Swain, R. B., and Wallentin, F. Y. (2009) 'Does Microfinance Empower Women? Evidence from sSlf-help Groups in India', *International Review of Applied Economics*, 23(5), pp. 541–556.

Syafei, A. W. (2010) 'The Responsibility and Independence of *Shari'ah* Supervisory Boards of the Indonesian Islamic Banks', paper presented at *The Third International Conference on Islamic Banking & Finance: Risk Management, Regulation & Supervision*, Jakarta, 23–24 February, 2010.

Tariq, A. A., and Dar, H. (2007) 'Risks of Sukuk Structures: Implications for Resource Mobilization', *Thunderbird International Business Review*, 49, pp. 203–223.

The Financial Express. (2016) Launching of Islamic Bond in the Offing. Dhaka: The Financial Express (Online Desk), retrieved from www.thefinancialexpress-bd.com/201604/08/25184/Launching-of-Islamic-bond-in-the-offing (on August 15, 2017).

Trester, J. J. (1998) 'Venture Capital Contracting Under Asymmetric Information', *Journal of Banking and Finance*, 22, pp. 675–699.

Ullah, H. (2014) 'Shari'ah Compliance in Islamic Banking: An Empirical Study on Selected Islamic Banks in Bangladesh', *International Journal of Islamic and Middle Eastern Finance and Management*, 7(2), pp. 182–199.

United Nations. (2005) *International Year of Microcredit. UN Department of Public Information*. New York, NY, retrieved from http://www.yearofmicrocredit.org (on January 5, 2018)

Venkataraman, S., and Shane, S. (2000) 'The Promise of Entrepreneurship as a Field of Research', *Academy of Management Review*, 25(1), pp. 217–226.

Venture Capital Bank Bahrain (various years) *Annual Report.*

Vinnicombe, T. (2010) 'AAOIFI Reporting Standards: Measuring Compliance', *Advances in Accounting*, 26(1), pp. 55–65.

Visser, H. (2009) *Islamic Finance: Principles and Practice*. London: Edward Elgar.

Wedderburn-Day, A. R. (2010) 'Sovereign Sukuk: Adaption and Innovation', *Law and Contemporary Problems*, 73(4), pp. 325–333.

West, P. M., Brockett, P.L., and Golden, L. L. (1997) 'A Comparative Analysis of Neural Networks and Statistical Methods for Predicting Consumer Choice', *Marketing Science*, 16(4), pp. 370–391.

Williamson, O. E. (1979) 'Transaction-Cost Economics: The Governance of Contractual Relations', *Journal of Law and Economics*, 22(2), pp. 233–261.

Williamson, O. E. (1985) *The Economic Institutions of Capitalism*. New York: The Free Press.

Williamson, O. E. (2000) 'The New Institutional Economics: Taking Stock, Looking Ahead', *Journal of Economic Literature*, 38(3), pp. 595–613.

Wilson, R. (2008) 'Innovation in the Structuring of Islamic *Sukuk* Securities', *Humanomics*, 24(3), pp. 170–181.

Wulandari, P., and Kassim, S. (2016) 'Issues and Challenges in Financing the Poor: Case of Baitul Maal Wa Tamwil in Indonesia', *International Journal of Bank Marketing*, 34(2), pp. 216–234.

Wydick, B. (2001) 'Group Lending Under Dynamic Incentives as a Borrower Discipline Device', *Review of Development Economics*, 5(3), pp. 406–420.

Yang, J. (2010). *Intelligent Data Mining using Artificial Neural Networks and Genetic Algorithms: Techniques and Applications*. Ph.D. thesis at University of Warwick, UK, retrieved from http://wrap.warwick.ac.uk/3831/1/WRAP_THESIS_Yang_2010.pdf (on January 11, 2018).

Yousef, T. M. (2004) 'The Murabaha Syndrome in Islamic Finance: Laws, Institutions and Politics, in Henry, C., and Wilson, R. (eds.) *The Politics of Islamic Finance.* Edinburg: Edinburg University Press, pp. 63–80.

Yumna, A., and Clarke, M. (2011) 'Integrating *Zakat* and Islamic Charities with Microfinance Initiative in the Purpose of Poverty Alleviation in Indonesia', paper presented at *8th International Conference on Islamic Economics and Finance,* Doha, Qatar, retrieved from www.assaif.org/ara/content/ . . . /33273/ . . . /Zakat%20 an%20Islamic%20Microfinance.pdf (on October 23, 2017).

Yunus, M., and Jolis, A. (1999) *Banker to the Poor: Micro-Lending and the Battle Against World Poverty.* New York: Public Affairs.

Yusoff, W. S. (2014) *Industrial Economics and Organization: Conventional and Islamic Perspective.* New South Wales: Xlibris Corporation.

Zaher, T., and Hassan, K. (2001) 'A Comparative Literature Survey of Islamic Finance and Banking', *Financial Markets, Institutions & Instruments,* 10(4), pp. 155–199.

Zeller, M. (2001) 'The Safety Net Role of Microfinance for Income and Consumption Smoothing', in Lustig, N. (ed.) *Shielding the Poor: Social Protection in the Developing World.* Washington DC, Brookings Institution Press and Inter-American Development Bank, pp. 217–237.

Zhao, Lu. (2012) 'Exploring Religiosity's Effects on Altruistic Behaviour', *Social Research Report.* University of British Columbia, Vol. 1, retrieved from http://ojs. library.ubc.ca/index.php/ubcujp/article/download/2433/182445 (on April 12, 2015).

Zulkhibiri, M. (2015) 'A Synthesis of Theoretical and Empirical Research on Sukuk', *Borsa Istanbul Review,* 15(4), pp. 237–248.

Index

Note: Page numbers in italic indicate a figure and page numbers in bold indicate a table on the corresponding page.